The Story of a Life

THE
STORY
OF A LIFE

St. Thérèse of Lisieux

Guy Gaucher

Translated by Sister Anne Marie Brennan ODC

1817

Harper & Row, Publishers, San Francisco
Cambridge, Hagerstown, New York, Philadelphia, Washington
London, Mexico City, São Paulo, Singapore, Sydney

Library of Congress Cataloging-in-Publication Data

Gaucher, Guy, 1930-
   The story of a life.

   Bibliography: p.
   1. Thérèse, de Lisieux, Saint, 1873-1897.
2. Christian saints—France—Lisieux—Biography.
3. Lisieux (France)—Biography.   I. Title.
BX4700.T5G37713   1987   282'.092'4   [B]
85-45715
ISBN 0-06-063095-7

87 88 89 90 91 RRD 10 9 8 7 6 5 4 3 2 1

In memory of Sister Geneviève
Dominican of Clairefontaine
who rejoined her friend Thérèse in eternal life
10 May 1980

Contents

Illustrations

Note

What Thérèse Martin said or wrote is printed in italics and the words she underlined in her writings are printed in small capitals.

All the illustrations in this book (with the exception of two, the ownership of which the publishers have been unable to trace) are reproduced by permission of the Office Central de Lisieux (OCL), 51 rue du Carmel, 14100 Lisieux.

Prologue

I can nourish myself on nothing but the truth.

You do not know me as I really am, wrote Sister Thérèse of the Child Jesus to Abbé Bellière, her spiritual brother, a few months before she died. This friendly reproach is undoubtedly justified for many of our contemporaries. Pilgrims, tourists to Lisieux or only readers of *Story of a Soul*, think they know 'the little saint': she is so simple! Yet it is a simplicity which fosters misunderstanding.

In her *Manuscrits autobiographiques* (the first part of *Story of a Soul*), two school exercise books consisting of 120 pages, Sister Thérèse has not told the story of her life. She clearly explains her intention to her prioress, Mother Agnès of Jesus (her sister Pauline): *You asked me to write under no constraint whatever would come into my mind. It is not, then, my life properly so-called that I am going to write. It is my* THOUGHTS *on the graces God has deigned to grant me.*

There are therefore many gaps in this account written under obedience. For example, she says that she has greatly abridged the story of her religious life. Speaking of the time of her novitiate she says: *Everything I have just written in so few words would require many detailed pages, but these pages will never be read on earth.* For us, this is not quite true. The young Carmelite could not have imagined that one day some of those details would be published in her *Letters*, or made known at the two canonisation processes. Neither would she have thought that she, who had lived hidden and wanted to be unknown, would one day be seen by millions of men and women thanks to the photographs taken inside the enclosure by her sister Céline.

As well as the two exercise books Thérèse Martin has also left us letters, poems, religious plays, prayers and various notes. All these fill out and complete the story of her soul which is told in them as clearly as it is in the memoirs.

Today anyone wishing to write the story of her life 'properly so-called' has first to put all these authentic texts back into chronological order, to show them in relation to each other and to collate them with all the evidence of her contemporaries to be found in letters, last conversations, personal notes and statements made at the processes, not forgetting the archives of the Carmel and those of the period, and so on.[1]

It has taken no less than eighty-five years for all the Theresian writings to be published in France. This considerable work was begun in 1956 by Father François de Sainte-Marie, a Carmelite. The original exercise books, *Manuscrits autobiographiques*, have been reproduced in a photocopied edition. The *Letters, Poems, Last Conversations*, and the evidence given at the two processes, have been published since 1971.[2]

This mass of documentation therefore calls for a short new biography for a wide public which still does not know Thérèse Martin 'as she really was'. Few saints have been as misunderstood as she was during her lifetime. After her death she was sometimes even more so. She fell victim to an excess of sentimental devotion which betrayed her. She was victim also to her language, which was that of the late nineteenth century and flowed from the religiosity of her age: a handicap to be overcome.

This book is based entirely, and scrupulously, on authentic documents. It contains no fiction. These pages try to be faithful to Thérèse who said on her death-bed: *I only love simplicity. I have a horror of pretence.*

She spoke out against the Lives of saints written in her day: *We should not say improbable things, or things we do not know. We must see their real, and not their imagined lives.*

We will therefore let Thérèse herself speak.

We hope the reader of this story, which contains only essentials, will rediscover the real truth about this mysterious

---

[1] A Centre of Theresian Documentation for research was opened at Lisieux in 1978.

[2] Not all the Theresian writings are yet translated into English (tr.).

young girl who died of tuberculosis when she was twenty-four.

On 30 September 1897 no one found anything special to say about this Carmelite who had been just like all the others in her hidden life in an unknown provincial monastery. Yet in 1899 her aunt Guérin said to her nieces, the sisters of the dead nun, that her family would be forced to leave Lisieux 'because of Thérèse'. Life was becoming unbearable! The Martin sisters, protected by their grilles, were unavailable and so the crowds wanted to see and question the Guérins. It became necessary to guard 'little Sister Thérèse's grave': pilgrims flocking from France and elsewhere were uprooting the flowers, taking away the soil from the cemetery, making relics of everything. Since 1898 *Story of a Soul* has overwhelmed millions of men and women of all languages, races, peoples and nations.[1]

Why? Why, in so short a time, did such a simple and hidden life unleash that 'storm of glory' (Pius XI) on a family with the very common name of Martin, in that quiet little town of Calvados?

> Who is wise?
> Let him pay heed to these things
> and understand God's love
> (Ps. 107:43)

GUY GAUCHER

---

[1] Some idea may be obtained from examples of the testimonies, which have been chosen from among thousands (p. 219).

Part I

Alençon
1873–1877

1 Thérèse aged 15 (April 1888)

1

Alençon
1873–1877

Everything smiled upon me on this earth.

THE LAST LITTLE ONE (2 JANUARY 1873)

At the beginning of the year 1873 Zélie Martin announced to her brother and sister-in-law the happy arrival of her ninth child:

My little girl was born, yesterday, Thursday, at half-past eleven in the evening. She is very strong and healthy. I am told she weighs eight pounds, let us put it at six, that is not bad. She seems quite pretty. I am very happy. However at first I was surprised. I had been expecting a boy because, for the last two months, the baby had felt much stronger than my other children. I was in labour for only half an hour and what I suffered beforehand is not to be counted.

In the afternoon of 4 January the Abbé Dumaine baptised Marie-Françoise-Thérèse Martin in Our Lady's church. The child was held over the baptismal font by her thirteen-year-old godmother Marie, her eldest sister, and by her godfather of the same age, Paul-Albert Boul.

This baby was to take her place in a family descended from peasants and soldiers, a family which had a rather unusual beginning.

LOUIS MARTIN

Louis Martin, born in Bordeaux on 22 August 1823, grew up in military barracks wherever his father happened to be

2 Louis Martin at 40 (1863)

stationed, and chose to become a watchmaker. When he was about twenty-two he thought of entering religious life at the great St Bernard Monastery, which was situated in remote solitude and provided help for travellers lost on the mountain. He was refused admittance because he did not know Latin but on his return began to study the language. He lived for three years in Paris. To a young country bachelor the capital seemed like a 'modern Babylon'. Then in 1850 he settled in Alençon with his parents who had a jewellery shop at 15 rue du Pont-Neuf. For eight years quiet meditative Louis lived a life of work, interrupted only by long fishing trips – *his favourite pastime* – a few hunting parties, and evenings spent with the young people of the Catholic Circle, which had been started by his friend Vital Romet.

He abandoned his Latin studies but his faith remained alive and active. He never opened his shop on a Sunday, and this must have caused him to lose good business. Weekday masses, nightly adoration, pilgrimages, this man was not ashamed to live as a Christian. His bearing, expression and agreeable manners did not pass unnoticed by some young girls of Alençon, but he did not seem to notice them. The purchase of a bizarre building, a hexagonal tower with two stories surrounded by a garden – the Pavillon, rue des Lavoirs – isolated him even more. Among the flowers he put a statue of the Virgin which a pious young lady had given him.

Mme Martin was worried that he was still unmarried at thirty-four. While attending a course on the making of Alençon lace she noticed a bright attractive, very Christian young girl who was extremely gifted in this art, which had made Alençon famous throughout Europe. Would she not be the perfect wife for Louis?

ZÉLIE MARTIN

Marie Azélie Guérin, born on 23 December 1831 in Gandelain (Orne), was in her mid twenties. Her father, Isidore, was a former soldier of Wagram who after travelling through Spain and Portugal with Masséna and Soult became a constable at Saint-Denis, and in 1828 married Louise-Jeanne Macé, a somewhat unlettered peasant. Zélie had not known a happy childhood and would one day write to her younger brother: 'My childhood, my youth were as sad as a shroud, for if my mother spoilt you she was, as you know, too strict with me. Although she was so good herself she did not understand me and I suffered from this very much.'

Intelligent, with a flair for writing, Zélie worked hard while retaining from her austere upbringing a certain anxiety, a tendency towards scrupulosity, which was not helped by the spirituality of her time. Her Visitandine sister would often reproach her with being 'ingenious at tormenting herself'. But her sound common sense quickly enabled her to overcome this difficulty. 'I want to be a saint. It will not be easy, for there is much wood to be pruned and it is as hard as flint.'

She too had thought of becoming a religious, but the superior of the Hôtel-Dieu had firmly discouraged the prospective postulant. Disappointed, she threw herself into

3 Azélie, Isidore and Marie-Louise (Sister Marie Dosithée) Guérin in 1857

making Alençon lace. She mastered the art of this very fine work so rapidly that in 1853 when she was twenty-two she set up her own business at 36 rue Saint-Blaise, working at first with her elder sister Marie-Louise. But soon after, her sister left her to enter the Visitation convent at Le Mans. Their correspondence would end only with the death of the Visitandine who was always her faithful counsellor.

Hardly three months elapsed between her first meeting with Louis and their marriage. On 13 July 1858 at midnight, as was the custom of the time, the lacemaker and the watch-maker exchanged vows in Our Lady's church. Their married life began in a surprising way: Louis proposed to his wife that they live together as brother and sister. Docile, and not knowing what to do, Zélie agreed. After ten months of this monastic life a confessor made them change their life style – radically. They had nine children: seven girls and two boys.

From 1860 to 1870 births and deaths followed in rapid succession. Infant mortality was a scourge in the second half of the nineteenth century. In three and a half years the Martins lost three children in infancy, and Hélène, a lovable child of five and a half.[1]

Between 1859 and 1868 Mme Martin also lost her parents and her father-in-law. We can then readily understand her writing after the birth of her last daughter: 'I have already suffered so much in my life.'

She therefore wanted another 'little Thérèse' to take the place of the one who had died in October 1870, knowing only too well that this would be the last child she would bring into the world. For about seven years she had suffered from a disease which was becoming progressively worse: a tumour in the breast. She did not slow down her intense activity but was worried: 'If God gives me the grace to nurse this child, it would only be a pleasure to rear it. I love children to the point of folly. I was born to have them, but soon the time for this will be over. I will be forty-one this month and this is the time when one is a grandmother!'

THE MARTIN FAMILY AT ALENÇON

The last little one to arrive in the family was the centre of love and affection. The four girls who preceded her all wanted to look after her. Marie, thirteen and her father's favourite, was independent and original: she would not hear of marriage or the convent. Pauline was twelve, a boarder at the Visitation convent at Le Mans, and like her sister determined and studious. She was her mother's confidante. At ten, 'poor Léonie' felt herself between the two eldest and her younger sisters. Her illnesses, unattractiveness and slowness at school separated her even more. There was hesitation about sending her in her turn to the Visitandine aunt. She stayed only six months. 'What was to be done? What a cross!' As for Céline, she was four, full of life but delicate. She was much nearer the new arrival.

[1] See genealogies of the Martin and Guérin families (p. 226). Note the absence of boys in these two families, who all died at birth (Guérins) or shortly after (Martins).

4 Thérèse's birthplace in Alençon

In the Martin family the mother played a leading role. But she never complained of Louis's peaceful goodness: 'My husband is a saintly man, I wish all women had husbands like him.' Through their work and good management the couple were financially secure. When they married they had between them 34,000F,[1] two houses and the Pavillon. Mme Martin employed up to twenty workers who each week brought along their piece of lace (it took about sixty hours to make a piece 8cm square). Rising early and retiring late, Zélie herself joined together this fine intricate work. Each Thursday she received her clients. 'I am completely enslaved', she was to write in April 1872, 'because of the orders which keep coming in and do not give me a moment's rest. I have nearly a hundred metres of Alençon lace to make up.' In 1870 her husband sold his watchmaking business to his nephew Adolf Leriche and undertook the management and successful marketing of his wife's business.

With the liberation of the region after the 1870 Franco-German war the memories of the conflict gradually faded. But the Martins did not forget the formidable 'display of warfare which had been unfurled over Alençon'. They had been obliged to take in nine soldiers 'neither wicked men nor looters', but who, to Zélie's indignation, devoured everything 'without bread'. After their departure business resumed as usual.

In 1873 Catholics were worried.[2] After the terrible days of the Commune they feared another revolution. In May 1872 Louis Martin had taken part in a pilgrimage of twenty thousand men to Chartres. He went there again in May 1873, and during the summer went to Lourdes. At that time of

---

[1] In Lisieux in 1874 a man in textiles earned 2.25F to 3.50F a day; women 1.60F to 2.50F; children 0.90F to 1.50F. A kilo of bread cost 0.30F; a kilo of beef 1.50F.

[2] Seven days after Thérèse's birth the death of the ex-Emperor Napoleon III was announced in the papers. For a short period Thiers presided over the destinies of the young French Republic. The majority of Catholics hoped the king would be returned but the obstinacy of the Count de Chambord, who was attached to the white flag, deceived them. Marshal MacMahon was soon to be elected President of the Republic. The construction of the Sacré-Coeur basilica on Montmartre was to begin. Prayers were offered for the liberation of Pope Pius IX, a prisoner in Italy.

5 Rose Taillé's farmhouse in Semallé

uncertainty there were many alarmist 'prophets' predicting
such diverse catastrophes that Zélie Martin reached a point
when she was no longer troubled by them.

Alençon had a population of 16,000; this peaceful 'City of
Dukes', which made lace and canvas, held three weekly
markets and seven annual fairs, was an attractive little town.
There were the two rivers, the Briante and the Sarthe, a castle
with battlements, a large pink-brick Henri IV house which
was now the Prefecture, a theatre and picturesque old houses.

The Martin family was rising lower middle-class. They
loved this quiet place near the open country. Little Thérèse
was to live there only three and a half years, but these childhood years are always decisive.

AT SEMALLÉ (MARCH 1873 TO 2 APRIL 1874)

The joy of her birth ('Everyone tells me she will be beautiful,
she laughs already') soon gave way to serious concern.
Feeding problems, intestinal troubles, restless nights – was
this beautiful baby going to die of enteritis like the others? 'I
often think of mothers who have the joy of nursing their

children themselves; and I have to see them all die one after another!'

There were crises in January and again in February. One night the baby was at death's door. Dr Belloc was adamant: the child would be lost if it was not breast-fed. Next day the distraught mother set out on foot for Semallé (8km), to find the wet-nurse Rose Taillé, who had nursed two of her dead babies. They came back together, again on foot. After she had been suckled the child slept and awoke smiling. Saved! But Zélie had to resign herself to letting her baby go to live with Rose and Moïse who already had four children. Their last one, Eugène, was thirteen months. The husband grumbled at the prospect but his wife stood her ground. In that very small brick house deep in Normandy Thérèse was to live for more than a year.

The healthy country life suited her perfectly, and she always retained her love of nature, water, flowers, trees and animals. By July she was a 'big baby tanned by the sun'. There were frequent comings and goings between the hamlet of Carrouges and the rue Saint-Blaise. Every Thursday 'little Rose' went to the market at Alençon to sell butter, eggs, vegetables, and the milk from her only cow, Roussette. The Martins used to go to see their youngest, and Marie, Pauline, Léonie and Céline enjoyed these trips to the country. They feasted on the Taillés' black bread while the nurse's children ate the city-dwellers' white bread.

Thérèse became a real country girl, 'taken out to the fields in a wheelbarrow, set on top of a load of hay', and she found it hard to readjust to town life. If, during one of her frequent visits home, one of her mother's smart customers picked her up she would scream, terrified by their hairstyles and above all their hats. She did not want to leave Rose, and to avoid screams and tantrums they had to let her go and sit at the market stall with her nurse.

RETURN TO RUE SAINT-BLAISE

At a year old, the little girl was walking. But her family had to wait some time before they saw her at home again. At last the date was set: 2 April 1874. For that happy family occasion

Thérèse wore a new dress, blue slippers and a white bonnet. 'Except for the first, I have never had such a strong child . . . She will be beautiful, she is already graceful.'

Her year in the country had left a deep impression on her. Now fifteen months, Thérèse discovered her family's world: the three rooms on the ground floor, the bedrooms upstairs, the little garden where her father had put up a swing. The baby was tied into it with a rope. 'When the swing would not go high enough, she cried.' Through the window she could see the Prefecture on the other side of the street. She used to go there with Céline to play with Genny Bechard, the Prefect's child, but was frightened by the big rooms, the balconies, the park, by all the luxury. She preferred her own little garden.

Nearly every Sunday Mme Martin wrote to the two daughters who were boarders at Le Mans, and to the Guérins at Lisieux. Her letters are full of details of the doings of the youngest and how she looked and behaved.

MY HAPPY DISPOSITION

The child's quiet life was enlivened by memorable occasions: for example, when the two older girls came home for the holidays shrieks of laughter and delight filled the house.

Thérèse showed a marked preference for Pauline, her *ideal*, and when she was bored used to think of this sister.

In sharp contrast to the austerity of provincial life, when normally only certain rooms were heated and breakfast consisted of soup, feast days were celebrations: at Christmas and the New Year the presents from parents and the Guérins were arrayed by the fireplace, to outbursts of such joy; and there were happy memories of family evenings together, not forgetting the first train ride from Alençon to Le Mans to the Visitandine aunt.

The child loved nature and was deeply impressed by picking strawberries at the Pavillon, fishing trips in a boat, walks through flowering meadows, and visits to Semallé when they were caught in terrible storms and returned home drenched but happy.

Thérèse Martin did not escape childish ailments. At two

6 Therese at 3½ (July 1876)

she fell on the leg of the table and 'cut her forehead to
the bone'. Toothache, measles and colds followed one after
another. These latter very much worried her mother: 'Since
she was born, she has had one cold after another, the nurse
told me this, but the worst part is that she becomes very ill
with them.'

At the same age she tried to run away to Our Lady's
church. Louise, the maid, overtook her in the rain, and an
hour later Thérèse was still crying about it.

Her first photograph was taken at three and a half. Usually
she was smiling but that day, because the photographer
frightened her when he hid under the big black cover, she
pouted.

She was a precocious little girl with blonde curls and blue
eyes. 'She is very advanced for her age,' noted her mother.
Marie agreed: 'She is amazingly clever . . . I think she will
be able to read fluently in six months.' Before she was three

she had learnt her alphabet and looked as if she was following the lessons Pauline was giving Céline, who was three and a half years older. 'She comes out with some unusual things for her age.' As in every family, her earliest sayings were remembered. With irresistible mimicry she said to her sisters: *You don't have to put on airs for Papa to take you to the Pavillon every day.*

She was observant and, without appearing to do so, took in everything. 'Her little imagination works non-stop.' She was very reflective. She *thought*. At four, she explained to Céline why God is all-powerful, and the meaning of a neighbour's unfortunate name.

Her good memory enabled her to recite poems at an early age and she had a gift for imitating people she met. They had to stop her imitating the gardener by telling her that his dead wife came 'and made him very sad' at night.

Her high spirits delighted the family. 'She laughs and enjoys herself from morning till night.' She sang with all her heart. 'Full of mischief', she loved to play tricks on her sisters. *I was* VERY OUTGOING, Thérèse was to say later.

VERY SENSITIVE

The warm and affectionate family atmosphere suited her sensitive nature. Everyone loved her. *My first memories are of smiles and the most tender caresses – but if (God) surrounded me with so much love, he had also put love into my little heart, making it warm and affectionate. I loved Mamma and Papa very much and expressed my love for them in a thousand ways.*

She did in fact adore her father, the only man in the family; and he worshipped her: his last little one was his 'Queen'. 'Her father spoils her and does whatever she wishes,' her mother wrote to Pauline. But it was the same with her mother, for Thérèse would call out to her at each step of the stairs as she came down. 'And if I do not answer each time, "Yes, my little one", she stops and will not go any further.'

She was very emotional, often cried, shrieked sometimes and kept it up for at least an hour. 'She is a child who is very easily upset.' There were tears in the parlour at the Visitation convent at Le Mans when she saw the grilles, silent tears during Pauline's lessons from which she was excluded, tears when she quarrelled with Céline; but also tears because she was sorry.

I WAS FAR FROM BEING A PERFECT LITTLE GIRL

She was a self-willed and proud child who knew what she wanted. Her mother asked her to kiss the floor for a sou just to see if she would be willing to do so. She always wanted things to happen immediately and by temperament she tended towards all or nothing. One day Léonie offered her two little sisters some pieces of ribbon and lace in a small basket. Céline took a pretty braid. Thérèse took up the rest, saying: *I choose all.*[1]

At twenty-two Thérèse, then a Carmelite, admitted: *I was far from being a perfect little girl.* She was prone to impatience and anger.

When she was three: 'Céline is playing with the little one with some bricks, and from time to time there is an argument. Céline gives in to gain a pearl for her crown. I have to correct poor baby who gets into frightful tantrums when she can't have her own way. She rolls on the floor in despair believing all is lost. Sometimes she is so overcome she almost chokes. She is a very highly-strung child.'

Her mother noted: 'Thérèse is not as gentle as Céline and has an almost unconquerable stubborn streak in her; when she says no, nothing can make her give in, and you can put her in the cellar for the day and she would rather sleep there than say yes.' A little later: 'Nothing can persuade her to read; all went well as long as she only had to name the letters, but now she has to spell out the words there is no way of getting her to do it. You can promise her everything, to no avail, but she is so little!'

With such a character Thérèse could have gone from one whim to another. But in the Martin family any inclination to act the spoilt child was firmly checked. One day her father called her to come and give him a kiss, and she replied

---

[1] Note that the interpretation Thérèse was to give to this significant phrase in 1895 applied to the choosing of *all sacrifices.*

from the height of her swing: *Come and get it, Papa!* Marie
immediately intervened: 'You naughty little girl. It is very
wicked to answer your father like that!' The lesson went
home.

When she had an accident (broke a vase, tore a piece of
wallpaper) she hurried to ask 'forgiveness, over and over
again'. 'There is no use telling her she is forgiven, she cries
just the same.' 'She has it in her little mind that she will be
forgiven more easily if she owns up.' In her own opinion her
chief fault was *a great self love.* She also admits to a certain
vanity. *Dressed in a pretty sky-blue frock trimmed with lace,* she
was sorry that, for fear of sunburn, her pretty bare arms had
to be covered.

TO PLEASE JESUS

The Martins were devout but they were not bigots. As the
older girls grew up they became dress-conscious. 'We are
truly slaves of fashion,' the mother complained. But she was
not sorry that 'Céline and Thérèse could be dressed better
than Marie and Pauline ever were'. When the aunt from Le
Mans criticised Marie's going to a worldly party, Mme
Martin reacted strongly: 'Should we therefore lock ourselves
up in a cloister? In the world, you can't live like wolves! The
blessed woman would have us pick and choose.'

However the neighbours noticed the pair of them going
down the rue Saint-Blaise each morning to the 5.30 mass for
'the poor and the workers'. Strict fasting was observed in the
family. The Sabbath rest, family prayers, the annual cycle of
liturgical ceremonies, were kept sacred. 'I belong to all the
societies,' declared Zélie. But she lost neither her common
sense nor her straightforwardness: 'For the past eight days
we have had two missionaries who give us three sermons a
day. In my opinion, they both preach badly. We go to listen
to them just the same out of duty and, for me at least, it is
one more penance.'

There was nothing rigid or pharisaical in this devoutness.
The Martins knew how to put their religion into practice.
They would welcome a tramp to their table and take steps
to have him admitted to the home for Incurables. They visited

42. - ALENÇON (Orne). - Rue St-Blaise,

Edit. Toutain, Alençon

7 Rue Saint-Blaise, Alençon

lonely old men, the sick and the dying. Zélie would help a mother in difficulties, and care for inexperienced maids. Not without fear, she exposed as impostors two nuns who were exploiting and terrorising Armandine V., a child of eight.

Thérèse plunged into the world. *To please Jesus* was her concern. *Is he pleased with me? It was enough for one to say a thing wasn't good and I had no desire to repeat it.* This did not spring from fear – she knew forgiveness was always possible – but from that instinct for truthfulness which was always hers. 'She wouldn't tell a lie for all the gold in the world.' Her very delicate conscience loved the light.

But she did not see herself as the exemplary little girl whom, much later, her sisters were to idealise. She was full of life, as the following account shows: Marie had put her into a cold bed without making her say her prayers. 'She began to cry saying that she wanted a warm bed. I listened to that music the whole time I was saying my prayers. Wearied of it, I gave her a little slap, and finally she got tired of it. When I had got into bed, she told me that she had not said her prayers. I replied: "Go to sleep, you can say them in the morning." But she would not let the matter drop.'

Another day she repeatedly begged to go to mass. 'I told her she was not good at church. On Sunday I had taken her to vespers and she had given me no peace, and besides, we were only going to benediction. Then she took me to task for not taking her to Lisieux. I told her it was because she was too boisterous. That did not please her and she began to cry.' At the age of four, during interminable sermons, she used to yawn. 'The little one was noticeably bored. She said: *It is more beautiful than usual, but it bores me just the same.* Then she sighed deeply. Finally the torch-light procession caught her attention.'

Her curiosity turned towards heaven. Would she go there? With expression and actions, she would recite:

> Little child with golden hair,
> where is God, now can you say?
> He's in this world everywhere.
> He's up there in the blue sky.

At four and a half she played nuns, and made herself the superior. Pauline had told her that one did not speak in the convent. Thérèse wondered how you could pray *without saying anything.* She concluded: *After all, Pauline, it's not worth troubling about now, don't you see, when I am big like you and Marie, before I enter the convent, someone will tell me how to do it.*

What contrasts there are in my character! she was to say before her death. Thoughtful and exuberant, meditative and outgoing, headstrong and gentle, she knew violent interior struggles which often passed unnoticed by those around her. *I had already firm control over my actions.* She *had acquired the good habit of never complaining,* even when someone took what was hers, or when she was accused unjustly. She preferred *to be silent and not to make excuses.*

In *Story of a Soul,* Thérèse devotes only fifteen pages to her childhood at Alençon. She concludes with these words: *Everything on this earth smiled on me. I found flowers under each of my steps, and my happy disposition contributed much to making life pleasant.* This appreciation, made in latter years, is confirmed by the description Marie sent to Pauline, just before misfortune was to strike the Martin family:

If you only knew how mischievous she is, but not silly. How I admire this little posy! Everyone in the house covers her with kisses, poor little thing! But she is so used to kisses that she scarcely notices them any more. When Céline sees her offhand manner she reproaches her: 'You'd think all those kisses were the little madam's right!' And you should see Thérèse's face!

MADAME MARTIN'S ILLNESS

Pauline was the only one still boarding at Le Mans, and her letters do not have the same joyful tone. They describe the slow decline of her aunt, Sister Marie-Dosithée, who was dying of tuberculosis. Zélie was very much affected by this long illness. Until that time, she had held her own. Despite her headaches, eye-strain and stomach trouble – especially during the Lenten fasts. But at the end of December 1876 she consulted Dr Prévost. His frankness left no room for hope: it was very serious, it would be useless to operate on that 'fibrous tumour'.

The family was stunned and dismayed (the two little ones were not told the truth). Louis was 'dumbfounded'. His wife calmly took stock of the situation: 'I am grateful (to the doctor) for his honesty, for I will set to and wind up my affairs, so as not to leave my family in financial difficulties.'

Her chemist brother made her go to Lisieux to consult Dr Notta, a noted surgeon. He too advised against an operation. It was too late. The sick woman wrote to her husband to reassure him: 'The doctor seemed to indicate that I could go on like this for a very long time. So let us put ourselves in God's hands, he knows much better than we do what is necessary for us: "He is the one who wounds, and who binds up our wounds".'

On her return to Lisieux Zélie kept busy, hid her pain and did her best to be cheerful. Her concern was directed more towards Le Mans where her sister died on 24 February 1877. For Zélie this was a vital link broken. 'It was after my aunt's death', Pauline wrote later, 'that her condition deteriorated.'

At one time she had considered selling her business. But she abandoned the idea and accepted, among others, an order for fifteen metres of lace to be made up in four months. ('I will therefore have to work until the end!') She suffered more and more, alternating between hope and fear. Her one great anxiety was to have her five daughters settled. Marie was wild and shy; she had always said she did not want to marry and protested loudly that she would never be a nun. However certain indications showed that she was thinking about it; as was Léonie, but their mother could not see the latter living in a community 'without a miracle'. Léonie would not leave the sick woman's side. She covered her with kisses, which restored her mother's hope: 'This is why I now have a desire to live, which I did not feel before. I am very necessary to this child.' At times the contrary was true, the cancer had made 'frightening' progress and she saw herself lost. But what clear-sightedness! 'I am like all the people I have known who do not see their own condition. Only others see it clearly, amazed that the sick promise themselves unlimited time when their days are numbered. It is indeed strange, but that is how it is, and I am just like the rest.'

Pauline, who was so close to her ('you are my friend'), also thought seriously of becoming a Visitandine nun. The two youngest did not worry their mother, especially not Thérèse: despite certain whims, 'she will be good, you can see the beginnings of it already, she speaks only of God'. 'This little one will manage.'

Spring restored the garden to the two 'inseparables', Céline and Thérèse: they counted their good deeds on a string of beads (Thérèse sometimes making a mistake: she counted even her mistakes); played wolf, blew soap bubbles, climbed trees. Life was stronger than misfortune.

PILGRIMAGE TO LOURDES (17–23 JUNE 1877)

Although she did not like travelling Zélie decided to go to Lourdes with her three elder children, leaving the little ones with her husband. The departure from Alençon was set for Sunday, 17 June.

There was a final consultation with Dr Prévost, with whom

she did not get on well. As soon as she got home she threw his prescription on the fire without reading it. Only a miracle could save her. She hoped for one.

At the Visitation convent at Le Mans she was surrounded by affection and prayer: all the nuns were praying for her cure and the chaplain was already preparing a mass of thanksgiving for her return.

'Tell me if anyone could have had a worse journey,' Zélie wrote to her brother on 24 June. Her sufferings grew worse from the fatigue of long hours in the train; there were delays and all sorts of mishaps (she lost her dead sister's rosary, the bottles of Lourdes water leaked, their provisions were uneatable, she tore her clothes, they missed the train, her daughters complained). Everything had conspired to make this pilgrimage an additional trial.

During the three days at Lourdes the sick woman had plunged four times into the icy water of the baths. As each hour went by the daughters asked her if she had been cured, whereas she was suffering terribly. Their disappointment affected her. On returning to Le Mans she had had to submit to a flood of questions, and at Alençon to the taunts of the sceptical. She told the Guérins about her trip: 'I am not cured, on the contrary the journey has aggravated the disease ... I am not sorry I went to Lourdes, although the fatigue has made me worse; at least I will have nothing to reproach myself with, if I am not cured. In the meantime let us hope.'

She had two months to live. With Marie's help she continued to run her business and the household. 'Mamma still wanted to go to early mass, but it took courage and extraordinary efforts for her to reach the church. Each step she took reverberated in her neck and sometimes she was forced to stop to regain a little strength.'

Her suffering, especially at night, became unbearable. She cried out. But she had to keep going to the end. At the beginning of August one of her last pleasures was to preside with Louis at the family distribution of prizes at 'the Visitation of Holy Mary of Alençon', organised by the two 'teachers'. 'Our two little ones were in white and you should have seen their triumphant faces as they came up to get their prizes and crowns.'

This interlude marked the beginning of the sad holidays.

The mother wanted her husband to take the younger children out in a boat. They were sent away from the house. *All the details of my mother's illness are still present in my heart. I remember the last weeks she spent on earth. Céline and I were like poor exiles. Every morning Mme Leriche came to get us and we spent the day with her.*

Thérèse would never forget the rite of the last anointing on Sunday, 26 August. *I can still see the place where I stood next to Céline. All five of us were in line according to age, and poor Papa was there too, sobbing.*

Summoned by telegram, the Guérins arrived at Alençon on the Monday evening, 27th. The dying woman could no longer speak to them.

HER MOTHER'S DEATH (28 AUGUST 1877)

Mme Martin died the following day at half-past twelve. Her husband and brother were with her. She was nearly forty-six.

The father took his four and a half year old daughter in his arms: *Come, kiss your poor little mother for the last time. And without saying anything I put my lips on my dear mother's forehead.* She who cried so easily did not remember crying very much. *I did not speak to anyone about the deep feelings I experienced – I looked and listened in silence.* In the general confusion in the house no one paid any attention to her. She saw *many things they would have preferred to hide* from her. *Once, I was standing in front of the coffin lid; I stood looking at it for a long time. I had never seen one before but I knew what it was. I was so little that, in spite of Mamma's small stature, I had to lift up my head to see the top of it, and it seemed to me to be so big, so dismal.*

This was her first brutal experience of death. No one knew then how deeply her mother's death had affected her. In the months that followed nothing showed. Later she was to say that the first part of her life ended that day. A pall had come down over a childhood that had been filled with love and happiness.

How does one live when a mother like that – who held such a place in the family – is gone? The balance of family life was disrupted; it would have to 'organise itself' in a new way. But nothing would ever be the same.

After the funeral at Our Lady's cemetery on Wednesday, 29 August Louise Marais (the maid) looked sadly at the two young orphans: 'Poor little ones, you no longer have a mother!' Céline threw herself into Marie's arms: 'Well, you will be my Mamma!' Then Thérèse ran to Pauline: *Well, for me, Pauline will be Mamma!*

THE GREAT DEPARTURE (15 NOVEMBER 1877)

Their father was fifty-four years old. His wife's death had hit him hard: how would he cope with five daughters? His sister-in-law, who had been with Zélie when she died and seen her last look, had taken it as an appeal to care for her children. She proposed a wise solution: the Martins should come and live in Lisieux.

Louis had no desire to uproot himself but gave in to the Guérins' reasoning. 'For us', Marie wrote, 'he would make any sacrifice. He would sacrifice his happiness, his life if need be, to make us happy. He did not shrink from anything, he did not hesitate for one moment. He believed it was his duty and for the good of all of us, and that was enough for him.'

The ever-active Uncle Isidore set out to find them a house. By 10 September he had sent an enthusiastic description of a house – one among twenty-five he had inspected. On the 16th after a family council M. Martin signed the lease of Les Buissonnets. Isidore Guérin was appointed deputy guardian of his five young nieces.

On 15 November 1877, after a last prayer at the cemetery, Louis Martin left the rue Saint-Blaise with his daughters, in black, and made the four-hour train journey to Lisieux where they spent the first night with the Guérins in the place Saint-Pierre. He went back to Alençon to wind up his affairs and finally rejoined his children at Les Buissonnets on 30 November. He had sold his business for 3,000F payable within five years.

Little Thérèse did not see her birthplace again for six years. She had left that happy world behind. *How quickly the sunny years of my childhood passed by!*

Part II

Les Buissonnets
1877–1888

8 Les Buissonnets

2

Before School
(16 November 1877 to 3 October 1881)

... the second period of my life the most painful of the three.

THE WAY TO PARADISE

I did not feel any great disappointment at leaving Alençon: children like change, and I came to Lisieux with pleasure.

Thérèse was to live in this new world for eleven years. The house was near the Jardin de l'Etoile, a park open to keyholders not very far from the Delauney barracks. To the left of a steep narrow road, which M. Martin called 'The Way to Paradise', the front gate stood opposite a street lamp: beyond the lawn was a middle-class house consisting of two stories and a belvedere, four bedrooms and three attics. At the back was a garden, the laundry, a shed and a greenhouse. It was surrounded by walls and trees and cut off from the town, which could be partly seen.

The family settled in. On the ground floor was the kitchen with its large fireplace. The well was a few yards outside. The windows and door of the dining room opened on to the front garden. A very narrow staircase led to the older girls' bedrooms. To one side was their father's bedroom. Céline and Thérèse's room was near Léonie's and had a door opening on to the back garden. From the belvedere the whole of Lisieux could be viewed, the cathedral towers and the bell-tower of Saint-Jacques, the Martins' parish church. From this third story the view was often hidden by the mist which rose up from the valleys of the Orbiquet, the Touques and the Cirieux, when it was not blotted out by smoke from the factories. The Martins arrived there in the winter.

LISIEUX IN 1877

With its 18,600 inhabitants, linen-thread and cloth mills, cider presses, tanneries and distilleries, Lisieux could claim to be the principal industrial city of Calvados. The Saturday markets filled the town with produce from the Norman countryside. Lisieux still looked medieval with its old streets lined with half-timbered houses: the rue aux Fèvres (Street of Fevers), rue du Paradis, rue d'Ouville, place des Boucheries (Butchers' place). On feast days the military band of the 119th Infantry regiment made a cheerful noise in the public gardens in the shadow of the cathedral.

After the 1870 war the town declined because of a recession in the textile industry. Several strikes broke out, and the birth-rate fell. But the Martins lived on the fringes of that world.

A NEW LIFE

To the four-and-a-half-year-old newcomer Lisieux meant holidays, the family atmosphere of the Guérin household, games with cousins Jeanne who was ten, and Marie, seven and a half. Uncle Isidore with his pince-nez and deep voice scared her somewhat, especially when he took her on his knee and sang 'Blue Beard'. But she listened attentively to all his stories. He met so many people in his chemist's shop.

The little girl felt the complete change of atmosphere. At Alençon the house was on the street. She saw everything that passed by. Women workers and customers brought life to the tiny rooms. At Les Buissonnets silence reigned. The garden, which was ever so much bigger, delighted her with its flowers and groves, and soon there were hens, ducks and an aviary. But where was the life her busy mother had brought to the home?

Here she found a completely different sort of existence, perfectly regulated. After that great sorrow the family closed ranks. There were few visits, they did not know anyone. Her father, cut off from his friends, was able to indulge his inclination for solitude. He made the belvedere his favourite retreat: there he read, wrote and meditated. He did the garden

– out of duty – and looked after the poultry-yard and the wood for the fire. He was not fifty-five and found himself retired, only having to manage his finances which amounted to about 140,000F. His white beard made him look old. To his daughters he was already 'the Patriarch'.

Marie, at seventeen, took charge of the running of the house. Pauline, now sixteen, helped her and took over the education of the two little ones, especially Thérèse. Léonie who was fourteen went as a boarder to the Benedictines at the abbey in the western section of the town. Céline presently became a day-pupil there.

Deprived of her playmate Thérèse spent long days with adults in that house which felt so big to her. A maid was engaged, Victoire Pasquer, who for seven years was to share the Martins' life. Others followed her.

In this new world a profound change came about in Thérèse. *After Mamma's death my happy disposition changed completely. I, who had been so full of life, so outgoing, became shy, quiet and oversensitive. A look was enough to reduce me to tears. I was only happy when no one paid any attention to me. I could not bear the company of strangers, and only regained my cheerfulness within the intimacy of my family.* Looking back over the years, Thérèse would see the move to Les Buissonnets as the beginning of the *second period of (her) life, the most painful of the three: it extends from the age of four and a half to fourteen, the time when I rediscovered my childhood character, and entered into the serious side of life.*

FROM FIVE TO EIGHT YEARS OLD

In this very feminine atmosphere the only men little Thérèse met were her father and her uncle.

She was to recall a typical day in those first three years. Pauline, her 'Mamma', called her and she got up and said her prayers, dressed and had breakfast (soup). In the morning there were writing lessons from Marie and reading and catechism from Pauline, which ended with a visit to her father up in the belvedere. The conscientious pupil had a good memory and she loved Scripture but grammar and spelling often caused tears to flow. In the afternoon if it was not too wet (Lisieux was often humid) there would be a walk with

Papa to the Jardin de l'Etoile, a visit to a church, the buying of a present worth one or two sous; and in the summer there were fishing trips to the surrounding green country towards Roques or Hermival.

The Lisieux people began to notice the daily walk of that 'handsome old man' and the child with the blonde curls. She called him her 'King'; he called her his 'Queen', his 'little grey wolf', 'the orphan of Beresina', his 'crowning glory', his 'blonde scatterbrain'. They returned in time for her to do her homework. After supper the family would gather round a blazing fire for the evening. Papa used to sing 'The Exiled Breton' or 'The Song of the Angels', recite Victor Hugo and Lamartine, and read from Dom Guéranger's recently published *Liturgical Year*. Thérèse and Céline played with small toys the former watchmaker made for them. After prayers and goodnight kisses it was early to bed in the large unheated room. One last kiss for Pauline; when the oil lamp was put out she was afraid of the dark.

Sundays and feast days fortunately broke this rhythm and added a little colour. She had a long sleep and breakfast in bed (with hot chocolate). Marie would dress Thérèse who cried when her hair got pulled during the curling process. They would all set out for mass at the cathedral, which they preferred to the parish church, for they saw the Guérins there. From his churchwarden's pew Uncle Isidore would smile at his niece. Some months after their arrival she understood Abbé Ducellier's sermon for the first time. He was a good speaker despite his husky voice. He spoke on the passion of Jesus.

The meal which followed at the Guérins' was a pleasure. What a lot went on in the heart of the town! Then Thérèse would stay on with them, sometimes with Marie, sometimes with Céline, and Papa came back for them on Sunday evening. At the beginning of 1878 the family circle was increased by the Fournets and Maudelondes, who were the Guérins' relations.

Such beautiful days passed all too quickly. Then it was Monday, and study again. Pauline took her role of mother seriously (perhaps too seriously). With her sister she let nothing go. It was her father who had to ask her not to cancel the afternoon walk when the morning lessons were not quite

9 The dining room at Les Buissonnets

up to the mark. There were never any compliments for the pupil; that might give rise to vanity.

The garden at Les Buissonnets, and nature in general, enchanted her. In the flower-strewn fields of Saint-Martin-de-la-Lieue or Ouilly-le-Vicomte she went quiet, looked about her, picked flowers: *My thoughts became very profound and, without knowing what meditation was, my soul became absorbed in real prayer . . . The earth seemed to be a place of exile and I dreamt of heaven.* Heaven was where her mother and four little brothers and sisters were. She could not bear the thought of death – especially the possible death of her father. She would have preferred to die with him. *I cannot say how much I loved Papa, everything in him made me love him.* He 'did everything she wanted'. He shared his thoughts with her. To know how to pray she only had to look at him in church or at home in the evening.

During the year, on 1 January and 25 August (St Louis's feast day), she would recite poems for her father which Pauline had written and in an unchanging ritual, wearing her best dress, her hair all curled, the little Queen would offer her greeting in the belvedere where 'the five diamonds had joined the beloved King'.

The first summer at Les Buissonnets M. Martin, a keen traveller, decided to visit Paris with his two eldest daughters. They went to the World Exhibition at the Palais de l'Industrie, to Versailles, and to the Bidel Circus. Thérèse stayed with her aunt from 17 June to 2 July. 'She is not at all bored, she is not hard to look after for she amuses herself with anything. She is even quite cheerful.' Her laughter won Mme Guérin who held her hand to finish a letter to Pauline.

The Guérins rented a house at Trouville (seaside resorts had only been in fashion for twenty years) and the sisters stayed there in turn. They went paddling with their cousins and fished for eels. Thursday, 8 August 1878 was a memorable day for her father was going to fetch Marie and he took Thérèse on the 30km train journey from Lisieux to Trouville. *Never will I forget the impression the sea made on me.* Neither did she forget that it was on that day that she attracted the attention and compliments of a couple who found her 'very pretty'. *It was the first time I had heard it said I was pretty and it pleased me, for I did not think that I was.* At home she was told rather the opposite.

Only one incident of her sixth year has come down to us: an outburst of anger against Victoire the maid, who enjoyed annoying Mlle Thérèse. On another occasion the teaser saw herself treated in a humiliating way: *Victoire, you are a brat!* Usually gentle and retiring, the little Martin retained both her temper and her dignity. But it did not prevent her one day from falling into a bucket of water and becoming stuck in it, or finding herself in the fireplace covered with ashes, luckily when there was no fire.

CÉLINE'S FIRST COMMUNION (13 MAY 1880)

Thérèse's first confession to Abbé Ducellier at the cathedral took place that year. She knelt in the confessional and was

10 Pupils at the Abbey in 1880. From the bottom: Marie Guérin is first on the left in the second row, Céline Martin third from the left in the same row. Léonie Martin is third from the left in the fifth row

so small that when the priest slid back the shutter he did not see her. She had to speak standing up. Carefully prepared by Pauline, she wondered whether she ought to tell him she loved him with all her heart, *since he was taking God's place. Since then I have gone to confession at all the big feasts, and each is a real feast for me.* At that time fear and scruples were unknown to her.

There were other feasts, and processions of the Blessed Sacrament in which she strewed rose petals. When Céline made her first communion, on Thursday, 13 May, Thérèse listened to everything Pauline told her sister. She had a heavy heart when she was sent away: she was too little. But Céline's joy became hers. *It seemed as if it was I who was going to make my first communion. I believe I received great graces that day and I regard it as one of the most beautiful in my life.* She decided then she had to begin, from that moment, a new life. Three years was not too long to prepare herself for her own communion. The following Christmas she very much wanted to go to communion, sneaking in among the grown-ups. *I am so little, no one would see me.* Marie did not allow it.

PROPHETIC VISION

In those still happy years a disturbing event made a deep impression on the little girl. One summer day (in 1879 or 1880) in the early afternoon, Marie and Pauline heard their little sister call out: 'Papa! Papa!' He was at Alençon at the time as he liked to go back occasionally to see his friends Boul, Romet, Leriche and Tifenne. From her window Thérèse said she had seen *a man dressed exactly like Papa*, bent over and covering his head with a sort of apron, cross the bottom of the garden and disappear behind a hedge. Had Victoire been playing a practical joke? The maid denied it; she had not left her kitchen. The shrubs were thoroughly searched. Nothing. The mystery remained. Her sisters tried to reassure the child. *It was beyond my power not to think any more about it.* It took fourteen years for the Martins, who were then Carmelites, to understand the meaning of that mysterious happening.

In all, her first three years at Les Buissonnets left Thérèse with a happy memory. The atmosphere was warm, very femi-

nine and maternal (her father's tender heart now felt motherly
love as well as the love he had always felt). This filled her
great need for affection. *I continued to be surrounded by the most
loving tenderness.*

That happy period came to an end.

At School with the Benedictines
(3 October 1881 to March 1886)

The five years I spent at school were the saddest in my life.

On 3 October 1881 Thérèse was eight and a half and it was her turn to go to the Benedictine school, which Léonie had just left. She went into the fourth or 'green' class, so-called because of the green sash worn over the uniform. She walked the 1.5km to the abbey with Céline, her cousins Jeanne and Marie and accompanied by Marcelline, the Guérins' maid. They arrived there at about eight o'clock. In the afternoon the father or uncle would pick up the little band. *I have often heard it said that the time spent at school is the best and happiest of one's life. It wasn't so for me. The five years I spent at school were the saddest in my life, and if my dear Céline had not been with me I could not have stayed there for a single month without falling ill.*

Marie and Pauline's lessons bore fruit. Except for writing and arithmetic Thérèse found herself top of the class. But she did not enjoy her new common life. Some backward pupils – one was thirteen – were jealous and bullied her. Thérèse cried, without daring to complain. The boisterous games at recreation frightened her. She did not like running and did not know how to play with dolls. She preferred to tell stories (she had a gift for it), bury dead birds or look after the little ones in the infants class. When she was 'attacked' by the older girls, Céline the 'Intrepid' came to her sister's defence. A former teacher described Thérèse in these words: 'She was obedient, meticulously faithful to the smallest detail of the rules. She got upset even at the prospect of a fault which sometimes made her seem overscrupulous. She was usually quiet, calm and reserved (generally thought to be too much so for her age), and sometimes seemed dreamy. Her face portrayed a certain sadness.'

What a relief to come home in the evening to Les Buissonnets! She was thrilled to be back with her father and sisters, her own world, her pet magpie which followed her about in the garden. *Then my heart expanded.* Sundays and Thursdays became her important days when she recovered her composure. With 'Loulou' – her cousin Marie – she invented a new game: living as hermits at the bottom of the garden: silence, prayers, various ceremonies, dressing-up near little altars erected in the laundry. One day however she told her Mamma Pauline that she would like to be a hermit and go off with her to a far desert place. The young girl had answered with a smile: 'I will wait for you.' Thérèse believed her.

On the other hand the 'social' gatherings with the Guérins and their Maudelonde cousins, the interminable Thursday afternoons when she had to dance quadrilles, bored her stiff. She admits that she did not know how to play like other children.

What she did like was reading. *It would be impossible for me to say how many books passed through my hands.* Tales of chivalry fired her with enthusiasm. She loved above all the French heroine Joan of Arc (not then canonised). She believed that she too had been born for glory. Not a spectacular glory like that of the Maid of Lorraine but a hidden glory: *to become a great saint.*

She also spent hours looking at pictures, some of which fascinated her, especially the one which depicted Jesus the 'Prisoner' behind a tabernacle grille.

How hard it was to go back to school! The only happy moments she experienced there were the ten minutes before the end of recreation when she could go and pray in the chapel.

THE LOSS OF HER SECOND MOTHER (15 OCTOBER 1882)

What Thérèse did not know was that her second Mamma, her father's 'fine pearl', had decided during mass at Saint-Jacques's church to become a Carmelite. It was a sudden inspiration, for Pauline had been thinking for a long time of

11 Céline, with Thérèse aged 8 (1881)

the Visitation convent at Le Mans. The same day she told Marie and her father, who gave his consent. A visit to the Carmel in the rue de Livarot followed, where the prioress, Mother Marie de Gonzague, approved the decision. This was a surprise, for Pauline had first thought of entering the Carmel of Caen. But there was a place for her at Lisieux. Everyone therefore heard the news – except her little sister.

During the summer of 1882 Pauline and Marie were talking about her forthcoming departure and Thérèse, by chance, overheard them.

It was like a sword piercing my heart. I did not know what Carmel was, but I understood that Pauline was going to leave me and enter a convent. I understood that she WOULD NOT WAIT FOR ME *and that I was going to lose my second mother! Ah! how can I express the anguish in my heart? In an instant I understood what life was; until then I had not imagined it could be so sad, but it appeared to me in its stark reality. I saw that it was only continual suffering and separation. I shed very bitter tears.*

Pauline, in the first fervour of her vocation, did not realise she had deeply hurt her sister. Very much later she would bitterly regret her behaviour 'Ah! if I had known it would cause her to suffer so much, I would have gone about it in another way. I would have told her everything!'

She then had to try and console Thérèse by explaining the Carmelite life to her. Through her tears the child listened intently. *I felt that Carmel was* THE DESERT *where God wanted me to go and hide too. I was so sure of this that there wasn't the least doubt in my heart.* Writing these lines thirteen years after the event Thérèse pre-empted the obvious objection: *It was not the dream of a child that lets itself be carried away, but the* CERTITUDE *of a divine call. I wanted to go to Carmel, not for Pauline* (to rejoin her lost mother), *but* FOR JESUS ALONE. *I thought very much about things which words could not express, but which left great peace in my soul.*

The next day she told Pauline her secret. One Sunday in the parlour of the Carmel the nine-year-old candidate devised a way to remain alone for a moment with Mother Marie de Gonzague. The latter *believed she had a vocation*, but said she could not accept a postulant under sixteen. Thérèse would wait. From then on she knew what she wanted to do with her life.

During the few weeks before Pauline's departure Thérèse devoured her with kisses, stuffed her with cakes and showered her with gifts. As the departure date drew near her heart ached.

Despite brilliant sunshine Monday, 2 October 1882 was a *day of tears*. While Louis Martin accompanied Pauline to the Carmel where she was welcomed by her director, Abbé Ducellier, and the superior, M. Delatroëtte, the parish priest of Saint-Jacques, the Guérins took the whole family to mass. The faithful were surprised to see all these young girls in tears. Full of sadness after that painful ceremony, Thérèse had to return to school to begin a new year. She set out miserably for the abbey. Did she notice the preparations busily under way for the third centenary of the death of Teresa of Avila, the foundress of the Carmelite Reform, and her patron saint?

She went up a class, into the 'violet class', which prepared children for first communion. Religious knowledge therefore had an important place. On Thursdays and Sundays M. Domin the chaplain, who was forty, gave instruction in the chapel, in addition to the three weekly lessons of the teacher in charge of communion candidates. Thérèse excelled in religious instruction. At this unhappy time the prospect of her communion, so long awaited, brought a ray of light. Alas, a recent episcopal ruling excluded her from the preparation: she had been born two days too late. M. Guérin did not hesitate to go to Bayeux to seek a dispensation from the bishop. The refusal was kind but firm; no exception could be made, not even for the niece of a well known and respected chemist of Lisieux. There were floods of tears; it was too much for the sensitive little girl.

THE ANGUISH OF THE PARLOUR VISITS

Even to see her Pauline again in the parlour every Thursday – a privilege given to the Martins by the prioress – became a source of torment for her. In that austere place with its double grilles and curtains (although the postulant was seen by her family), the half hour, timed by an hour-glass, passed too quickly. Marie and the Guérin ladies talked and talked. Thérèse could only get two or three short minutes at the end. Pauline, now Sister Agnès of Jesus, entirely caught up in the conversation, paid no attention to her sister, she did not notice her new skirt. Thérèse sulked and left the parlour in tears. *Ah! how I suffered in this* PARLOUR *of Carmel . . . I must say that the sufferings which had preceded Pauline's entrance were nothing in comparison with those which followed it.*

When reading these lines much later Pauline would say again: 'Ah, if I had known!' The child was in despair: *I said in the depths of my heart: Pauline is lost to me!!!* This shock reawakened in her the trauma caused by her mother's death which had remained latent until then. At ten years old she had already lost two mothers.

DISTURBING SYMPTOMS

In about December the pupil in the 'violet class' who had made a good start to the school year began to suffer from continual headaches and pains in her side and stomach. She broke out in a rash, lost her appetite and slept badly. In the parlour Sister Agnès was worried about her 'baby's' face 'which was always so pale'. Even her personality was disturbed. This time Thérèse did not choose Marie to be her third Mamma; the eldest sister assumed this role, undoubtedly with some severity. Thérèse always 'answered her back' when she was told to do something. There were 'little tiffs' with Céline! The Carmelite was lavish with little notes which combined affectionate reprimands with good advice. Mother Marie de Gonzague went one better, without suspecting that she was aggravating the trouble, and put her finger on the secret wound: 'I heard that my little daughter Thérèse of the Child Jesus[1] was not sleeping very much and that she was ill. I want to tell my angel child that she must not think all day long about my Agnès of Jesus; that would weary our little heart and could damage our health!'

[1] Thérèse had chosen this name herself and, without knowing this, Mother Marie de Gonzague gave it to her.

SUCH A STRANGE ILLNESS (25 MARCH TO 13 MAY 1883)

The prioress had been right. Without complaining the child, who was just ten years old, continued her life as usual. In her relationship with Céline the roles had been reversed: the latter had become a mischievous little imp of fourteen, Thérèse just *a sweet little girl who cried too much*. When word of any squabbles reached Sister Agnès's ear she advised the older girl to give in.

For the Easter holidays of 1883 Louis Martin decided to spend Holy Week in Paris with Marie and Léonie. Thérèse and Céline would stay with the Guérins. Their daughter Marie said a cruel thing one day, as children will. Thérèse had called her aunt 'Mamma' and her cousin reacted quickly: 'My Mamma is not your Mamma. You no longer have one.'

On 25 March, Easter Sunday night, Isidore Guérin, equally tactless at dinner, recalled memories of his sister and life at Alençon. Thérèse burst into tears. She was quickly put to bed while her uncle and his daughters went to the Catholic Circle. She began to tremble all over, felt cold and was very agitated. On his return the chemist was gravely concerned when he saw his niece's condition. The next day he called in Dr Notta whose diagnosis was vague but pessimistic: it was a 'very serious illness which had never before attacked a child'. He prescribed hydrotherapy. A telegram summoned 'the Parisians' who returned in all haste. When they arrived Aimée the cook greeted them with such distress in her face that for a few moments, they thought Thérèse was dead. She could not be moved so was looked after by her aunt and her sister Marie.

The maid, Marcelline Husé, gave testimony of 'a nervous trembling, followed by seizures of fright and hallucination which recurred several times a day. In the intervening periods the sick child was in a very weak state and could not be left alone. After the crises she remembered clearly what had happened.' Jeanne Guérin also gave her account: 'At the worst time, there were also several attacks when the motor nerves were affected and she was able to wheel her whole body round which she would have been absolutely incapable of doing when well.' *The illness became so serious that, according to human calculation, I would not recover from it.*

There was general consternation. This was only increased by Thérèse ceaselessly repeating that she wanted to go to Pauline's reception of the habit, which was fixed for 6 April. They avoided speaking of the Carmelite in front of her.

Contrary to all expectation, after a more than usually violent crisis on the morning of Friday, 6 April the sick child got up 'cured' and went to the Carmel with all the family. They would not let her attend the ceremony but in the outside parlour afterwards she sat on the knee of her re-found mother and covered her with kisses. All that day she appeared to be full of joy and life. Those around her thought they were dreaming. She returned to Les Buissonnets in a carriage and despite her persistent assertions – *I am perfectly cured* – was put to bed.

The next day there was an even more serious relapse.

I said and did things that were not in my mind, I seemed to be almost always delirious, saying things that had no meaning, and nevertheless I am sure that I was not DEPRIVED OF THE USE OF MY REASON *for a* SINGLE MOMENT. *I often appeared to be in a faint, not making the slightest movement and at those times anyone could have done anything to me, even killed me, and yet I heard everything that was said around me.*

Marie, who was often with her, caring for her and comforting her with *a mother's tenderness*, witnessed her hallucinations. Dr Notta remained evasive and worried: 'It is not hysteria.' Was it St Vitus's dance? M. Martin wondered if his *poor little girl who was like an idiot* was going to die or remain in this condition for the rest of her life.

All the family prayed together with the Carmel. A novena of masses was offered at Our Lady of Victories, the Paris shrine so loved by the Martins and Guérins. A miracle was sought. The statue of the Virgin Mary which had always followed the family was placed in Marie's room, where Thérèse had been moved.

The only moments of remission were when Thérèse received a letter from Pauline. Those letters were read, re-read and learnt by heart. The chemist uncle was annoyed when he saw one of his niece's dolls dressed as a Carmelite. It would be better to make this child forget Carmel.

It was an impossible situation.

YOU WHO CAME AND SMILED ON ME IN THE MORNING OF
MY LIFE (13 MAY 1883)

On Whit Sunday during the novena to Our Lady of Victories,
while Léonie was looking after her, the sick child was continually calling out: 'Mamma', 'Mamma', as was her custom.
Marie who was in the garden finally went up to her. Then
Marie, Léonie and Céline knelt at the foot of the bed and
turned towards the statue. Thérèse recounts:

> *Finding no help on earth, poor little Thérèse also turned towards
> her heavenly Mother and prayed with all her heart for her to have
> pity on her at last. All of a sudden the blessed Virgin appeared to
> me beautiful, more beautiful than anything I had ever seen before.
> Her face expressed an ineffable goodness and tenderness, but what
> went right to the depths of my soul was* THE BLESSED VIRGIN'S
> RAVISHING SMILE. *Then all my pain vanished, two large tears
> welled up on my eyelashes and silently rolled down my cheeks, but
> they were tears of pure joy. Ah! I thought, the blessed Virgin has
> smiled at me, how happy I am – but I will never tell anyone, for
> then* MY HAPPINESS WOULD DISAPPEAR.

The three sisters witnessed this scene and the relaxed
condition of the sick child. The next day she resumed her
ordinary life. During the following months, in the garden,
Léonie opposed her twice. She fell down and remained
stretched out for some moments, her body rigid. But there
was no delirium or violent spasm. From that time there was
no recurrence of any trouble of this kind.

But Thérèse remained psychologically delicate, and those
around her were deeply affected by that dramatic illness. The
doctor had warned the family to avoid any violent emotion
which could be harmful to the child, and each did their best
to coddle her more. 'Beware of a relapse! Do not oppose her!'
was the implicit order, but this was not going to help Thérèse
to grow up.

Twelve years later Thérèse gave her interpretation of her
illness: *It certainly came from the Devil who was infuriated by your
entrance into Carmel. He wanted to take revenge on me for the wrong
our family was to do to him in the future.* She added: *My soul was
FAR from mature.*

At the end of May she was finally able to return to the

parlour at Carmel, looking very pretty all in black, in mourning for her grandmother Martin who had died during her illness (8 April).

TWO INNER TRIALS

The cure itself was the source of a twofold inner martyrdom for her.

She had promised herself that she would keep the Blessed Virgin's smile a secret. But her sister Marie forced her to tell and had told the Carmelites. A miracle was proclaimed. In the parlour the community gazed on the child who had been miraculously cured and assailed her with questions: 'What was the Blessed Virgin like? What colours did she wear, the same as at Lourdes? Was there light?' The child was distressed. Her joy turned to anguish. She felt a traitor and could not look at herself *without feeling profound horror*.

Her sense of guilt was increased by another doubt which was to torment her for five years. Given the symptoms of her strange illness, had she not brought it on herself? She believed she had lied. She tried in vain to talk about it to Marie, to Abbé Ducellier, her confessor, but nothing would set her mind at rest. *Ah, what I suffered I shall not be able to say except in heaven!*

FIRST ENTRANCE INTO THE WORLD: ALENÇON (20 AUGUST TO 3 SEPTEMBER 1883)

It was thought prudent not to let the convalescent go back to school. To celebrate her recovery she went on her first long holiday from the closed world of Lisieux, and made her 'entrance into the world'.

For the first time she revisited the places of her childhood at Alençon. The pilgrimage to her mother's grave passed without incident. Introduced into her father's circle of friends, the respectable middle-class of Alençon, she went *from château to château*: from the Romets at Saint-Denis-sur-Sarthon to Mme Monnier at Grogny, where she went riding side-saddle; and to the Rabinels – Langhal's Manor – at Semallé where she joyfully met Rose Taillé's family again. *Everything was a festivity around me: I was entertained, coddled, admired.* On all sides the friends exclaimed: 'We saw a baby leave, and an attractive young girl has returned!' Her father was considerably proud of her. He wrote to his friend Nogrix: 'I assure you, my little Queen is a fine young lass.'

At ten and a half, with her long fair hair and grey eyes, Thérèse made quite an impact. Her serious illness was referred to in veiled terms but she appeared well restored to health, happy and very much at ease in this new world. *I must admit this life had charms for me. At the age of ten the heart allows itself to be easily dazzled.* She felt she could easily have taken that road which young girls around her in Alençon were following. She thought of Pauline in her poor little Carmel. This holiday was to provoke the following comment: *Perhaps Jesus wanted to show me the world before his FIRST visit to me so that I might choose more freely the life I had promised him to follow.*

On 22 August she met Father Almire Pichon, a Jesuit from Orne, whom Marie had chosen for her spiritual director, and whom she praised to the skies. The priest remarked how well the young Thérèse looked, and at M. Martin's suggestion she kissed him to thank him for his prayers for her during her illness.

In October 1883 another school year began at the abbey; the 'violet' class still, but in the second division. At last it was the year of her first communion. She entered wholeheartedly into the preparation and was always first in catechism. Abbé Domin appreciated his 'little doctor', but Thérèse had great difficulty in accepting some points of his teaching; she got indignant at the idea that little children who died without baptism might be deprived of heaven!

From Carmel also, her preparation was just as intense. From February to May 1884 a letter from Pauline arrived each week at Les Buissonnets. The Carmelite had put together a little book of daily sacrifices to be made for Jesus, with prayers to offer him. At home Marie complemented this in her own way. She made Thérèse meditate on a leaflet on 'Renunciation', far too advanced for her years. Thérèse took all this literally. She wrote to Agnès: *Every day I try to perform as many acts as I can, and I do my best not to let a single occasion pass by.* From 1 March to 7 May she made 1,949 sacrifices, an average of 28 a day. She repeated 2,773 times invocations suggested by her sister, a daily average of 40.

The Carmelite was also preparing for her own profession. The two ceremonies were set for 8 May. For Thérèse there were no clouds in the sky.

THE FIRST KISS OF JESUS TO MY SOUL (8 MAY 1884)

When that flame which is called love was kindled in my young heart, you came to claim it.

Still delicate, Thérèse was exempted from the obligation of boarding at school for the month before 'the most beautiful day of her life'. She only made the three-day retreat from 4 to 8 May, with many precautions and privileges. At the slightest headache or cough she was taken to the infirmary. Céline even had permission to visit her each day.

In a small exercise book the retreatant made brief notes on Abbé Domin's instructions. The titles are eloquent: Hell, Death, Sacrilegious Communion, The Last Judgment. The stories which illustrated these chapters frightened Thérèse. 'Who knows', threatened the preacher, 'whether any of you who are making this retreat will die before Thursday?' In the event the abbé was unable to continue his terrifying lessons because Mother Saint-Exupère, the prioress, died suddenly!

After four years preparation the day at last arrived. Thérèse forgot the record-keeping suggested by Pauline, and the fears awakened by the chaplain took flight. Her language describing her first meeting with Jesus is in a totally different register:

Ah, how sweet was that first kiss of Jesus! It was a kiss of LOVE, *I* FELT *that I was* LOVED, *and I said: 'I love you, and I give myself to you forever!' There were no requests, no struggles, no sacrifices; for a long time Jesus and poor little Thérèse* LOOKED *at each other and understood each other. That day it was no longer simply a* LOOK, *it was a* FUSION, *there were no longer two, Thérèse had vanished like a drop of water lost in the depths of the ocean. Jesus alone remained. He was the Master, the King.*

She no longer feared separations: when she received Jesus she was united with her mother in heaven, and with Pauline in Carmel. Her companions misunderstood the copious tears during the mass. They were tears of joy, not sorrow. Sister Henriette recalled:

> At the two-hour party which followed, a child said to me: 'Do you know, Sister, what Thérèse asked God during her Thanksgiving – to die, Sister. How frightening!' But Thérèse looked at them with pity and said nothing. I then said to them: 'You don't understand. Thérèse did indeed ask, like her holy patron, to die of love.' Then she came up to me and looking me in the eye said: *Sister, you understand – but they –.*

That depth which escaped those around her undoubtedly came from her habit of *praying without knowing it*. She had been instructed in secret, much better than by M. Domin. Several times she asked one of her teachers: *Marguerite, I would so much like you to teach me how to meditate.* Marie, finding her 'so pious', would not allow her to make half an hour's prayer as she had asked to do. Not even a quarter of an hour. But who could have forbidden Thérèse to withdraw into the space between her bed and the wall, and there, hidden by a curtain, think *about God, life* – ETERNITY?

The profoundness of that first communion did not stop her being of this earth. She enjoyed the family celebration, the beautiful watch and the numerous other presents, among them that 'pale cream woollen dress trimmed with garnet-red velvet and a straw hat of the same shade with a large garnet-red feather'.

She was motherless, and had come first in catechism; it was her right to read the consecration to the Blessed Virgin in the name of her five companions during vespers. But two nieces of Abbé Domin were among the group and the abbey nuns wanted to please their chaplain by giving this honour to one of them. Thérèse would not hear of it. Mme Guérin and Marie had to go to Mother Saint-Placid, then all the family went to the chaplain to plead Thérèse's right. She was finally given permission.

Thérèse was a Norman, a mystic and a realist. She noted abruptly in one of her notebooks: *Lent 20 francs to Céline. Oh! Jesus, you alone, and that is enough.* She developed a great hunger

for the Eucharist. *Only Jesus could satisfy me.* At that time
the confessor's permission was needed for communion, and
Thérèse's must have been liberal since his penitent noted all
her communions from 8 May 1884 to 28 August 1885: twenty-
two.

THE SECOND VISIT OF JESUS: ASCENSION THURSDAY, 22 MAY 1884

Her second communion, on Ascension Thursday, was no less
important than the first. Contrary to all expectations Abbé
Domin allowed her to receive communion after barely a fortnight. Again there were tears of *ineffable sweetness*. A sentence
from St Paul impressed itself on her mind: 'It is no longer I
that live, it is Jesus who lives in me' (Gal. 2:20). The next
day she received *one of the greatest graces of her life.* Later, after
another communion something her sister Marie had said to
her came back to her mind. Still thinking of her as a baby,
the young twenty-four-year-old woman had predicted that
God would spare her the way of suffering. It would be difficult
to be more completely mistaken, for it was to be just the
opposite. On that day Thérèse felt born within her heart *a
great desire to suffer*, and an assurance that a great number of
crosses awaited her.

After communion she used to repeat a prayer from the
Imitation of Christ (her bedside book): 'O Jesus, ineffable
SWEETNESS, change all the consolations of this earth into
BITTERNESS for me.' She repeated these words without fully
understanding what they meant, *like a child who repeats words
that a loved one prompts him to say . . . Until then, I had suffered
without* LOVING *suffering, but since that day, I have had a real love
for it.*

During the twelve months she was receiving these
numerous eucharistic graces, her inner trials, which resulted
from her illness, vanished completely.

THE HOLY SPIRIT MUST BE THE LIFE OF YOUR HEART (14 JUNE 1884)

Three weeks later she embarked with joy on a two-day retreat
at the abbey: Mgr Hugonin was going to confirm her and

Léonie would be her godmother. The *sacrament of love* filled her with wonder. The Holy Spirit gave her the *strength to suffer*.

On the 26th of the same month she joyfully welcomed 'the furry animal' she had asked her father for: a beautiful spaniel, Tom, who would not leave her. He became the guardian of Les Buissonnets and the companion of her walks.

The summer of 1884 was splendid. Since May Thérèse had been coughing a lot and developed whooping-cough. In August she was sent on holiday to the home of Mme Guérin's mother, Mme Fournet, at Saint-Ouen-le-Pin (10km west of Lisieux). Great was her joy to rediscover the countryside of Normandy, its rivers and fields. Each day at the neighbouring farm she drank a bowl of warm milk. She drew, played with the dog Biribi, walked in the Theil wood, and even went as far as the castle of Guizot, Louis-Philippe's former minister, who lay buried in the village cemetery. Mme Guérin wrote to her husband: 'Thérèse's face is always radiant with joy.'

After this excellent holiday she went into the second, the 'orange' class. Her teacher was Mother Saint-Léon. The time of concentration for the first communion was over. Still the youngest in the class, Thérèse suffered from girls who regularly amused themselves at her expense. She loved history and catechism, in which she always came first; arithmetic and spelling remained her weak points. If she did not get the bright red badge, the first prize, she burst into tears. 'It was impossible to console her.' She also had a tendency to whisper to her companions when they did not answer questions. Mother Saint-Léon had scarcely any more to say about that sweet and sensitive pupil when she recalled her memories.

The Easter holidays, from 3 to 10 May, enabled her to rediscover the sea at Deauville, at the Chalet des Roses which M. Guérin rented. She was twelve and a half. Marie, who remained at Les Buissonnets, still called Thérèse her 'big baby'. And that was just what she was; seeing Marie Guérin made much of by her mother, Thérèse began to whimper hoping that she in turn might be petted. But it did not work. She remembered her lesson and declared that she had been cured *for life of desiring to attract attention*. Her headaches were probably caused by the strong sea air.

THE TERRIBLE DISEASE OF SCRUPLES (MAY 1885 TO
NOVEMBER 1886)

Thérèse returned to Lisieux to prepare for what was then
called 'the second communion' or renewal. There was another
retreat with Abbé Domin. Thérèse went back to her little
notebook of the previous year. The tone of the instructions
had not changed. Hence the second entry: *What Monsieur the
abbé told us is very frightening. He spoke to us about mortal sin.* The
third door after death. This time no death would come to
interrupt those instructions, which were so different from
what Thérèse experienced at her communion.[1]

It proved too much for someone so delicate. Her inner
trials quickly returned and she sank into *the terrible disease of
scruples. You would have to endure this martyrdom to understand what
it was like. It would be impossible for me to say what I suffered for
eighteen months.*

Her only recourse was Marie, her last mother, who was
still at Les Buissonnets; for how could she confide her troubles
to Pauline in the Carmel parlour? Especially as some of the
scruples may have concerned chastity.[2] Pauline was a
Carmelite, therefore a saint. She had become so distant that
her sister regarded her as *dead* to her.

To Marie, now her *one indispensable adviser*, Thérèse, in tears
every day, poured out her troubles during the hairdressing
session. (Marie curled her hair every day to please her father.)
Thérèse forced herself to tell everything, even her most absurd
thoughts. She was troubled by the simplest actions and
thoughts. It is an astonishing fact that her confessors (Abbé
Domin; then after leaving school Abbé Lepelletier), were
completely ignorant of her *ugly malady*. She blindly obeyed
her sister who told her what she had to accuse herself of in
confession.

The long holidays brought a happy diversion. In July she
returned to Saint-Ouen-le-Pin and carefully hid her suffering.

[1] Thérèse renewed her three resolutions of the previous year: (1) I will not
become discouraged. (2) I will say a *memorare* to Our Lady each day. (3)
I will try to humble my pride.
[2] This subject was taboo at the time and the silence gave rise to scruples.
Marie, Céline, Léonie and Marie Guérin all experienced difficulties in
this matter.

12 Thérèse's drawing of the Villa Rose at Trouville (May 1885)

'Thérèse is delightfully happy,' wrote her aunt Elisa, 'I have never seen her so gay.' This rustic sketch follows: 'Yesterday she and Marie (her daughter) came home all decked out in little posies. Marie had knapweed and Thérèse forget-me-nots. They were wearing their Breton aprons with little very well-made posies at each corner, on their heads, at the end of their plaits and even on their shoes. One was 'Little Reddy', the other 'Little Bluey.'

There followed a stay in Trouville at the Villa Rose, rue Charlemagne. A fortnight at the seaside with Céline! What a delight! On the beach, with sky-blue ribbons in her hair, Thérèse looked very pretty. But, thinking she had been too vain, she accused herself of it in confession.

At this time Louis Martin undertook a long trip in Central Europe as far as the Balkans via Munich and Vienna, in the company of Abbé Charles Marie the curate of Saint-Jacques. At Constantinople they abandoned their plan of going on to Jerusalem. The return journey was through Athens, Naples, Rome and Milan. The Martin girls found the time from 22 August to mid-October very long. Tom, in his kennel, cried for his master. The whole family hurried to the station to welcome the great traveller home, and he would fill the winter evenings with tales of the marvels he had seen. His youngest daughter wrote on 3 December 1885, in an essay: *I love the long evenings when we gather as a family round the crackling fire.*

Thérèse returned to school on Monday, 5 October. She was filled with dread, for what she had long feared now came to pass; she was alone at the abbey. Céline had finished her studies.[1]

Marie Guérin, who was often ill, did not go back to school. Céline the Intrepid, who became president of the Children of Mary, was no longer there to be with her sister and defend her when necessary. Thérèse was even more tense because the year began with a retreat. M. Domin fortunately gave only one instruction. But according to her notes the preacher who replaced him also went on about sin, death, hell and the last judgment.

Thérèse was more than ever on the verge of tears. 'I remember very well', noted Mother Saint-Léon, 'that the child's face expressed a melancholy which surprised me.' Thérèse tried in vain to overcome her solitude by making friends with companions her own age and with a teacher. *My love was misunderstood.*

In February 1886 she was received as a candidate into the sodality of the Children of Mary. But her continual headaches forced her to be often absent. At the beginning of March M. Martin decided to remove his daughter from the abbey. So, unlike Céline, she did not complete her normal schooling, which would have required two more years of higher studies.

WITH MADAME PAPINAU (MARCH 1886)

A new life began for the thirteen and a half year old pupil: she had a governess to teach her several times a week. Mme Papinau was fifty and lived near the Guérins. Three or four times a week Thérèse went to her house. *A very good person, well educated*, reported the pupil, *but a little old-maidish in her ways. She lived with her mother and her cat.* In the drawing-room, furnished with antiques, Mlle Martin discovered a world very different from that of the abbey. Visits often interrupted the lessons. There were snippets of Lisieux gossip; someone asked, 'Who is that very pretty young girl? What beautiful hair.'

---

[1] *If I had not had my dearest Céline with me, I could not have stayed there for one month without becoming ill.* And this was precisely what happened.

With her nose in her book the young girl heard everything and blushed with pleasure.

With more free time on her hands, Thérèse did up an attic on the third floor of Les Buissonnets to her own taste. *It was like a bazaar*, with a large aviary full of birds, plants, an aquarium with goldfish, statues of saints, various boxes, baskets, dolls, books; and a picture of Pauline on the wall. There she spent hours studying, reading the books she loved so much, meditating, and praying.

In June she went to Trouville again, to the Chalet des Lilas. It was a short stay. Alone (that is, without anyone from Les Buissonnets), Thérèse fretted and became ill. Her aunt was worried and sent her back to Lisieux, but when she got there she recovered. Thérèse acknowledged that it was *only an attack of homesickness for Les Buissonnets.*

MARIE'S DEPARTURE: THE LOSS OF HER THIRD MOTHER (15 OCTOBER 1886)

Her emotional fragility could not withstand another separation. Her one support, her only intimate friend, was going to leave her. In August Thérèse learnt that Marie, in her turn, was going to enter the Lisieux Carmel. Fr Pichon had authorised it. It was too much! *When I learned that Marie was leaving my room lost all its attraction for me.*

Thérèse might have hated that Carmel which had claimed all the people who had supported her; she could well have detested the convent parlours where she had suffered so much during visits. Yet she still thought of entering there herself, not to find Pauline and Marie again, but because Jesus was calling her there.

For the moment she relived what she had experienced at Pauline's departure: she did not want to leave Marie, she knocked repeatedly at her door, kissed her at every moment. M. Martin hid his own sorrow. He had hoped that his favourite, 'the Diamond', would never leave him. The surprise was no less great in the chemist's family. No one had expected to see the independent 'Bohemian' (another name her father had given her) set out for the convent.

Thérèse went back to her lessons at Mme Papinau's in

October. A trip to Alençon this time brought only *sadness and bitterness*. At her mother's grave Thérèse cried because she had forgotten a bouquet of cornflowers. Her frequent tears made some friends think she had a *weak character*. The Guérins shared this opinion. She was regarded as *a little dunce, good and sweet, with good judgment but incompetent and clumsy*.

Another calamity! Léonie went to the Poor Clares in the rue Demi-Lune and persuaded the abbess to admit her on the spot to the enclosure. It was 7 October. M. Martin tried to calm Marie's anger. There was general embarrassment when they returned to Lisieux. Uncle Isidore predicted that Léonie would not be long in returning to Les Buissonnets.

Eight days later, on the feast of St Teresa of Avila, Marie joined Sister Agnès of Jesus in Carmel. She was to become Sister Marie of the Sacred Heart.

For Thérèse those weeks were very dismal. The warm atmosphere at Les Buissonnets, so necessary to her, was disappearing. Now only she and Céline remained with their father. Céline, who was seventeen and a half, became the mistress of the house. After that 15 October Thérèse reached rock bottom.

SECOND CURE (END OF OCTOBER 1886)

To whom could she now confide the scruples which obsessed her? She made difficulties out of everything. Her spiritual crisis came to a head. Was she going to have a relapse? Once again she obeyed an instinctive reflex: not finding anyone on earth, she turned to heaven. In her loneliness Thérèse suddenly remembered her little brothers and sisters who had died before she was born.

> *I spoke to them with the simplicity of a child, pointing out that, as the youngest in the family, I had always been the most loved, the one who had been showered with my sisters' tender care. Their going to heaven did not seem to me to be a reason for forgetting me; on the contrary, finding themselves in a position to draw from the divine treasures, they had to get* PEACE *for me and thereby show me that, in heaven, they still knew how to love.*

From the pit of her distress this was Thérèse's spontaneous

prayer. *The answer was not long in coming, for soon peace poured into my soul and I knew that I was as loved in heaven as I was on earth. Since then, my devotion to my little brothers and sisters has increased.*

She never forgot that healing experience. All of a sudden her scruples disappeared; but her over-sensitiveness remained. In the parlour on Thursdays she still cried. Marie reproached her for it. Moreover she cried about everything, *then cried for having cried.* All arguments were useless. *I was really unbearable because of my extreme touchiness.*

She was however nearly fourteen. She had grown very much and was given some physical exercises to do so that she would not become hunch-backed. But she was not inclined to be very active. It was Céline who tidied up their bedroom. Thérèse took practically no part in the housework. Sometimes she *tried* to make the bed and to bring some potted-plants in from the garden in the evening. If Céline did not thank her she started crying. *I was still only a child who appeared to have no will except that of others.* She *was turning in a narrow circle, not knowing how to get out,* imprisoned *in the swaddling bands of infancy.*

And this was the adolescent who was still dreaming of entering on the austere life of Carmel! For she was thinking about it, while admitting that she did not know how she would be able to live there with strength, as the Spanish mother vigorously exhorted her Carmelites. How could she, who was so delicate and so emotional, become a worthy daughter of St Teresa who wanted strong and resolute postulants? It would take a miracle to change her.

The proof that religious life was not easy was demonstrated on 1 December when, covered in eczema and hiding her short hair under a mantilla, Léonie, now twenty-three, came home. Seven weeks of the Poor Clare regime in Alençon had got the better of her. Her two sisters did everything to help her get over her failure and humiliation.

The family rituals continued. But at the end of 1886 there was very little heart left in them. On Christmas eve M. Martin and his three daughters went down to the cathedral for midnight mass.

MY COMPLETE CONVERSION: CHRISTMAS NIGHT 1886

'A baby'; that was how Céline then regarded her sister. The proof: the custom of putting presents into slippers in front of the fireplace! At fourteen Thérèse still wanted to do it. While she was going up the narrow stairs she heard her father, who was tired, say to Céline: 'Well, fortunately this will be the last year!' Seeing Thérèse's tears, her sister realised that the midnight supper was spoilt. She advised her not to go back downstairs immediately. But it was then that everything suddenly changed. In an instant Thérèse recovered herself, dried her eyes, went down and, full of joy, opened the parcels. Céline could not believe it!

On the stairs a complete transformation had taken place in her sister. A new unknown strength suddenly came upon her. She was *no longer the same. Jesus had changed her heart.* The night in which she had been living was changed into brilliant light. The account which we have of this *conversion* is dated 1895. Nine years later Sister Thérèse of the Child Jesus could judge the permanence of her sudden transformation. For she could not doubt: it was a *little miracle. In an instant Jesus, content with my good will, accomplished the work I had not been able to do in ten years.* On that 25 December 1886 Thérèse passed a major milestone in her life which marked the beginning of the third period of her existence, *the most beautiful of all.* After nine sad years (1881–6 in particular) she had *recovered the strength of soul she had lost* when her mother died and, she said, *she was to retain it for ever.*

An admirable exchange had just taken place between the Infant in the manger who had taken upon himself frail human nature, and little Thérèse, who had become strong. It was a eucharistic grace: *I had the happiness*, on that night, *of receiving the strong and powerful God.*

Suddenly she was freed from the faults and imperfections of childhood. This grace made her grow up and mature. Her tears dried up. Her over-sensitiveness was cured. At last she was equipped to live. *Since that blessed night, I have not been vanquished in any battle, but on the contrary, I have marched from victory to victory and begun, so to speak, 'TO RUN A GIANT'S COURSE'* (Ps. 19:5).

That night another Thérèse Martin was born.[1] *Jesus changed me in such a way that I no longer knew myself.* Or rather, he had just returned her to herself, out of a bad dream which had lasted for years, the most dramatic moments of which had been her strange illness and her crisis of scruples. It was not her real nature to be weepy, dreamy and weak-willed. In Alençon she had not been like that. After the smile of the Blessed Virgin, the intercession of her little brothers and sisters, the Infant of Christmas – the strong God – had at last set her free. Thérèse became herself. It was a decisive fundamental happening. Henceforth she was to know, for ever, that God had saved her, Thérèse, from shipwreck. It was an irreversible experience. Now she was *armed for war*!

---

[1] That 25 December, during vespers at Notre-Dame Cathedral in Paris, a young man, an atheist, was converted. Paul Claudel learnt much later of this coincidence. It was also 'the first Christian Christmas' of Vicomte Charles de Foucauld who was on the way to real conversion.

4

'The Third Period of my Life, the Most Beautiful of All'

We enjoyed the most beautiful life young girls could dream of . . .
our life on earth was the ideal of happiness.

If this profound transformation was not immediately apparent
to those around her – Céline excepted – Thérèse's physical
development was evident to all. On 2 January 1887 she was
fourteen. 'My baby is so tall', sighed Marie behind her grille.
Their cousin Jeanne now spoke of 'tall Thérèse'.[1] On the
beach at Trouville in June, with her blonde plaits, she was
called 'the tall English girl'.

That year of 1887 saw her develop in every way: physical
maturity and emotional development went hand in hand. *I
was at the most dangerous age for young girls.* Her desire to love
and be loved was great, and her maternal instinct came to
the fore when two orphans were looked after at Les Buissonnets; they were not six years old. Their openness and
confidence towards 'the tall lady' amazed her.

Her intellectual development was also great. *Freed from
scruples and excessive sensitiveness, my mind developed. I had always
loved the great and the beautiful, but in this period of my life I was
filled with an ardent desire to learn.* The standard of Mme Papinau's lessons was moderate. In her attic Thérèse accumulated
science and history books. Everything interested her. But the
anti-intellectual counsels of the *Imitation of Christ* prevented
her from succumbing to the dizzy heights of knowledge. She
kept herself well in hand.

In her written exercises, the young girl sometimes slipped

[1] Thérèse, 1.62m, was the tallest of the Martin sisters. Pauline, the shortest,
was 1.54m.

in some of her own preferences. The hubbub of cities was not to her liking, and she often returned to the joys of nature. *If my dreams come true, one day I will go and live in the country. When I think about my plan I am carried away in spirit to a delightful sunlit little house, all my rooms would look out on to the sea.* She saw herself there, living alone with a cow, a donkey, some sheep, poultry and an aviary. Her little house would be near a church where she would hear mass every morning. Then she would ride on her donkey to visit the few poor inhabitants, bringing them *food and medicine.* In short, a solitary life of prayer and charitable works, in a fine Norman tradition.

From January to May Céline, a pupil of Mlle Godard's, taught her drawing. Thérèse applied herself to still-life, portraits and country scenes. Together they modelled clay.[1] But Thérèse would have very much liked to have had lessons from Mlle Godard as well. When she was told she was not as gifted as her sister, she remained silent.

Twice a week, out of duty, she went to meetings she had to attend if she wished to join the sodality of the Children of Mary (she was finally received on 31 May). At the abbey she no longer knew the pupils. Her one refuge was the gallery of the chapel, where she spent long moments before the Blessed Sacrament. There she found her *only Friend.* The standard of those meetings was scarcely on a par with the sort of questions she was then asking herself. Once in May, contrary to her usual custom, she dared to ask her father to lend her a recently published book which he had borrowed from the Carmel: *The End of the Present World and the Mysteries of the Future Life,* nine lectures of Abbé Arminjon, Canon of Chambéry Cathedral and former Professor of Scripture (1881).

In those 280 pages – especially the seventh lecture, 'Eternal Beatitude and the Supernatural Vision of God' – the adolescent discovered a much fuller synthesis of revelation and tradition than that given in M. Domin's lessons. *All the great truths of religion, the mysteries of eternity plunged my soul into a state of joy not of this world.* She copied out the pages which touched her most, especially those on 'perfect love'. This reading was *one of the greatest graces of (her) life.*

Thérèse henceforth shared all these discoveries with Céline,

[1] Modelling clay used for earthenware crockery.

her new confidante. Her sudden transformation had brought them closer together. *It was, so to speak, the same soul which animated us both. For some months, we enjoyed the most beautiful life young girls could dream of. Everything around us was in accord with our tastes, we were given the greatest liberty. I would say our life on earth was the* IDEAL OF HAPPINESS.

During that summer, in the evenings, they went up to the belvedere and talked in the moonlight. *It seems to me that we were receiving graces like those granted to the great saints.* She gives as an example Augustine and Monica conversing at Ostia. *Doubt was impossible, already faith and hope were no longer necessary. Love made us find on earth the One whom we were seeking.*

Thérèse even seemed to outstrip her older sister. All her femininity was awakened; and expressed in the romanticism of a girl of the period.

Abbé Lepelletier allowed her to receive communion four times a week, and even five, when there were feast days. It was an unusual permission which made her weep for joy, and she took full advantage of it in her youthful ardour.

> *I felt within my heart certain aspirations unknown until then, and at times I had veritable transports of love. One evening, not knowing how to tell Jesus that I loved him and how much I desired that he be loved and glorified everywhere, I was thinking he would never receive a single act of love from hell. Then I said to God that to please him I would consent to see myself plunged into hell so that he might be* LOVED *eternally in that place of blasphemy. When we love, we experience the desire to say a thousand foolish things.*

Was this the elation of adolescence? No, for it was not a question of feelings only. Her attitude had completely changed. These graces bore abundant fruit. *The practice of virtue became sweet and natural to us* (she charitably includes Céline). *Immediate renunciation became easy for me.*

Not without a certain audacity, she did not feel she needed outside assistance like her sisters, who each had a director. Her way was straight and clear. *I was only a very short time in confession and I never spoke a word about my inner feelings.* She would go on to write: *Ah! if the learned who spent their lives in study had come to me, undoubtedly they would have been amazed to see a child of fourteen understanding the secrets of perfection.*

THE THIRST FOR SOULS

There is another sign which shows that she was not trapped in the pleasure of introspection: a small seemingly chance event was to turn her permanently towards others.

One Sunday in July, at the end of mass a picture of Jesus crucified slipped from her missal. No one was collecting the blood he had shed. Thérèse decided that she would henceforth remain, in spirit, at the foot of that cross to collect that blood for sinners. *Charity entered into my heart.* She too would be a fisher of human beings. She thirsted like Jesus. Her vocation to Carmel became clear and deep. She felt the need to forget herself. The Pranzini affair provided her with the opportunity to put her desires into practice.

A GREAT CRIMINAL: HENRI PRANZINI (MARCH TO AUGUST 1887)

On the night of 19 to 20 March two women and a little girl were murdered, in a horrible way, at 17 rue Montaigne in Paris. One, Régine de Montelle (her real name was Marie Regnaud), was known in fashionable Parisian society for her fast living; the other was her maid. The child, who was twelve years old, undoubtedly belonged to the former. Jewellery had disappeared.

This triple crime aroused universal interest. Two days later the police arrested a suspect in Marseilles; he was Henri Pranzini, thirty years old and born in Alexandria. The charges mounted against this tall and handsome adventurer. He repeatedly denied them and did not seem to be a common criminal. Boldly he faced witnesses and judges. All the press in France and abroad followed the case from March to June and gave the most sordid details. The hearing began on 9 July and on the 13th Pranzini was condemned to death.

Thérèse heard about him. She had but one desire: to save his soul. When all the newspapers – including *La Croix* – were speaking only of 'the sinister scoundrel', 'the monster' or 'the vile brute', the young girl adopted him as her *first child*. For

13 Cast of Henri Pranzini

him, she prayed; she increased her sacrifices and asked Céline to have masses offered for him, without telling her of the intention! Her sister finally drew the secret from her and they united their efforts.

I was convinced in the depths of my heart that our desires would be granted, but to give me courage to go on praying for sinners I told God I was sure he would pardon poor unfortunate Pranzini and that I would believe it even if he did not go to confession or show any sign of repentance. I had such confidence in Jesus' infinite mercy, but I was asking for a 'sign' of repentance, just for my own consolation.

On 31 August at dawn, in the Grande Roquette prison, Pranzini protested his innocence to the foot of the guillotine and refused the services of Abbé Faure, the chaplain.

However at the last moment he called for the crucifix and kissed it twice before he died.[1]

The next day, disregarding her father's ruling not to read the newspapers, Thérèse opened *La Croix* and read the account of Pranzini's death. She had to hide to conceal her tears. Her prayer had been *heard to the letter!* The sign she had asked for had been granted. It corresponded exactly to the grace Jesus had given her to draw her to pray for sinners: Pranzini had kissed the wounds of Jesus crucified whose blood Thérèse wanted to gather up for all the world.

This *unique grace* increased her determination to enter Carmel: to pray and to give her life for sinners. If the Lord had given her Pranzini as her first child, it was so that she would have a great many others.

OBSTACLES TO HER ENTERING CARMEL (MAY 1887 TO JANUARY 1888)

There was little time to lose. Thérèse attached great importance to dates and had already fixed the day for her entrance: 25 December 1887, the anniversary of her conversion.

But a series of increasingly difficult obstacles were to arise to thwart her plan. She had to overcome them one by one. *The divine call was so strong that had I been forced to pass through flames, I would have done it to be faithful to Jesus.* She had to *conquer the fortress of Carmel at the point of the sword.*

CONVINCING HER FATHER (29 MAY 1887)

The first step to be taken was to obtain her father's consent. She chose Whit Sunday to confide her secret to him. Would he allow her to enter the convent at fifteen, when he had already accepted Pauline's and Marie's vocations, and when Léonie, after her unhappy attempt with the Poor Clares, had just asked him if she could enter the Visitation at Caen? On 1 May he had suffered a slight stroke which had paralysed his left side for several hours. His brother-in-law's quick inter-

---

[1] *La Croix* said: 'twice'. Thérèse wrote 'three times' in 1895.

vention had restored him to health. But Thérèse had to make her request to a man who was tired and not well. She was nervous and hesitant. Throughout the day she prayed for courage to speak.

In the evening after vespers, in the garden of Les Buissonnets she asked him. Her father simply objected that she was so young. But she quickly convinced him of the sincerity and urgency of her vocation. 'Her King' said that God was doing him 'a great honour' asking his children of him in this way. Then from the low garden wall he picked a saxifrage, a small flowering rock plant, and gave it to Thérèse. He explained to her how that little white flower symbolised her whole life. She received it as a relic and put it in her *Imitation* which never left her. Overjoyed by her father's consent, she little suspected her joy was quickly to come to an end.

The summer holidays came round again, the last, Thérèse hoped. The Guérins and friends knew nothing about all these events. Life continued: the Martin girls went for walks in the country with their father and Abbé Lepelletier, aged thirty-four, Thérèse and Céline's confessor. He drew a sketch of the three sisters in the fields: the youngest, as was her wont, picking flowers, Léonie browsing through a book, Céline painting. Then there was a pilgrimage to Honfleur followed by a visit by steamboat to the International Maritime Exhibition at Le Havre. Finally a week in Trouville at the Chalet des Lilas, rented by the Guérins.

The 'tall English girl' took full advantage of her holidays. With Jeanne, she went to see the Colombe girls. Twice a day they went to the beach. 'Yesterday we went to the rocks to get some seawater. Thérèse took off her shoes for a moment.' 'Tall Thérèse is very well and enjoying herself too, I believe.'

From 6 to 15 October Fr Pichon, the Jesuit who was so highly esteemed by Sister Marie of the Sacred Heart, preached the retreat at Carmel. He visited Les Buissonnets. Céline in her turn asked him to direct her. Léonie having left, on 16 July, for the Visitation at Caen, Thérèsita[1] knew only too well that her early entrance into Carmel would not receive the family's unanimous approval. Marie, who had been a

---

[1] She was called by this name in the Carmel after Teresa of Avila's niece who entered Carmel at the age of eight as a boarder.

14 Céline, Thérèse and Léonie drawn by Father Lepelletier
on 16 June 1887

Carmelite for a year and knew what the life was like, did all she could to put off the entrance date. Pauline, on the other hand, was in favour of it. But she too restrained the postulant's eagerness. Céline, learning her sister's resolve, felt it deeply; she would then be alone at Les Buissonnets. But she supported her. Thérèse already saw Céline in Carmel with her and had even chosen her religious name: Sister Marie of the Trinity!

UNCLE ISIDORE'S OPPOSITION (8–22 OCTOBER 1887)

All these plans came up against a major obstacle: Uncle Isidore. The Martin girls' guardian put his veto on his niece's desire. On Saturday, 8 October, six months after she had spoken to her father, Thérèse *in trepidation* entered the chem-

ist's study. Kindly but uncompromisingly he countered Thérèse's tears with prudent reasoning: she was far too young for
'that philosopher's life'. The whole town would be talking
about it. A well known person in Lisieux must avoid scandal.
Let his niece – who undoubtedly did have a vocation – not
mention it to him until she was seventeen. It would take a
miracle to make him change his mind.

On the same day Thérèse wrote to Sister Agnès (who had
advised her to speak to him) to tell her about the failure of
the interview. They had again become very close to each
other. *Pray for your Thérèsita. You know how much she loves you.
You are her confidante.* Pauline once again came to the fore and
guided her young sister's struggles. The postulant felt full of
confidence, certain that God would not abandon her.

Nevertheless for three days (from 19 to 22 October), for
the first time she experienced inner dryness, the silence of
God. *Night, the dark night of the soul like Jesus in his agony in the
garden. I felt that I was alone, finding no consolation either on earth
or from heaven. God seemed to have forsaken me!!!* This was a new
and bewildering experience for one who had known so much
light since Christmas. She could no longer understand. Seeing
her in this sad state in the parlour on Thursday, 21st, Sister
Agnès no longer held back: she wrote to her uncle. Naturally
she did not wish to argue with him, but to explain to him
the situation as she saw it. In her opinion it was much 'more
than childish fretting'.

M. Guérin had always had a high regard for his godchild.
From that Saturday he changed his opinion. Let Thérèse
enter Carmel!

M. DELATROËTTE, THE INTRACTABLE SUPERIOR OF THE
CARMEL (23 OCTOBER 1887)

The postulant's joy was short-lived. On the Sunday evening
she met with another insurmountable refusal: M. Delatroëtte,
aged sixty-nine, ecclesiastical superior of the Carmel since
1870, would not hear of her entering before she was twenty-
one.

Thérèse's immediate reaction was to go and see him and
make him change his mind. On Monday, 24th she set out,

accompanied by her father and Céline. The churchman, who had all too recently had his fingers burnt over an affair of this kind which the whole of Lisieux was still talking about, did not want to take another risk. He remained immovable. Of course the final decision rested with the bishop; if he agreed . . .

Thérèse went out into the rain in tears. Her father, trying to console her, promised he would take her to see the Bishop of Bayeux. His daughter went one better: *If he will not consent I will ask the Pope!* I AM DETERMINED TO REACH MY GOAL. And why not indeed, since her father, despite his fatigue, had booked them on a pilgrimage to Rome organised by the diocese of Coutances in honour of Leo XIII's jubilee.

There was another gloomy Thursday parlour visit: M. Delatroëtte was holding firm to his position. So a veritable general movement was set in motion: Sister Agnès of Jesus, Mother Marie de Gonzague 'and all the Carmelites' including Mother Geneviève the saintly foundress, who was ill, and the chaplain, Abbé Youf, joined together to beseech heaven: 'She is such a delightful child, I do want her to enter!' said this good priest. But his juridical powers were nil. He advised them to speak to Mgr Hugonin as soon as possible, without waiting for the pilgrimage to Italy.

AT BAYEUX WITH THE BISHOP (31 OCTOBER 1887)

On Monday, 31 October Thérèse put on her best white dress and arranged her hair in a knot on top of her head to look older. Her father took her to the bishop's palace at Bayeux. *For the first time in my life I had to make a visit unaccompanied by my sisters, and that visit was to a bishop!*

She remembered the smallest details of that day: the torrential rain; the visit to the cathedral where her white dress and hat in the midst of a funeral caused a sensation; the good meal at the hotel while they were waiting for the audience; the welcome given by the Vicar General, M. Révérony, and finally, after walking through long corridors, the meeting with the bishop.

She sat opposite him in an enormous armchair and shyly explained, in a tearful voice, the reason for her visit. Kindly and without interrupting, Mgr Hugonin listened to her. He would have to see M. Delatroëtte. Then the tears flowed freely. The interview was over. In the garden the bishop was surprised to see her father's eagerness to give his daughter to Carmel. 'I will give you my answer on the pilgrimage to Italy.' The story of Thérèse putting her hair up in order to make herself look older amused his lordship very much. After asking about some details of protocol for a papal audience M. Martin mentioned the possibility of appealing to the Holy Father.

Once outside his daughter wept bitterly: *It seemed my future had been ruined for ever. The nearer I approached my goal the more involved my affairs seemed to become. My soul was plunged in sadness, but also in peace, for I was seeking only God's will.*

The day after this set-back there was another very sad parlour visit. Only one hope remained: Pope Leo XIII. After discussing this unusual step (which Sister Agnès shortly afterwards advised her against), Thérèse left the Carmelites. She had only two days to prepare with Céline for 'the event': the pilgrimage to Italy.

WHAT A JOURNEY THAT WAS! (4 NOVEMBER TO 2 DECEMBER 1887)

Under the leadership of Mgr Germain, Bishop of Coutances, a hundred and ninety-seven French pilgrims, seventy-five of whom were priests, went to celebrate Leo XIII's sacerdotal jubilee. It was a tribute which did not pass unnoticed at the time, when Franco Crispi's Italian government's anti-clerical measures were alarming Christendom. The press, both French and Italian, gave wide coverage to this pilgrimage which was a political statement of ultramontane faith. The majority of French Catholics were royalist, hostile to the Republic and strongly opposed to Freemasonry. Thérèse herself had but one purpose: to fight for her vocation, to speak to the Pope. But during the trip she would hear conversations and discover the importance of political problems mixed with religion. In Rome outside the station the Italian police were arresting young printers for demonstrating and shouting: 'Down with Leo XIII! Down with the monarchy!'

She was newly grown-up and the trip did her good. But in Lisieux tongues wagged. It was rumoured that Louis Martin had taken his youngest daughter on this journey to make her forget the convent.

THE WONDERS OF PARIS (4–7 NOVEMBER 1887)

Although the first gathering of pilgrims was to be in the crypt of the Montmartre basilica[1] on Sunday, 6 November at nine o'clock, the three Martins left on Friday, 4th at three in the morning. They wanted to see Paris.

Two days were not long enough to exhaust the wonders: the Champs-Elysées with its Punch and Judy show, the gardens of the Tuileries, the Arc de Triomphe, the Bastille, the Royal Palace, the Louvre, the shops with their spring collections and their lifts, the Invalides, and so on. The Martin girls were worn out. The horse-drawn carriages and the trams somewhat alarmed them, and wherever they went they risked being crushed.

Yet *all the beautiful things* Thérèse saw in Paris *did not bring happiness*. In her memory the capital stood out above all as the place where she received a very important grace. M. Martin had arranged to stay at the Hôtel du Bouloi near the church of Our Lady of Victories, a sanctuary especially dear to the family since 13 May 1883. During mass on 4 November Thérèse was completely freed from her doubts about the Virgin's smile. For four years she had borne that trial. There, at Our Lady's feet she re-found her happiness in all its fullness. *It really was her who had smiled at me and cured me.* Mary was truly her mother, and she asked her to let her enter Carmel quickly. She confided her purity to the Virgin, for – as she had been told – she expected this trip to bring with it some tests for her vocation. She was not mistaken.

The next day the pilgrims met at Montmartre for their first mass together and to organise the groups. The two Martin sisters, who were fifteen and eighteen years old and pretty

---

[1] Under MacMahon, the National Assembly had voted on 24 July 1873 in favour of the construction of 'The Church of the National Vow' dedicated to the Sacred Heart. Work had begun in 1875.

and cheerful in their light dresses, did not pass unnoticed: they were the youngest on the pilgrimage.

The cost of the trip (660F first class, 565F second class) had made it rather exclusive. A quarter of the pilgrims belonged to the nobility. Thérèse, formerly so shy, was surprised to find herself perfectly at ease in 'society'.

The Lubin agency had organised the trip very well: nights on the train were avoided and the pilgrims stayed in the best hotels. All this luxury astonished the young Martin girls, used to the simple life-style of Les Buissonnets.

ITALY (8–28 NOVEMBER 1887)

The special train left the Gare de l'Est on Monday, 7 November at 6.35 a.m., in the rain. The next day the travellers saw the Swiss Alps. Thérèse ran from one side of the carriage to the other, stunned by the snow-capped summits, the lakes, the waterfalls, the bridges over gorges. The future Carmelite, far from closing her eyes to the wonders of nature, enjoyed them to the full.

After the customs, there was Italy at last! That same evening they went all together to Milan, which was all lit up. After the seven o'clock mass at the tomb of St Charles in the cathedral with six thousand statues, Thérèse and Céline climbed the four hundred and eighty-four steps of the dome. On Thursday, 10th, in sunshine, the Martin trio passed beneath the Bridge of Sighs, but Thérèse found Venice *sad*. There was a short trip to Padua before going on to Bologna.

The young girl did not forget that city. Her special train was met by a crowd of Italians, many of whom were students. As the ladies alighted they were greeted with whistles and hoots. Two attractive young girls were especially noticed. Céline later recounted: 'We stood together on the station platform waiting for Papa to get our transport. Thérèse looked very pretty and a number of times we heard admiring whispers from the passers-by. Suddenly a student rushed up to her and took her in his arms with some words of flattery. He was already carrying her off.' *But*, Thérèse reported, *I gave him such a look that he took fright, let me go and fled shamefacedly.*

Thérèse had never been so close to young people and men.

During the trip she saw on numerous occasions that she had made an impression, especially in Italy. But on the pilgrimage itself she learnt much on this subject. 'Marriages were hatching,' again Céline noted.

After a pilgrimage to Loreto in the evening of Sunday, 13th they finally reached their goal. 'Roma! Roma!' The Martins were booked in at the Hôtel du Sud and stayed there ten days. Visits began immediately. At the Colosseum the two girls boldly ignored the barriers blocking the entrance to the arena. Despite their father's calls to come back, Thérèse wanted at all costs to kiss the sand where the martyrs' blood had flowed. She dragged her sister along. Kneeling down, she asked for the grace to be a martyr for Jesus. *I felt in the depths of my soul that my prayer had been heard.*

The days were too short to see and admire everything. They were deeply impressed by the Roman countryside, the catacombs, the church of St Cecilia (this young saint became from that time her friend), and St Agnes-outside-the-Walls.

I was indeed far too bold. Although she knew she was being watched and listened to by M. Révérony, who would report back to the bishop on his return, the postulant did not hold back. She was fully herself, eager to see all, to touch everything, so as to collect relics. There was not a tower, not a dome she did not climb, not a dungeon she did not enter. In the Carmelite Monastery of Santa Maria della Vittoria she found herself inside the enclosure. An elderly religious tried in vain to show her the exit: *I cannot understand why women are so easily excommunicated in Italy, for at every moment someone was saying to us: 'Don't go in here! Don't go in there, you will be excommunicated!' Ah, poor women, how they are misunderstood!*

The youthful enthusiasm of the two Martin sisters did not please certain clerics. For in the evenings they used to sit on the floor of their hotel room and discuss the day's events late into the night. Fr Vauquelin would knock on the dividing wall to make the two chatterboxes keep quiet.

PRIESTS ARE WEAK AND FEEBLE MEN

The future Carmelite was about to make an important discovery: priests are neither angels nor gods. They are simply men. Until this time she had met them only in the exercise of their priestly ministry. At Les Buissonnets priests were not usually invited for a meal.

She now found herself for a month in the company of seventy-five clerics, in the train, in hotels, at table. She heard their conversations – not always edifying after a good meal – and saw their shortcomings for herself. In all the shrines she met Italian priests. Abbé Leconte, a twenty-nine-year-old curate, was with the Martin sisters so often that Céline's warm manner set a few tongues wagging. Such things happen even on pilgrimages.

Thérèse was to draw valuable lessons from this experience. *I understood my vocation in Italy.* She had understood that she had to pray and give her life for sinners like Pranzini. But Carmel prays specially for priests and this had surprised her since their souls seemed to her to be *as pure as crystal!* But a month spent with many priests taught her that they are *weak and feeble men.* For *if the most saintly have great need of prayers, what is to be said of those who are lukewarm?* It was not too far to go to gain such useful knowledge.

THE FIASCO OF SUNDAY, 20 NOVEMBER 1887

The purpose of the trip was not forgotten. The long-awaited papal audience was fixed for Sunday, 20th. *That day which I had both longed for and dreaded. My vocation depended on it.* For Mgr Hugonin had not sent any answer.

The copious correspondence exchanged between Lisieux and the pilgrims makes no secret of the fact: the Carmel and the Guérins knew Thérèse wanted to speak to the Pope. Sister Agnès had changed her mind again. On the 10th she had written and told her sister how to go about it. And Marie Guérin told her that at Lisieux they were praying for her 'enough to break the kneelers'.

On Saturday, 19th Thérèse replied: *Tomorrow, Sunday, I will speak to the Pope.*

On the morning of the 20th heavy rain fell on Rome. It was a bad sign, for Thérèse had noticed that in all the important events of her life nature reflected the state of her soul. On days of tears heaven wept with her, on days of joy the sun shone. At 7.30 the pilgrims, including those from the diocese of Nantes, filled the papal chapel. Leo XIII entered, an old man of seventy-seven, with a stern, pale, emaciated face. He blessed those present, celebrated mass in a moving way before assisting, kneeling, at a mass of thanksgiving. Then, one by one, the pilgrims entered the audience room. Each bishop presented his diocese. After the faithful of Coutances had passed through M. Révérony, in Mgr Hugonin's absence, presented the Pope with a lace rochet which represented eight thousand days work. Then the procession of those from the Bayeux diocese began: ladies, priests, men. At the beginning Leo XIII had a kind word for each. But time was pressing. The Vicar General now forbade them to speak to the Holy Father who was tired. The order ran along the ladies' line. Céline was last. Her sister, in front of her, felt her courage fail. 'Speak!' whispered Céline the Intrepid.

Like everyone else, Thérèse Martin knelt down, kissed the Pope's slipper, but, instead of kissing his hand, she said to him crying: *Most Holy Father, I have a great favour to ask of you.* His deep black eyes looked searchingly at her. She repeated her petition. The Pope turned towards Mgr Révérony: 'I do not understand very well.' Displeased, the Vicar General wanted to end the conversation. 'Holy Father, it is a child who wants to enter Carmel at fifteen, but the superiors are looking into the matter at this moment.' 'Ah well, my child,' said the Pope, 'do what the superiors say.' *Oh! Holy Father, if you say yes, everyone else will too.* 'There, there, you will enter if God wills it!'

Her hands joined on Leo XIII's knees, Thérèse wanted a positive answer. Two papal guards, after having tried in vain to make her get up, forcibly lifted her and carried her to the door. Then Céline, feeling very moved, knelt down. She asked the Pope for a blessing for the Lisieux Carmel. M. Révérony, furious, kept his temper: 'The Carmel is already blessed.'

Louis Martin, in the men's group, saw nothing of the scene. When he passed before Leo XIII the Vicar General presented him as the father of three religious. He did not say that he was also the father of the two young girls who had just caused an incident. The Pope blessed the 'Patriarch' and put his hand on his head.

15 Golden Jubilee card of Pope Leo XIII. The 1887 Jubilee was the occasion of the pilgrimage to Rome in which Thérèse took part

The father found his Queen in tears. He tried to console her. No, it was finished, this great trip had been for nothing. Why had she overcome so many obstacles, her uncle, M. Delatroëtte, the bishop, only to stumble at her last hope, the sovereign pontiff? That same evening a letter left for Lisieux,

telling the Carmelites of what Céline, twenty years later, was
to call a 'fiasco', an 'almost shameful humiliation'. Her sister
gives her version of the facts and comments:

> *The Pope is so old that you would think he was dead . . . He can*
> *say almost nothing, it was M. Révérony who spoke . . . Pauline, I*
> *cannot tell you what I felt. I was completely crushed. I felt aban-*
> *doned, and so far away, so far. I could cry writing this letter, my*
> *heart is so sad. Yet God cannot give me trials that are beyond my*
> *strength. He has given me the courage to bear this trial. Oh! it is*
> *very hard. But, Pauline, I am the Child Jesus' little ball, if he*
> *wants to break his toy, he is free. Yes, I will all that he wills.*

The trip continued. While M. Martin remained in Rome
his two daughters visited Pompeii and Naples. The whole
pilgrimage now knew Thérèse's secret. *L'Univers*, Louis Veuillot's newspaper, reported the incident at the audience. But
after Wednesday, 23rd a ray of hope appeared. M. Martin,
taking advantage of his stay in Rome, went to see Brother
Siméon, principal of the Brothers of Christian Schools, whom
he had met two years before on his European trip. He told
him of Sunday's events. The seventy-three-year-old brother
marvelled at such a vocation. Then there was a surprise! M.
Révérony arrived too and was very friendly. M. Martin took
the opportunity to plead his daughter's cause.

On 24 November in the morning, it was farewell to Rome.
At Assisi Thérèse, who had lost the buckle of her belt, was
late. All the carriages had left but one, that of M. Révérony.
Graciously, he took the lost sheep with him; she made herself
very small in the midst of all those great personages.

The return trip passed through Pisa and Genoa. At Nice
the Vicar General promised the young girl he would support
her request to enter Carmel. A hope then remained.

With the ascent to Notre-Dame-de-la-Garde at Marseilles
and the thanksgiving mass in the Fourvière basilica, the long
and complicated journey came to an end on 2 December at
the Gare de Lyon in Paris, at one in the morning. This time
the Martins hurried back to Lisieux. No sooner had they
arrived than they went in all haste to the Carmel. How much
there was to tell!

In twenty-three days it would be Christmas, the first anniversary of the great grace of conversion. How could she still

hope to be a Carmelite after the 'failure' of Rome? There was no time to lose.

DIPLOMATIC BATTLES (3 DECEMBER 1887 TO 1 JANUARY 1888)

In the parlour it was less a matter of recounting all the recent happenings than of discussing a strategy. Abbé Lepelletier, alerted by the article in *l'Univers*, was abreast of the news: so his young penitent wanted to enter Carmel that year? Without taking offence at her silence, he admired her determination. On the other hand the situation remained very tense with the superior. He did not wish to be manipulated by the Carmelites: he was suspicious of their diplomatic manoeuvres. On 8 December in front of the whole community he replied sharply to Mother Geneviève who asked him to allow Thérèse to enter before Christmas: 'You are still speaking to me about that! Are we to think from all these requests that the community's salvation depends on this child's entry? There is no danger in delay. Let her stay with her father until she is twenty-one. I ask you, do not speak to me of this affair any more.'

On the 10th, after a very unpleasant parlour visit with M. Delatroëtte from which Mother Marie de Gonzague went out in tears, M. Guérin also took up the cause. But his meeting with the superior failed in its turn. Thérèse made a rough draft of a letter to Mgr Hugonin which was read and corrected by her uncle. Ten days before the fateful day, the letter was posted, as well as one to M. Révérony, reminding him of his promise at Nice. There remained but to hope.

Every day after mass, when she prayed fervently, the postulant went to the Post Office with her father to look for a reply. Nothing.

And then it was Christmas 1887. There were tears at midnight mass. But Thérèse discovered that the trial was increasing her faith and her self abandonment to the will of God. We cannot impose a date on God. However despite her bitter disappointment she was pleased to be wearing for the first time a pretty navy-blue cap decorated with a white dove.

Then at last, on 1 January, the eve of her fifteenth birthday, a letter from Mother Marie de Gonzague brought Mgr Hugonin's answer. It was yes! He had written to the prioress on 28 December: let her make the decision herself.

Was her joy finally to burst forth? No, for the last obstacle arose – from the Carmel. The young postulant's entrance could be only after the strict Lenten regime, in April. *I was unable to hold back my tears at the thought of such a long wait.* As for M. Martin, he was very annoyed with Pauline who was so changeable. For she was the one who had persuaded the prioress to delay her little sister's entrance.

I do not think I would have seemed unreasonable in not accepting joyfully my three months of exile, but I also believe that, without appearing to be so, this trial was very great and made me grow very much in abandonment and in the other virtues. After this long struggle which had called for so many different strengths, this respite enabled her to take stock and to prepare herself peacefully for that unusual step unforeseen by the Reformer of Carmel, the great Teresa of Jesus: to enter the cloister at fifteen years and three months of age, in a monastery where two of her sisters were already living.

EVALUATION OF A JOURNEY AND A LIFE (1 JANUARY TO 9 APRIL 1888)

On top of all these emotions came Léonie's return home; she could not endure the life of the Visitandines at Caen. After this second attempt her spirits and health were affected. Thérèse did her utmost to make the re-adaptation easier for her.

Life went on peacefully at Les Buissonnets. Thérèse resumed her lessons with Mme Papinau. She thought about her trip, which had *taught her more than long years of study.* She who was so interested in history had grasped something of the history of nations, and that of the Church. To be sure she had hardly been given much solid information – later in Carmel she would humourously mimic the Italian guides' mistakes – but she had laid in an ample stock of deep impressions. For the first, and last, time beyond her native Normandy, she had seen the splendours of nature: Swiss and Italian mountains, the Roman and Umbrian country, the

Riviera and Côte-d'Azur. She saw Paris, Milan, Venice, Bologna, Rome, Naples, Florence, Genoa, Nice, Marseilles, Lyons. She made many discoveries, came into contact with other social classes: *What an interesting study the world makes when you are about to leave it.* 'High society' with its titled people did not dazzle her at all. *I understood that true greatness is to be found in the soul and not in the name.*

What she discovered about herself was just as important. She had thought she was shy and self-conscious but realised how much she had changed when she found herself very much at ease with other people. She was lively, happy to be alive and full of a humour she shared with Céline. She became aware of her femininity and beauty. The way to a splendid marriage could have opened out before her. *My heart could easily have let itself be caught by affection.* Now she could freely choose to make herself a *prisoner for love* behind the grilles of Carmel, that desert where God wanted her to be, and also to be hidden.

Those twenty-nine days had been decisive, and sufficed to confirm her decision. She recognised this: it was enough to shake a vocation that was not strong. Her sister Agnès was justified when she wrote: 'She is only fifteen but I think the impression made by this trip will last all her life, for *her soul is old already.*' She had changed so much in one year!

To fill in the waiting time her father, always eager to travel, proposed to her THE pilgrimage: 'Little Queen, do you want to go to Jerusalem?' She longed to see the places where her beloved had lived but that would have delayed her entrance into Carmel. She refused. It was more pressing to find Jesus there where he was waiting for her.

Tempted to take it easy before facing the austere Carmelite life, she quickly stopped herself. She understood the *value of time* and prepared herself for her entry by the practice of little *nothings*: breaking her own will, biting back a retort, rendering little services without drawing attention to them, and so on. At the end of March – that month would remain in her memory as the most beautiful in her life – she learnt finally the date set for her departure: Monday, 9 April, the feast of the Annunciation.

That day Céline aged nineteen received a proposal of marriage.

A young pupil of Mme Papinau kept this clear memory of Thérèse Martin, a few days before her farewell to 'the world':

That day Thérèse was waiting for her father who had popped into Bouline's grocery shop in the Grande-Rue. I can still see her on the pavement mechanically turning the point of her umbrella in the groove of one of the kerb stones. She was wearing a green dress edged with astrakhan and frogged trimmings, and her hair was tied with a sky-blue ribbon. I have always kept this memory of her.

Part III

Carmel
1888–1897

16 Entrance to the Lisieux Carmel in the rue de Livarot (1890)

5

Postulant
(9 April 1888 to 10 January 1889)

*I did not come to Carmel to live with my sisters,
but only to answer Jesus' call.*

What Pauline had gone through at twenty and Marie at
twenty-six, Thérèse experienced at fifteen; the preparation of
the trousseau, taking leave of her own room, the last walk
round the garden with Tom bounding beside her. The final
meal in the dining room on Sunday, 8 April, with the Guérins
all present. The goodbye to Les Buissonnets where she had
spent more than ten years. She had to leave Léonie, Céline
– Papa above all.

The following morning they all went to the seven o'clock
mass in the chapel of the Carmel in the rue de Livarot; only
Thérèse did not cry. But her heart was pounding. *What a
moment that was! You would have to have experienced it to know how
it felt.*

In front of the door with two locks and two bolts the young
girl knelt down before her father. He too knelt to bless her,
with tears in his eyes. The door opened slowly: the whole
community – their big black veils lowered – was assembled.
M. Delatroëtte was not resigned to Mlle Martin's entrance.
His words of welcome cut short the family's sobs and froze
all present: 'Well! Reverend Mothers, you can sing a Te
Deum! As the bishop's delegate I give you this fifteen-year-
old child whose entrance you have wished for. I hope she
does not disappoint your hopes, but I remind you that if she
does you alone will bear the responsibility.'

Thérèse crossed the threshold. The heavy door closed.
Mother Marie de Gonzague led her to the choir before
showing her her cell on the second floor: a room 2.10m by

3.70m, a bed with a brown couverture, a small stool, an oil lamp, an hour-glass. A plain wooden cross hung on the white wall. Through the window a slate roof and the sky could be seen.

Everything delighted the postulant on her tour of the convent: *With what deep joy I repeated these words: 'I am here for ever and ever!'*

The following day her father wrote to his friends the Nogrixes: 'My little Queen entered Carmel yesterday. God alone could have asked such a sacrifice, but he is helping me so powerfully that in the midst of my tears my heart is overflowing with joy.'

THE LISIEUX CARMEL IN 1888

'Small and poor' was how Marie had described it when she entered. The red brick cloisters, the refectory, the garden with the chestnut 'alley': this monastery which was soon to celebrate its fiftieth anniversary was indeed small and poor.

The community of twenty-six nuns (their average age was forty-seven) who welcomed Thérèse Martin were no strangers: for six years she had visited them. But living there was a different thing. God gave her *the grace not to be under* ANY *illusion* when she entered Carmel.

The Carmelite life had been reformed in the sixteenth century by St Teresa of Avila, the postulant's patron saint. This exceptional woman, who was both a mystic and a very practical person, founded little 'deserts' where enclosed religious sought God privately (two hours of mental prayer daily) and in communal prayer, while working in an atmosphere of friendship and joy. The Spanish foundress, full of common sense and with her feet on the ground, laid down a balanced way of life where love must take precedence over all, including the practices of mortification, which are only means. Three centuries later some Carmels had been diverted towards indiscreet ascetical practices, sometimes towards a narrow moralism. The Lisieux Carmel had not escaped these tendencies which the general climate of French Christianity – with its Jansenist learnings – encouraged. The spirit of penance and mortification was in danger of taking precedence

17 South side of the cloister. Standing at the open window, Mother Agnès of Jesus with Mother Marie de Gonzague seated

over the dynamism of love. More than one Carmelite was terrified of God the Judge.

The young postulant's heart went out to Mother Marie de Gonzague, who was now fifty-four and had been born Marie-Adèle-Rosalie Davy de Virville. The prioress had shown so much interest in her 'Thérèsita' and had fought so hard for her entry! Her bearing, height and natural attractions, her good relations with the Martins, and her sound judgment which was valued by the priests of Lisieux, all drew the new sister to her. Thérèse already loved the old Mother Geneviève of Sainte-Thérèse also, one of the foundresses of that Carmel (in 1833), who had been ill for four years. She suffered, and was silent. Many, including the community's doctor, regarded her as a saint. Besides Mother Geneviève and the elderly nuns, Sister Saint-Joseph of Jesus (the oldest there) and Sister Fébronie of the Holy Infancy (sub-prioress), the community also had five lay-sisters – called white-veiled sisters – who did not recite the office in choir, and two externs,

18 Community recreation in the chestnut alley, 20 April 1895.
Thérèse is standing on the left

sisters outside the cloister, who kept contact with the outside
world.

But for the time being Thérèse's life was connected with
her four sisters of the novitiate: Sister Marie of the Angels,
the novice mistress, born Jeanne de Chaumontel, aged forty-
three, who assembled the little group each day; Sister Marie-
Philomène, aged forty-eight, 'very holy and very limited';
Sister Marie of the Sacred Heart, who was happy to be with
her godchild again; and Sister Marthe of Jesus, aged twenty-
three, an orphan, who had been a white veil postulant for
three months, 'a poor little unintelligent sister', according to
Mother Agnès.

In this community, rather poorly endowed with natural
talent, the prioress, the Martin sisters and two or three other
nuns stood out. At a time when women finished their studies
at fifteen, these few privileged ones seemed very 'learned' to
the group from the country, where extremely hard manual
labour began at an early age.

Wearing a long blue dress and black cape, with a small dark bonnet holding back her thick blonde hair, the postulant began her acquaintance with the Carmelite life. Six hours of prayer in choir, meals at ten and six o'clock (never any meat, except in a case of sickness), followed both times by an hour's community recreation. Seven hours sleep in winter. Apart from the recreation room with its fireplace, no room had a stove. Five hours of manual work (making hosts, painting pictures, sewing, housework, washing). All members of the well-regulated group spent their lives in silence and solitude.

THE BEGINNINGS (APRIL TO JUNE 1888)

For the postulant work consisted of mending. At Les Buissonnets Thérèse had hardly held a needle. Her novice mistress found her slow. She also swept the 'dormitory'[1] and a staircase, and did a little gardening in the afternoon for exercise. She did not study any longer. In the novitiate each day Sister Marie of the Angels explained the Rule, the customs of the common life: the way to dress, eat, move about. Sister Marie of the Sacred Heart, assigned to be her 'Angel',[2] completed this initiation. Did she show her how to hold the heavy Latin breviaries for chanting the office?

The harsh contrast with 'life' at Les Buissonnets did not seem to affect the young newcomer. But this little Carmelite who had been so wanted did, nevertheless, cause division in the community. Surrounded by her two sisters, was Thérèse now going to become 'the Carmel's toy'?

On 17 May the prioress wrote to Mme Guérin: 'This *Loulou*[3] is perfect. Never would I have expected to find such sound judgment in a fifteen-year-old! Not a word has to be said to her. Everything is perfect.'

The first three months in fact filled Thérèse with happiness. *'My dearest Céline, there are moments when I wonder if it is really true that I am in Carmel.'* To her great joy – she who loved

[1] Name given to the corridor on to which the nuns' cells opened.
[2] This is the name given to the nun who initiates the newcomer into the customs of the monastery.
[3] A nickname given to Thérèse by her cousin Marie Guérin, which Mother Marie de Gonzague also used for her.

flowers so much – spring burst upon the garden. And there was festivity. On 22 May her sister Marie made her profession in the presence of Fr Pichon. According to the custom Thérèse crowned her with roses.

The Jesuit preached to the Carmelites for several days. Until then Thérèse had never had a spiritual director. She remembered the desire she had revealed the previous October: *I thought that since you are directing my sisters (Marie and Céline) you would be willing to take the youngest one too.* 'The Martins' family director' accepted.

LIBERATION (28 MAY 1888)

Thérèse had never known how to speak about her inner life and her meeting with her new counsellor on 28 May caused tears because of this difficulty. She made a general confession. The previous evening, having seen her praying in the choir, the Jesuit had taken her for a child without problems. Now he told her: 'In the presence of God, the Blessed Virgin and all the saints, I declare that you have never committed a single mortal sin.' This solemn formula can doubtless be explained because he wished to reassure a person inclined to scruples. He himself had suffered from this problem and been freed from it. A former victim of the destructive effects of Jansenistic scrupulosity, he now preached a God of love. He added: 'Thank God for what he has done for you, for if he abandoned you, instead of being a little angel you would become a little demon.' Thérèse comments: *I had no difficulty in believing it.* The confessor concluded: 'My child, may our Lord always be your superior and your novice master.' On that day Thérèse found herself finally freed from the distress of soul which had tortured her for five years. From now on she was *perfectly at peace*.

After this happy inner liberation, what did she care about the prioress's harshness (*unmeant* – as Thérèse said later). This was a different Marie de Gonzague from the one of the parlour, who had been so kind. Thérèse saw little of her, but at each meeting the prioress humiliated her in one way or another. Thérèsita kissed the ground very often.[1] Did Mother

[1] Act of humility then in use.

Marie de Gonzague, who was moody and ill, want to 'break' that young girl in whom she had noticed tendencies to pride? Or was it to counterbalance the support which the presence of her two sisters gave her?

Thérèse, who felt spontaneously drawn to her, sometimes hung on to the banister of the stairs when she passed in front of the prioress's cell, so as not to knock and ask her for a permission, and so find a *few crumbs of comfort*.

The interviews with her novice mistress were, on the whole, a trial for her. She did not know what to say, and Sister Marie of the Angels kept talking and questioning her. One day, no longer knowing what to do, the postulant threw herself on her neck and kissed her!

She also discovered that community life with twenty-six enclosed women had many difficulties. There were such differences in temperament, social background and everyday behaviour! *Of course, one does not have enemies in Carmel, but still there are natural attractions, one feels drawn towards a certain sister, whereas you go a long way round to avoid meeting another.* After nine years of common life she said baldly: *The lack of judgment, education, the touchiness of some characters, all these things do not make life very pleasant. I know very well that these moral weaknesses are chronic, that there is no hope of a cure.* Later, three sisters left the community, one of them to enter a home for mental patients.

Some early *pin-pricks* wounded her keen sensibility. Sister Saint-Vincent-de-Paul, a lay-sister with a sharp manner, did not spare the newcomer whom she called 'the grand lady'. Thérèse, who sometimes heard the formidable old nun's criticism, just smiled back at her. This same nun, a very good embroiderer, did not refrain from telling the prioress that the young girl was not naturally gifted at manual work and would never be useful to the community. And the sisters, Agnès of Jesus and Marie of the Sacred Heart, wanted to look after the baby of the family as they had at Les Buissonnets. This caused friction. One day Marie received a reply from her godchild which hurt her somewhat: *Thank you . . . I am happy to be with you, but it is better that I deny myself, for we are no longer at home.* For her part Sister Agnès made a resolution (which she did not keep) no longer to fuss over the 'little reed'. 'We have enough to do looking after ourselves . . . let us keep to our own path. Otherwise we would find so many causes for trouble that it would be unbearable.'

It was a difficult situation for one who, coming to Carmel for Jesus, found two attentive 'mothers' there. She felt in danger of being suffocated and wanted to find her own freedom. She did not want always to follow her two sisters.

THE FATHER'S FLIGHT (23–7 JUNE 1888)

Upon the calm summer sky of 1888 burst a thunderclap.

Céline was nineteen on 28 April, and her birthday had been celebrated in the parlour of the Carmel. She had been worried by the proposal of marriage she had received. Not without a struggle, she made her decision. On 15 June she told her father in her turn of her wish to enter Carmel.

Already unsettled by the recent sacrifice of his youngest child, Louis Martin foresaw the departure of this daughter to the contemplative life and his own lonely old age. Léonie too was thinking of re-entering, and had not Pauline written to him last summer: 'I want nothing for you on earth but to see all five of us in the Lord's house! In this I believe I am pleasing you since you yourself desire nothing more.'

Since the trip to Italy M. Martin had aged. 'Our poor little Father', wrote Céline to Thérèse, 'seems to have got so old and worn out. If only you could see him at the communion table, leaning over and supporting himself at best he can; it makes me weep. It breaks my heart. I think he will die soon.' At Alençon an insect had stung him behind his left ear; the sting had never healed properly and now it spread. This epithelial tumour, as big as the palm of a hand, was painful. Much more serious were his arterio-sclerosis and attacks of uraemia (final stages of serious kidney trouble) which caused dizziness, loss of memory, sudden mood changes and gave him the urge to run away.

On the morning of 23 June there was panic at Les Buissonnets: Léonie and Céline, with the help of the maid, searched everywhere for their father. He had disappeared. The Guérins were informed, but they had not seen him at the pharmacy. An anxious night followed. On the 24th a telegram arrived from Le Havre. Louis Martin was asking for money. The Carmel was finally told. On the 25th Céline, accompanied by her uncle Isidore and Ernest Maudelonde, set out for Le Havre to look for her father; they had no address.

The following day there was a further alarm for Léonie, who had remained at home alone. The Prévost's house near Les Buissonnets was destroyed by fire. The firemen put out a fire on the roof of the Martins' house, which fortunately was not badly damaged.

After four days of terrible anxiety M. Martin was found at the Post Office in Le Havre. His mind had cleared, but he was dogged by an obsession: 'to withdraw into solitude and live as a hermit', hardly a reassuring proposal.

These events shocked the whole family. The youngest of the Martin sisters, who loved her father very dearly, was shaken to the core. At a time when her father needed her she was a 'prisoner'. How could she avoid the indiscreet questions of some of the nuns, the tactless remarks, the echoes of Lisieux gossip. If M. Martin had gone 'mad', was it not due to the departure of his daughters into religion, especially the youngest, whom he loved so much?

Strength was not wanting in the postulant through these very difficult beginnings. She was determined that her letters to her father should be light and amusing, cheerfully reminding him of the happy moments during their Italian trip, the mischievous games they had played; but to Céline she wrote in a very different vein. And adding to these serious worries she was experiencing her first dryness in prayer. Until then prayer had been her joy. All of a sudden she felt a terrible blackness: *Life is often burdensome, what bitterness – but what sweetness. Yes, life is an effort, it is hard to begin a day's work . . . if only we could still be aware of Jesus. Oh! we would do anything for him, but no, he seems a thousand miles away . . . He is hiding.* But the fighter *armed for war* is revealed. There were no outward signs of her inner struggles.

In a letter to Marie Guérin, who was spending her first holiday at the magnificent La Musse estate (near Evreux), which her father had just inherited,[1] the young girl made

---

[1] A hundred-acre estate where the Guérins would henceforth spend all their holidays.

jokes. She even astonished her novice mistress; one evening in June when the latter went into her cell to give her some encouragement, she found Thérèse in a long nightdress, with her hair down. She received this reply: *Yes I am suffering very much, but I feel that I can bear still greater trials.*

RECEPTION OF THE HABIT DELAYED (OCTOBER 1888 TO JANUARY 1889)

On 12 August, after a short stay at Alençon with Céline and Léonie, their father had another attack. The family situation was uncertain. Thérèse should normally have received the habit after the six months postulancy, that is, in October. The chapter had, in fact, with Mgr Hugonin's authorisation, voted for her admission. M. Delatroëtte, still cautious, had advised them of it in a rather curt letter. They still had to find a date. M. Martin, ever generous to the Carmel, had already sent some Alençon lace to adorn his Queen's dress for the ceremony.

Fr Pichon's departure for Canada did not help these plans. Céline, who was now responsible for running the house and had to look after her father (Léonie was now completely taken up with thoughts of re-entering the Visitation), grieved for the loss of her director. Thérèse wrote to her: *Jesus is still with us!* From then on Thérèse was to send a monthly letter to Canada to report on her inner development, to the Jesuit she never saw again.[1]

On 30 October together with her father and Léonie, Céline went to Le Havre to say goodbye to her director as he was leaving for the new world. At Honfleur M. Martin suffered a serious relapse. It was a terrible journey. The sick man sobbed. He recited a poem: 'Death alone attracts me overwhelmingly.' At Le Havre there was no Fr Pichon. They finally caught up with him in Paris. M. Martin's mental condition moved him: 'The venerable old man, who has reached his second childhood, will surely not be long in leaving for heaven' (letter to Marie).

[1] In eight years Fr Pichon must have received about fifty letters from Thérèse. He did not keep any of them.

In these circumstances the reception of the habit had to be delayed. The bishop would only be free in January. 'It will be said that the little lamb (another of Thérèsita's nicknames) suffers set-backs at every step,' remarked the Jesuit.

The sick man's condition improved in December. The parish priest of the cathedral had started a fund for the purchase of a central altar and M. Martin paid in full the required sum of 10,000F.[1] His brother-in-law (who had just sold his pharmacy) found this liberality excessive. Thérèse approved of her father's generosity. It was too bad that he had just lost 50,000F on his Panama Canal shares at the time of the financial scandal that shook the young French Republic.

Finally the date for the clothing was fixed: Wednesday, 9 January 1889. Nine months to the day after her entry into Carmel on the feast of the Annunciation. Always on the lookout for coincidences of dates, the postulant was delighted.

A PAINFUL RETREAT (5–9 JANUARY 1889)

She celebrated her sixteenth birthday on 2 January and on the evening of the 5th went into retreat. Fourteen notes exchanged with her sisters speak of the difficulties, the *sadnesses*, of those days of solitude. The aridity which she had experienced for some months grew worse during the three or four hours of daily prayer. *It is nothing in comparison with Jesus! Dryness! Sleep!* She was not getting enough sleep despite permission to rise later. *Deprived of all consolation – in darkness . . . Jesus is not doing much to keep the conversation going!*

Abbé Domin's retreats had had such a strong effect on her that she always dreaded retreats, whether private or preached. But 'the little ball', as Sister Agnès called her, rose above all these troubles. Her love urged her to strenuous action.

Since Jesus wants to sleep, why should I prevent him, I am only too happy if he does not stand on ceremony with me . . . I want so much to love him! To love him more than he has ever been loved! . . . It

---

[1] He gave the same amount for Thérèse's dowry in 1890.

is incredible how large my heart seems to be . . . I would like to
convert all the sinners on earth and save all the souls in purgatory!

She was undergoing a tough emotional battle. She thanks the
One who will soon be (her) fiancé for not allowing her to become
attached to ANY *created thing. He knows well that if he gave me a*
shadow of happiness I would cling to it with all my energy, all the
strength of my heart.

In the middle of her retreat she learnt that a death had
delayed the ceremony until the 10th. What did the date
matter! Jesus was Master.

The *pin-pricks from creatures* were worse. She smiled at Sister
Saint-Vincent-de-Paul, who seldom missed an opportunity to
make an unpleasant remark to her. *Those around me are really*
good, but there is something, I don't know what, that repels me.

There was still anxiety for her father's health. Would he
be able to stand the emotional strain of the ceremony? No
one dared mention it. Twenty-five years later Mother Agnès
of Jesus remembered her own fears. 'Our poor father was in
danger of an attack at any moment, I was afraid of some sort
of accident during the ceremony. I still tremble to think of it
and remember that, on the evening before, I asked God not
to let him cry in the chapel.'

Returning later to the first nine months of her life in
Carmel, Sister Thérèse of the Child Jesus declared that the
first steps of *the little sixteen-year-old fiancée* met *more thorns than*
roses. The new diet, the lack of sleep, the cold, but above all
the humiliations, the repressed feelings, the sufferings of the
communal life; all that would have been nothing without her
father's illness. She simply took up the pet-names given her
by her companions: little lamb, Jesus' toy, little ball, little
reed, atom. For her they were an invitation to the hidden life,
to littleness, to abandonment, to silence. But there was fire
in her heart.

She saw the taking of the habit as a total gift of herself to
her love: Jesus. What did it matter if he slept. This was how
she saw the difficult days she had just lived through: *I believe*
Jesus' work during this retreat has been to detach me from all that is
not himself.

And so ended her postulancy. On entering Carmel: *Suffering*
held out its arms to me and I threw myself into them with love. After

such a beginning, many another young girl might have given up.

THE TAKING OF THE HABIT (10 JANUARY 1889)

In her white velvet dress with its long train, with her hair down over her shoulders and crowned with lilies given by her aunt, Thérèse Martin went down the aisle of the Carmel chapel on her father's arm. Mgr Hugonin gave a short talk and made a mistake in the ceremonial: in place of the *Veni Creator*, he intoned the *Te Deum*. (Was this the fulfilment of M. Delatroëtte's prophecy made nine months before?) Thérèse who was about to enter the novitiate was radiant. As for her father, *he had never been more handsome, more* DIGNIFIED. *He was admired by everyone.*

Re-entering the enclosure Thérèse discovered with delight that nature was in tune with her: snow blanketed the garden. She loved it so much that she had asked for it. The temperature that morning had given no warning of such a surprise. The little fiancée saw it as the kindness of her beloved who fulfilled her smallest desires. *The snow at my clothing seemed a small miracle, the whole town was surprised.*

From that time she wore the habit of Carmel joyfully: rough homespun and brown scapular, white wimple and veil, leather belt with rosary, woollen 'stockings',[1] rope sandals. After the celebrations daily life resumed.

But a small, very significant change appears in her letters. Henceforth Thérèse would often sign her letters 'Sister Thérèse of the Child Jesus *of the Holy Face*'. Since 26 April 1885 she had been enrolled in the Archconfraternity of the Holy Face of Tours, a devotion spread by Sister Marie of Saint-Pierre and M. Dupont. In the choir of the Lisieux Carmel a lamp burned day and night in front of a picture of the Holy Face. But it had taken those nine months for her to discover that the Child Jesus whose name she bore had begun, right from the manger, to live a life of sacrifice which would

---

[1] For summer these 'stockings' (like leggings) were made of cloth. 'Sister Thérèse never complained,' reported Sister Marie of Jesus. 'One day when she was asked if the stockings she was wearing were not too short, she answered simply: "I think they are" ' (1907).

lead him to Calvary. Since 25 December 1886 she knew that
Christmas was not a sorry story, but a mystery of strength.
By choosing, at the dawn of her religious life, thus to complete
her name, she was truly setting out to follow in the steps of
Jesus. Fr Pichon, writing from Canada, confirmed her choice:
'What makes your profession glorious is the seal of the cross
. . . Jesus has given you his childhood and his passion. How
fortunate you are! What a matchless dowry!'

6

Novice
(10 January 1889 to 24 September 1890)

He was humbled so that his face was hidden
and no one recognised him; and I too want to hide my face.

The novice was given a new duty: to prepare the water and
the 'beer'[1] in the refectory, and the bread in the recess called
Saint-Alexis, under the stairs where the big black spiders
terrified her. Henceforth she took her turn at community
tasks; ringing the various bells, reading during meals,
intoning verses in choir. As Sister Agnès of Jesus was also in
charge of the refectory the temptation for the two sisters to
speak together was great. The novice resisted this firmly. She
was always afraid of reviving the family atmosphere in her
convent life.

On 13 February Mother Marie de Gonzague was re-elected
prioress for three years. Sister Marie-Philomène left the
novitiate and Sister Marthe and Sister Marie of the Sacred
Heart remained there with Sister Thérèse.

Two photographs taken in January 1889[2] show the novice
rather bundled up in her large new homespun, her cheeks
chubby, smiling near the cloister cross. The Carmelite diet,
rich in starchy food, had made her put on weight (she did
not fast until she was twenty-one). In fact she suffered daily
from indigestion. As Sister Marie of the Angels had ordered
her to tell her when she was ill, Sister Thérèse knocked on
her door every day. Having forgotten her instructions,

---

[1] A drink of hops that was made at the monastery.
[2] Taken by Abbé Gombault who had entered the enclosure for some work.
A small favour for M. Martin that Sister Agnès asked to be kept secret.
For a photograph taken about the same time see p. 191.

19 Lisieux Carmel. The refectory

Sister Marie then complained of her novice's endless ailments!
Dialogue between them remained difficult.

THE GREAT TRIAL OF HER FATHER'S HUMILIATION
(12 FEBRUARY 1889)

Scarcely twelve days after their father's *triumph*, Céline was
greatly concerned about his state of health. He was confined
to bed. Suddenly the drama began. There was an unexpected
crisis: 'In his imagination the sick man saw terrifying things:
Slaughter, battles; he heard cannon and drum.' He grabbed
hold of his revolver – to defend us, Céline said – and would
not put it down. Isidore Guérin was summoned, and feared
for the lives of his nieces and Maria Cosseron, the maid.
Helped by his friend Auguste Benoît, he disarmed his brother-
in-law. The doctor decided on immediate confinement in the
Bon Sauveur asylum at Caen.
      Under pretext of going for a walk the sick man, who had
become calm again, was taken away. It was snowing. There

was a brief stop at the Carmel where Pauline alone saw him. He gave her a few small fish which he had wrapped in his handkerchief. How often he had brought his catch to the extern sisters!

At Caen Louis Martin was placed in the care of Sister Costard who looked after one section of the asylum. He was to remain there for three years. A week later Léonie and Céline became boarders with the Sisters of Saint-Vincent-de-Paul near the Bon Sauveur and, from 19 February to 5 May, went there each day to ask for news. They could see their father only once a week. Frequent letters were exchanged between Caen and Lisieux.

This had really happened, even though it had been inconceivable before: the respected 'Patriarch' was living with 'the insane'. *I did not know that on 12 February, one month after my reception of the habit, our dear father was to drink the most bitter and most humiliating of all chalices. That day I did not say I could suffer still more! Words cannot express our anguish.*

The Martin family was scattered. The pitying conversations and ill-natured gossip going the rounds of Lisieux sometimes tactlessly echoed within the enclosure. Each of his daughters tried to stand fast and support the others. What was the meaning of such a trial?

The sick man had regained his peace after two crises and astonished the medical team by his gentleness and submissiveness. Who could tell of his suffering, his humiliation? To a doctor he said: 'I have always been accustomed to command and I see myself reduced to obeying, it is hard. But I know why God has given me this trial: I have never had humiliation in my life, I needed it.' To which the other replied: 'Well! that may be it!'

Separated from Céline and not seeing her[1] for fifteen months, Sister Thérèse of the Child Jesus plunged into silence, pondering the word of God which the liturgy and her reading lavished upon her. The young girl's courage was amazing, even if, sometimes, she could not hide her tears. The whole period of her novitiate was marked by this great trial which cut her to the heart.

---

[1] In the strict sense, for building works in the extern area had cut off access to the usual parlours.

In April the Guérins bought a house in Lisieux at 19 rue de la Chaussée. While waiting to move they stayed at Les Buissonnets with Léonie and Céline who had returned. It had become pointless to remain at Caen. In July they all moved into the new house.

On 18 July M. Martin's *passion* reached its culmination: he had to sign an act renouncing the administration of his goods. His brother-in-law feared he would ruin himself financially by his reckless liberality. That day the sick man was perfectly lucid. He sobbed: 'Oh, my children are abandoning me!'

YOU HAVE HIDDEN ME FOREVER

During this long period of inner suffering (her letters show her sometimes on the verge of breaking down), an unexpected grace at the beginning of July was to enlighten Sister Thérèse for a whole week. In a small grotto at the bottom of the garden – in a hermitage in honour of St Magdalene – she experienced something new: *it was as though a veil had been cast over all things of this earth for me; I was entirely hidden beneath the Blessed Virgin's veil . . . At this time I was placed in charge of the refectory . . . I recall doing things as though not doing them; it was as if someone had lent me a body. I remained that way for a whole week.*

It was a very special grace, for normally she experienced difficulties at prayer when sleep – she was still not sleeping well – often overpowered her. Working with Sister Agnès in the refectory – when they had permission to speak – Sister Thérèse did not respond to her confidences. She listened. Recalling this period one day, she said to her sister: *You had come to the point where you no longer knew me.*

The fear of sin still tried her, and she sometimes had attacks of scruples. One of Fr Pichon's letters testifies to this: 'I forbid you in the name of God to question your state of soul. The Devil is laughing heartily. I protest against this wilful distrust. Believe, come what may, that God loves you.'

However it was the same Thérèse who wrote two letters 'of direction' to her cousin Marie Guérin, who was beset by scruples. On a trip to Paris with Léonie and Céline, she had visited the International Exhibition[1] and certain galleries, where some 'nudes' disturbed her. She stopped receiving communion. The young novice, recalling her own experience, wrote to her firmly:

> *I understand everything . . . your poor little Thérèse can guess it all and she assures you that you can go without any fear of receiving your only true Friend. She too has passed through the martyrdom of scruples but Jesus gave her the grace to receive communion just the same . . . Your heart is made to love Jesus, love him passionately, pray hard that the most beautiful years of your life may not be spent in imaginary fears . . . receive communion often, very often. Therein lies the only remedy if you want to be cured.*[2]

Now that her father was living at a distance in the night of his trial, she entered more deeply into her desert vocation. She wanted *to disappear in order to love. To be that grain of sand, hidden, unknown, of no account, trodden underfoot. What a joy to be so hidden that no one thinks of you! To be unknown even to those with whom you live.*

Who was she thinking of? The 'battles' of community life continued. Often the young Thérèse had to tread her *self-love beneath her feet.* She was finally to win over old Sister Saint-Pierre (who was very difficult because of her many ailments), by accompanying her every evening to the refectory, and finishing off that small service and its complicated ritual with her most beautiful smile. She already knew that love must be put into the smallest things. Poverty had a special attraction for her and she chose the ugliest and most inconvenient objects for her use. *I applied myself to practising little virtues, not having the aptitude to practise great ones.*

When the bonds with Sister Agnès (with whom she was living) became strained, those which linked her to Céline 'in the world' paradoxically became stronger. Parlour visits and letters repeat the favourite theme of these exchanges: suffering accepted for Jesus. To suffer in poverty, poorly, without sensible courage. The two sisters spoke of the shortness of life, the joy of heaven, the final reunion of all the scattered family: *Life will pass very quickly. In heaven we will not mind seeing that*

---

[1] Organised for the centenary of the French Revolution.
[2] Pius X, the Pope of frequent communion, read this letter in 1910 and was very enthusiastic about it.

all the relics of Les Buissonnets have been taken here or there! What does earth matter?

THE END OF LES BUISSONNETS

She had to renounce everything. All that had still kept her childhood so near, disappeared. Her family was separated, Les Buissonnets deserted. In October the neighbours saw a very sad expedition leave: the furniture was being moved out. The Carmel inherited a few pieces. A low cart went into the Carmelites' garden through the workmen's entrance. Faithful Tom had followed. Bursting in, he broke the enclosure, where several sisters, their large veils lowered, awaited the convoy. Instinctively the white spaniel threw himself on his young mistress to lick her tears.

From that time the Carmelites' prayers would be made to the sound of the ticking of Les Buissonnets' clock. The lease of the house would be up at Christmas, the third anniversary of Thérèse's conversion. When she made her last tour of the garden Céline picked an ivy leaf for her sister. A page was definitively turned in the life of the novice, now nearly seventeen. Truly, only Jesus remained for her. She did not indulge herself in self-pity over her sufferings. She offered them to *save souls. Let us be apostles, above all, let us save priests' souls . . . Alas! how many bad priests there are, priests who are not holy enough . . . Let us pray, let us suffer for them.* Her letters as a novice repeat these exhortations unceasingly. To see her smiling under her white veil, who would have dreamt the depth at which this young girl was living?

POSTPONEMENT OF PROFESSION (JANUARY TO SEPTEMBER 1890)

Her cries of love for Jesus – which she confided continually to Céline – expressed her desire to consecrate herself totally to him as soon as possible. At the beginning of 1889 she had made a private vow of chastity.

Usually the novitiate preceding profession lasted a year. Sister Thérèse had hoped to make her final commitment on or after 11 January 1890. There was another obstacle: Mother Marie de Gonzague, with Sister Agnès's consent, asked her to renounce that joy. They found the novice beyond reproach, but felt M. Delatroëtte might oppose the request. The superior had not relented: Thérèse was too young for a final commitment. Besides, would not her father's illness be another reason for not daring to mention it?

The novice felt deeply disappointed: waiting always seemed to be her lot. But during prayer she realised that her *intense desire to make (her) profession was mixed with great self-love.* She surrendered to her beloved. *I will wait as long as you desire.* She must not waste this time but fervently prepare herself for her wedding. How? By abandoning herself to the will of Jesus.

Yes, I want to be forgotten, not only by creatures, but also by MYSELF. *I'd like to be so reduced to nothingness, that I have no desire. The glory of my Jesus that is all, as for my own, I abandon it to him, and if he seems to forget me, well, he is free since I am no longer mine, but his. He will grow weary of making me wait quicker than I of waiting for him!*

When a Jesuit, Fr Blino, came to preach at the Carmel she confided to him her lifelong hope: to become a great saint and to love God as much as Teresa of Avila. The preacher was shocked by these remarks, coming from such a young nun. He found there traces of pride and presumption. 'Moderate your desires.' *Why, Father, since our Lord has said: 'Be perfect as your heavenly Father is perfect'.* This scriptural argument did not convince the Jesuit. However later at the Carmel in the rue de Messine in Paris he spoke highly of this novice.

But Fr Blino's objections did not make her change her mind. To Céline, who had returned from a pilgrimage to Tours[1] and Lourdes, she confided: *Do you think St Teresa received more graces than you? As for me, I shall not tell you to aim at her* SERAPHIC *sanctity, but rather to be perfect as your heavenly Father is perfect. Oh! Céline, our infinite desires are not dreams or fancies, since Jesus himself gave us this commandment!*

At seventeen she spoke out. She had always been the same and dared to say what she thought: *You know, I do not see the*

---

[1] To the Oratory of the Holy Face of M. Dupont, 'the holy man of Tours'.

Sacred Heart like everyone else (her sister had been to Paray-le-
Monial), *I think the heart of my spouse is mine alone, as mine is his
alone, and so I talk to him in the solitude of that delightful heart-to-
heart, while waiting for the day when I shall gaze upon him face to
face!*

Two important influences helped her greatly during this
long novitiate: two readings which enlightened her and
grounded her firmly in the word of God and the Carmelite
tradition.

NO FORM OR COMELINESS

For some months Sister Thérèse contemplated the face of
Jesus with his eyes lowered (*for if we saw his eyes we would die
of joy*). The face of her beloved fascinated her. The liturgical
texts heard during Lent gave her a new insight. She read, re-
read and meditated upon them and they only appeared in
her letters in July. She sent Céline a sheet of paper on which
she had copied out some texts which *say so much to (her) soul*.
With a very sure biblical instinct (she had not received any
education in this field),[1] certain passages from the prophet
Isaiah (Chapter 53) gave her a key to reading the life of Jesus
'the suffering servant'. *These words of Isaiah have been the whole
foundation of my devotion to the Holy Face, or, to be more exact, the
foundation of all my devotion.* At the same time they gave
meaning to the terrible trial of her father, now exiled and
alone. He too was the just man who suffered, confined at
Caen. *Papa! Oh! Céline, I cannot tell you all I am thinking . . .
How can I say things which are in the innermost depths of my soul!
. . . Jesus has sent us the best-chosen cross he was able to find in his
immense love. How can we complain when he himself was looked upon
as a man stricken by God and afflicted.*

Her father had always been an image of the heavenly
Father for her. Now she discovered that the Son, humiliated,
despised, unrecognisable, was also the image of her father.
Suffering sent her back to the Son's self-abasement, to the
mystery of the cross. Love himself has been down to these
bottomless depths: *Now we are orphans, but we can say with love:*

---

[1] The novices did not have a whole Bible at their disposal.

'Our Father who art in heaven'. Yes, he is still all in all for our souls!
This purification of her heart enabled her to cross a decisive
threshold.

OUR FATHER ST JOHN OF THE CROSS

On the same sheet of paper Thérèse quoted, for the first time,
a passage from St John of the Cross. *Oh! what insights I have
gained from the works of our holy father, St John of the Cross!
When I was seventeen and eighteen (1890–1), I had no other spiritual
nourishment . . . I begged God to accomplish in me what he wrote.*

In the Lisieux Carmel this was somewhat unusual reading
for a novice who was so young. At recreation one day Mother
Coeur de Jésus was surprised at a comment made by Sister
Thérèse on the Spanish Carmelite's work. Sister Marie of the
Angels felt the same surprise during times of spiritual direction. At that time St John of the Cross was little read in
the French Carmels. But the third centenary of his death
(1591–1891) aroused fresh interest in his writings.[1]

'The doctor of love' satisfied the deepest aspirations of the
young novice's eager heart.

> *My dear little Marie, for my part I know of no other means to
> arrive at perfection except love. To love, how well our hearts are
> made for that! Sometimes I try to find another word to express love,
> but on this earth of exile words are powerless to communicate all
> the vibrations of the soul, and so I have to be satisfied with this one
> word: love!*

The fear of God, which she found in certain sisters, paralysed
her. *My nature is such that fear makes me recoil, with* LOVE *not only
do I go forward, I fly.*

After an eight-month extension of her novitiate M. Delatroëtte finally wrote to the novice to say that, despite his reservations, he would not oppose her writing to the bishop for
permission to make her profession.

The community, three times consulted according to the
custom, approved this step. At the beginning of August Mgr
Hugonin sent his consent.

---

[1] The Carmelites of Paris published a second edition of his works at that
time.

At that time a Carmelite's profession consisted of two ceremonies: the first, inside the enclosure in the chapter room, was fixed for Monday, 8 September; the second, in the presence of the faithful, called 'the taking of the veil', for Wednesday, 24 September.

Sister Thérèse of the Child Jesus of the Holy Face was at last nearing her goal. Soon, at seventeen and a half, she would finally be a Carmelite.

A RETREAT OF GREAT DRYNESS (28 AUGUST TO 7 SEPTEMBER 1890)

This irrevocable commitment had to be prepared for by a ten-day retreat which began on Thursday, 28 August. Once again, this time of solitude did not bring the retreatant any consolation. *Absolute dryness and almost total abandonment were my lot.* She compared her *wedding journey* to an entrance into *an underground passage where it is neither hot nor cold . . . Where I see nothing but a half-veiled light, the light which comes from the downcast eyes of my spouse's face! He says nothing and I say nothing to him either except that I love him more than myself.*

On the evening of 7 September, while making her way of the cross in private after the office of matins, panic seized her: a terrible doubt about her vocation, an anguish which she had never known till then: *I have not got a vocation! I want to deceive everyone!*

When all the community was praying till midnight in the choir on the eve of that profession, she asked the novice mistress to come out so that she could tell her her fears. Sister Marie of the Angels reassured her. But Thérèse wanted the prioress's confirmation also! In her turn, she came out of the chapel and simply laughed at her novice.

The following morning *a river of peace* flowed into her as, prostrated on the ground and surrounded by her community, she pronounced her final vows. Near her heart she carried a note of twenty-three lines which explained her step. She offered herself totally to Jesus (whom she addressed with the familiar 'tu'), and asked him to keep her from committing the smallest voluntary faults. She asked for *martyrdom of the*

heart or body, or rather, both. And *that today* many souls might
be saved!

A graphologist has described this note as 'touching'. 'You
can judge the extent of her impressionability, weakness, fears,
mood changes, lack of confidence in her own powers, anxiety
and anguish.' But also, 'an iron determination, a will to fight,
fierce energy: a child's fears and a warrior's resolve'.

On 2 September the young Carmelite went into the outside
chapel. (Céline took this opportunity to kiss 'her cheeks which
were so very soft and fresh'.) She had to answer the questions
of the canonical examination. 'Why have you come to
Carmel?' *I have come to save souls and especially to pray for priests.*
Her life's goal remained; it was inflexible.

Mother Marie de Gonzague suggested that she asked for
her father's cure. But the professed nun's prayer was: *My
God, I beg you, let it be your will that Papa be cured!* She did not
stop thinking of her father. At the beginning of September
she had received Leo XIII's blessing – asked for by Brother
Siméon in Rome – for herself and for 'the saintly old man
who was greatly tried by suffering'.

In anticipation of the public ceremony Thérèse and Céline
had conceived a foolish hope: to bring M. Martin from Caen.
In the parlour on Tuesday, 23rd they disclosed their plan.
But Uncle Guérin would not hear of it.

A DAY COMPLETELY VEILED IN TEARS: THE TAKING OF THE
VEIL (24 SEPTEMBER 1890)

The young fiancée had drawn up, half in fun, half seriously,
an invitation to her wedding. The idea had come to her from
her cousin Jeanne Guérin, who was to marry Dr Francis La
Néele on 1 October. *Almighty God, creator of heaven and earth,
sovereign ruler of the world, and the most glorious Virgin Mary, queen
and princess of the heavenly court, invite you to be present at the
marriage of their Son, Jesus, King of kings and Lord of lords with
Mlle Thérèse Martin . . .*

But the wedding day was completely veiled in tears.
Thérèse wept because her father was not present. Just before
going into the ante-choir her sister Agnès scolded her: 'I
cannot understand why you are crying! How could you have

hoped to have our poor father at your ceremony? If he were here, we would be in danger of far greater sufferings than that caused by his absence.' Yes, Thérèse would be alone when she committed herself to follow Jesus. Her father was confined, her spiritual father was in Canada, the bishop was kept at Bayeux by illness. *Everything was sadness and bitterness. Nevertheless* PEACE, *always* PEACE *reigned at the bottom of the chalice.* Yet this did not prevent her from crying again with Céline in the parlour in the afternoon. *Left to her own resources* the seventeen-year-old Carmelite felt that she was still *very weak*.

The character-sketch which Mother Marie de Gonzague drew the day after the profession shows that the prioress, despite her inconsistencies of character, was clear-sighted. In a letter to the prioress of the Tours Carmel, she speaks of 'a child (she) offered to God yesterday. This angelic seventeen-year-old has the judgment of a thirty-year-old, the religious perfection of an old and accomplished novice, and self-mastery. She is a perfect nun. Yesterday there was not a dry eye at the sight of her great and total sacrifice.'

On the 24th a young girl of twenty, present at the ceremony, was convinced of her own vocation. That day Marie Guérin decided that she would become a Carmelite like her young cousin.

The young Thérèse Martin, on the eve of her entering Carmel, had written to her sister Agnès: *I want to be a saint. The other day I read something which pleased me greatly. I don't recall which saint said it, but it was: 'I am not perfect, but I* WANT *to become so.'* The young girl had written the word 'want' in very large letters, and underlined it. She had expressed the same idea to her father: *I will try to bring you glory by becoming a great saint.*

For the past two years in Carmel she had been carrying on this struggle for sanctity. The sufferings, which were not lacking, seemed to her a privileged way to prove her love for Jesus. Did not her *Imitation of Christ* tell her: 'Love can do all things, the most impossible things do not seem difficult to it.'

Stretched to the limits of her own strength – her profession note shows this – anxious about her weakness, and concerned for her inner purity,[1] she began to have a presentiment that sanctity is not so easily conquered.

---

[1] Anxiety as to her state of grace would continue until the end of 1892, or even to the beginning of 1893.

7

The Burial
(24 September 1890 to 20 February 1893)

Christ is my love. He is my whole life.

Henceforth Sister Thérèse of the Child Jesus plunged ever more deeply into the wilderness where she wished to hide herself with her beloved who was hidden. Silence enveloped her father whose health remained precarious. Léonie and Céline went to see him regularly at Caen. There was no sign of an imminent return to Lisieux. In the Carmel his name was only whispered, as if he was in disgrace. The Guérins were full of the happiness brought by Jeanne and Francis's marriage, and visited the parlour less frequently. It was a hidden year for the young Carmelite.

Her prayer was very often that of St Peter,[1] or she remained in inner darkness. Abbé Youf scolded her, but Mother Marie de Gonzague reassured her; keep going without any consolation: 'You will thus become a true Carmelite in the remoteness of the wilderness and darkness of the night.' The winter of 1890–1 was very severe. *I felt cold enough to die*, Thérèse would confide much later.

She continued to fill the little acts of everyday life with love. *I loved to fold up the mantles forgotten by the sisters, and to render them all the little services I could.* She tried not to *let one small sacrifice escape her, not one look, one word, taking advantage of all the smallest things and doing them for love.*

No one noticed this heroism in little things. Sister Thérèse did not get involved in the 'tales' which sometimes went round the community. Neither did she defend herself when she was accused unjustly. She smiled at the sisters she found

[1] That is, she slept, like St Peter in the garden of Gethsemane.

least agreeable. She ate everything she was given, without protest. Sister Marthe did not hesitate to serve her with the left-overs that no one else wanted. Thérèse remembered, among other things, a *dried up omelette, fit for the bin*. Sister Saint-Raphaël, who sat next to her in the refectory, used to take, without realising it, almost the whole bottle of 'cider'.

This was how she lived, day after day. Quite naturally, she remained flexible, genuine and smiling. It is true that sometimes she had to struggle strenuously to check the anger that rose within her. For she was impetuous.

Shortly after her eighteenth birthday she had a change of work. She was appointed assistant sacristan to Sister Saint-Stanislas, a kind old nun who nicknamed her 'little Sister Amen'. No longer working in the refectory, she did not see Sister Agnès. In July 1891 Sister Marie of the Sacred Heart left the novitiate. Thérèse still had to complete the three years training there with Sister Marthe. She had noticed that the latter showed an attachment to the prioress that was too exclusive. In silence and prayer she came to realise that one day she would have to speak to her about it. For this attachment *was like that of a dog to its master*. But it was not yet the time to intervene.

Her solitude increased. She willed it for Jesus alone, to save souls for him, especially those of priests. Just at that time one priest in particular was causing a great stir in France.

THE 'RENEGADE' CARMELITE

Father Hyacinthe Loyson, a brilliant preacher at Notre-Dame in Paris, had been a Sulpician and a Dominican novice before becoming a Carmelite and provincial of his order, but he left the Catholic Church in 1869. Three years later he married a young American widow, a Protestant, by whom he had a son. In 1879 he founded the Catholic Anglican Church which rejected papal infallibility (proclaimed by the Vatican Council in 1870), proposed the election of bishops by priests and people, was in favour of a married clergy, and wanted the liturgy to be in French. After major excommunication had been pronounced against him, he continued to travel round France giving lectures. In 1891 he was in Normandy, at Coutances then at Caen. His presence was given wide coverage in the local press. Thérèse received several articles which Céline had cut out of *La Croix du Calvados*. While the clerical papers were calling Fr Loyson the 'renegade monk', and Léon Bloy was furiously lampooning him, Sister Thérèse of the Child Jesus wrote and told Céline that she was praying for her *brother*. What God had done for Pranzini the murderer, could he not repeat for the rebel priest? *Let us not stop praying; confidence produces miracles.* From that time until her death, she was not to cease praying for him. She offered her last communion, 19 August 1897, for Father Hyacinthe whose name no one dared to mention in the Carmel. Sister Agnès was to say: 'This conversion filled her whole life.'

She also gave her attention to the family of the Guérins' cousin Marguerite-Marie (Maudelonde) who had married René Tostain, a magistrate who was an atheist. The young woman had been influenced by her husband's views and was having doubts about her faith. Thérèse asked Céline to lend her Arminjon's book which had helped them so much four years before. There was always the same concern: *Oh! Céline, let us not forget souls, but forget ourselves for them.*

CÉLINE'S FUTURE

Céline was causing her sister concern. People she knew were marrying. There had been four weddings in five years. Céline was an attractive girl of twenty-two and Henri Maudelonde, a solicitor from Caen, was infatuated with her. He did not hide his feelings at La Musse château where the Guérins held splendid parties. Every summer Céline joined her cousins there. On 8 December 1889 she had taken a vow of chastity and said she intended to become a nun. But she experienced strong temptations, and her health was affected as a result. She prayed earnestly to the Virgin of the Smile. Thérèse was worried. But she remained firmly convinced that her sister would join her in Carmel, and did everything she could to make this happen. Jesus was calling her there.

Sister Thérèse also fought for her companion in the novitiate, Sister Marthe. For her sake, she put off the date for her own annual retreat so that their times of solitude would coincide. This was a real sacrifice for the younger nun, for Sister Marthe frittered away her companion's rare free time during the sisterly conversations together which the prioress permitted.

A way to forget herself even more would be by going to Indo-China, to the Carmel of Saigon which had been founded from Lisieux in 1861. Thérèse had thought about it. There, she would truly be hidden, exiled, forgotten by all.

ON THE WAVES OF CONFIDENCE AND LOVE (7–15 OCTOBER 1891)

The times of retreat remained a source of uneasiness for the young professed sister. The preachers of that time did not refrain from terrorising scrupulous souls by stressing sin, the sufferings of purgatory, and even those of hell. One phrase heard during a sermon made Sister Thérèse weep: 'No one knows if they are worthy of love or of hate.' At that time she experienced *great inner trials of all kinds, even wondering sometimes whether heaven existed.* How was it possible to become holy if sin threatened on every side?

The chaplain himself, Abbé Youf, was a very scrupulous person. One day Sister Thérèse of Saint-Augustin, a strict and austere nun, came out of the confessional in tears and went and knocked on the prioress's door: 'Mother, the chaplain has just told me that I already have one foot in hell, and if I go on like this I will soon put the second one there!' 'Don't worry,' replied Mother Marie de Gonzague, 'I already have both feet there!'

Was Sister Thérèse nervous about this retreat of 1891? 'All through these exercises', Sister Agnès of Jesus said later, 'she looked pale and drawn. She could neither sleep nor eat and would have fallen ill if that had continued.'

That year the retreat did not look very promising. The prioress had engaged as preacher Father Bénigne de Janville, the Franciscan provincial. But at the last minute he was prevented from coming and sent Father Alexis Prou, a Franciscan from Saint-Nazaire, to replace him. This popular forty-seven-year-old preacher received a rather cold reception at Lisieux. He specialised in large crowds (he preached in

factories), and did not seem the right person to help Carmelites. Just one of them found great comfort from him: Sister
Thérèse of the Child Jesus.

Fr Prou's zealous preaching on abandonment and mercy
expanded her heart. Even more so his spiritual direction. She
who normally had so much trouble speaking about her inner
life, after a few words to the Franciscan felt herself

> *understood in a marvellous way. My soul was like a book which the*
> *priest read better than I did. He launched me full sail on the waves*
> *of confidence and love which held such an attraction for me, but upon*
> *which I had not dared to venture. He told me that my faults did not*
> *offend God, and, taking God's place as he did, he told me in his*
> *name that God was very pleased with me.*

This brought her great light and joy! She had never heard
that faults could not offend God. As for confidence and love,
they attracted her so much! But in the climate which
surrounded her, she had not dared to go that way. After this
first conversation, which had been so liberating, she had but
one desire: to speak again with Fr Prou. Why did Mother
Marie de Gonzague, overriding her authority, forbid her to
see the heaven-sent preacher again? It was a torment for her,
the assistant sacristan, to hear Fr Prou walking up and down
reading his breviary, when she had only to make a sign to
speak to him, as she had the right to do. But she preferred
obedience to another interview. No one could take away from
her the peace and hope which this passing priest had given
her, and whom she would never see again.

For her 'Canadian' director brought her scarcely any help.
Busy in his active ministry, he only replied once to her twelve
annual letters. In the end Jesus became her *director*.

THE DEATH OF A SAINT (5 DECEMBER 1891)

During the severe winter of 1891–2 death came to the Carmel.
First it took Mother Geneviève of Saint-Thérèse on Saturday,
5 December 1891 after a severe final illness. She was eighty-
seven. The foundress, regarded by all the sisters as a saint,
had just celebrated sixty years of religious life. Since 1884 she
had had great sufferings, both physical and spiritual.

From the time of her entry Thérèse had been drawn to this nun, then aged eighty-three, whose experience, discernment and gentleness were a light on her road. The old nun had taught her many things.

It was a priceless grace to have known our holy Mother Geneviève and to have lived with a SAINT, *not one who could not be imitated, but a saint who had become holy by the practice of the ordinary hidden virtues. Jesus was living in her and making her act and speak. That kind of sanctity seems to me to be the most authentic, the holiest, and it is what I desire because it is free from any illusion.*

Mother Geneviève had sometimes supported her in her 'night' by reminding her that 'our God is a God of peace'. And Thérèse had carefully written down some of her sayings.

That death, the first she had seen in Carmel, far from frightening her, seemed to her *ravishing*. When no one was looking she gathered up her old friend's last tear. Some time later she dreamt that Mother Geneviève three times said to her: 'To you, I leave my *heart*.'

DEATH REIGNED SUPREME (WINTER 1891–2)

Mother Geneviève was only just in her grave when the influenza that was ravaging France hit the community of the Lisieux Carmel. Deaths followed in quick succession: the senior nun (aged eighty-two) died on Thérèse's nineteenth birthday, then the sub-prioress (on the 4th) and a lay-sister, whom Thérèse found dead in her cell (on the 7th).

The whole community was confined to bed with the exception of three young sisters: Marie of the Sacred Heart, Marthe, and Thérèse of the Child Jesus. Community life was disrupted: there were no bells rung, no office, no meals in the refectory.

Sister Thérèse, who had always been an assistant in all her duties because she was thought to be slow, showed her presence of mind and intelligence. At last free to take the initiative, she showed what she could do. Far from depressing her, this atmosphere was stimulating. She went about calmly with a certain eagerness. She had to look after everything, prepare the dead nuns for burial, care for the sick,[1] arrange for the funerals. But her strength stood by her. *Death reigned supreme,* all customs gave way. Though the sick were deprived of communion, the able-bodied sacristan had the great joy of being able to receive it daily. One of her great desires had at last been fulfilled!

The superior, M. Delatroëtte, who had had reservations about the young sister for four years, was finally won over. The ordeal had revealed the nineteen-year-old nun's ability; from then on he said: 'She shows great promise for this community.' It had taken this trouble for the 'little Amen' to be able to demonstrate her true mettle as a strong woman.

Reduced to twenty-two nuns, the Carmel slowly recovered from its distress. The election of a prioress should have taken place on 2 February, but in these exceptional circumstances the superiors decided to extend Mother Marie de Gonzague's mandate for another year.

HER FATHER'S RETURN (MAY 1892)

Another great trial was coming to an end. On 10 May Uncle Isidore went to bring his brother-in-law home, after thirty-nine months at the Bon Sauveur asylum in Caen. On 12 May M. Martin saw his daughters again in the parlour. It was his first visit in four years, and would be the last. They found their father greatly altered and emaciated. That day his mind was clear but he did not speak. As he was leaving with tears in his eyes, he pointed his index finger upwards and managed to say: '*Au ciel* – to heaven!' That was her last heart-rending sight of her afflicted father.

The old man stayed at first with the Guérins then in July moved with Léonie and Céline to the rue Labbey. The two sisters were helped by a maid and a manservant, who were very necessary as the sick man could no longer stand. He had to be moved about, fed, and could not be left alone. However

---

[1] Thérèse would have liked to have been infirmarian but was never given this work.

20 Louis Martin in his invalid chair at rue Labbey. From left to right: Marie Guérin, Léonie, maidservant, Céline, manservant, Isidore Guérin, Mme Guérin, a friend and Thérèse's spaniel Tom (1892)

the three Carmelites knew he was out of that formidable place, the Bon Sauveur, and permanently surrounded by family affection. Céline devoted herself to looking after him. She still thought of Carmel but her duty was at home for the present. Thérèse gave her continual motherly support both in the parlour and by letter. One day she begged her sister not to dance at Henri Maudelonde's wedding. (The solicitor had grown tired of waiting for Céline.) But Céline sometimes found her enclosed sister very strict and somewhat extreme. During the reception, after being a voluntary wallflower, she found herself quite unable to waltz with a young man who, blushing with embarrassment, left the ball. Thérèse was delighted by this incident. Céline must not give her heart to a human being. Jesus was waiting for her.

But Céline also knew that the superior would absolutely forbid the entrance into the Carmel of a fourth Martin sister, and that Fr Pichon had other plans for her. Active and dynamic as she was, he saw her as the one to set up a new foundation he was planning in Canada and told her to say nothing about it, even to Thérèse. From the château La Musse where Céline was spending her holidays, she wrote uncomfortable letters. Her inner state was darkness.

Replies full of light came back from the Carmel. More and more Thérèse was finding her spiritual nourishment in the word of God. What could be more natural for a Carmelite, the central teaching of whose Rule is 'to meditate day and night' on that word? Yet the piety of her day was fed more on commentaries than by the actual sources of revelation. Not having a Bible at her disposal Thérèse asked Céline to get the Gospels and the Epistles of St Paul bound into a single small volume which she could carry on her heart. Some of the nuns were surprised at this, but several followed her example. *It is especially the Gospels which sustain me during my hours of prayer, in them I find all that my poor little soul needs. I am always gaining fresh insights and finding hidden and mysterious meanings.* She admitted that all other books left her cold.

It seems to me that Jesus' word is himself. He, Jesus, the incarnate Word, the word of God! She read, re-read and meditated on that word. She sought her way through Scripture. 'Your word is a lamp for my feet.' The different translations grieved her: *If I had been a priest, I would have really studied Hebrew and Greek so as to be acquainted with the divine thought which God deigned to express in our human language.*

More and more she realised that she felt no attraction towards the exalted heights of *great souls*. Her private retreat of October 1892 pointed out to her a 'downward' path. *Let us listen to what Jesus tells us* (as he told Zacchaeus): *Make haste and come down so that I can stay with you today . . . he the King of kings humbled himself in such a way that his face was hidden and no one recognised him and I too want to hide my face, I want my beloved alone to be able to see it.*

A FIGHT FOR TRUTH

A short time later Sister Thérèse finally took a step that could have cost her dearly, but she decided to act only after months of patience and prayer. It was an act which gave proof of her love of truth and her strength of character. *My God, make me see things as they really are.* It was time to speak to Sister Marthe about her inordinate attachment to Mother Marie de Gonzague. In following out the evangelical counsel: 'If your brother has committed a sin, go and tell him his fault between you and him alone' (Matt. 18:15) Thérèse was taking a great risk, which she confided to Sister Agnès: *Pray for me. The Blessed Virgin has inspired me to enlighten Sister Marthe. I am going to tell her what I think of her.* 'But you risk being betrayed, then our Mother will not be able to bear the sight of you and you will be sent to another monastery.' *I know that very well, but since I am now certain that it is my duty to speak, I must not worry about the consequences.*

That same evening she explained to Sister Marthe, with great affection (*I can only speak with my heart*), what true love is. It is not the attachment but the sacrifice of one's self for the good of the other. Tenderness becomes strong and disinterested when love does not seek itself. Sister Thérèse was speaking from experience. This sisterly correction bore immediate fruit. Sister Marthe understood perfectly and would never forget that day of inner liberation. Five years later Thérèse herself did not hesitate to tell Mother Marie de Gonzague about it, and on another occasion in a letter to her, Thérèse asked Jesus to enlighten her 'shepherdess', who heard around her only flattering untruths. Nothing is a greater destroyer of community than *these poisonous praises*.

Sister Thérèse of the Child Jesus of the Holy Face had just turned twenty (2 January 1893). Behind her she had five years of Carmelite life, five years of suffering undergone. Slowly she was emerging from that long winter, from that 'burial' which she had accepted, indeed welcomed, because of her love for him. An important event was about to give her a springtime.

8

Towards Maturity under Mother Agnès of Jesus' Priorate
(20 February 1893 to March 1896)

*It has been above all since the blessed day of your election
that I have flown in the ways of love.*

MY SISTER – MY MOTHER (20 FEBRUARY 1893)

After a year's delay the elections for prioress were to take
place. Mother Marie de Gonzague had come to the end of
her term and was not eligible for re-election. Thérèse did not
vote. With restrained joy she learned the result: her Sister
Agnès had been elected prioress. But the secrecy of the ballot
had not been complete, and it was quickly learnt that the
votes had been very divided. Pauline, very upset, did nothing
but cry in the parlour when her family congratulated her.

And so the mother she had chosen at Alençon and lost at
Les Buissonnets had become once again – in her thirty-second
year – Thérèse's 'Mother' in the deepest sense of the word.
But Thérèse did not think at all of her personal benefit.
She immediately realised that this election would make the
situation of the Martin sisters inside the enclosure more
delicate. That same evening she wrote to her new prioress:
*My dearest Mother, how easy it is for me to give you this name! . . .
Today God has consecrated you. You are truly my Mother and you will
be so for all eternity. Oh, what a beautiful day this is for your child!*

With clear-sightedness, she adds: *Now that you are to penetrate
the sanctuary of souls, you will pour out on them the treasures of grace
with which Jesus has filled you to overflowing. Of course, you will
suffer.*

Mother Agnès quickly discovered the truth of this
prophecy. She was young and inexperienced and it was not

easy for her to assert her authority in the face of the ever-present influence of the former prioress. She would have to be miraculously flexible and diplomatic. That would not be too difficult for her. But clashes between these two 'personalities' in the community were inevitable, and Mother Agnès, distressed by Mother Marie de Gonzague's scenes, often cried.

Respecting the custom of alternation, she named the retiring prioress mistress of novices. But she took an unexpected initiative: she ordered Sister Thérèse of the Child Jesus 'to help' Mother Marie de Gonzague in her task. The 'little gun-dog' was very well aware of her delicate position. She would have to act with great tact so as not to offend the former prioress who was still very moody and touchy. Especially as Mother Marie de Gonzague, who had at first been in favour of the election of Mother Agnès whom she had hoped to influence, soon realised the independence of her personality. Sister Thérèse was thus between hammer and anvil.

The two novices she had to care for did not make her task easy. There was Sister Marthe whom she knew well, but a newcomer who arrived on 22 July was a lay-sister: Sister Marie-Madeleine of the Blessed Sacrament. She was very introverted and for a long time eluded the 'senior novice's' influence.

Sister Thérèse was no longer involved in the sacristy, so as well as the novices she was put in charge of the art work. She had always loved drawing and was pleased to be given this job. She had to make pictures and paint on material. She even tried a fresco. That summer she painted the wall around the tabernacle in the oratory for the sick. Among the dozen little angels which are flying about the Blessed Sacrament, there is a child asleep near the tabernacle: Thérèse painted herself sleeping at prayer near Jesus!

All these changes had little effect on the rhythm of her everyday life. Yet, imperceptibly, Sister Thérèse was emerging from a long period of obscurity. Within her community she was called upon to express herself more, not only through 'painting', but also through 'poetry'. Her first attempt in this field is dated 2 February 1893. At Sister Thérèse of Saint-Augustin's request she wrote an amateurish poem, but it marked the beginning of a fruitful 'career'.

Mother Agnès, who was too busy with her new duties, gave up writing poems, hymns and plays for community recreation, which she had done till then.

In the language of pious clichés called religious 'poetry', Thérèse unburdened her innermost heart. The means at her disposal were meagre but under obedience she managed to express more and more of what was burning inside her.

A character sketch which Sister Marie of the Angels sent to the Visitation at Le Mans – one among twenty-three – gives an accurate description of Thérèse at this period of her life:

> Tall and robust, childlike, with a tone of voice and expression to match, hiding the wisdom, perfection and discernment of a fifty-year-old. She is always composed, and in perfect control of herself in everything and with everyone. An innocent little thing to whom you would give communion without confession, but her head is full of tricks to play on whoever she pleases. A mystic, a comic, she has everything going for her – she knows how to make you weep with devotion or die with laughter at recreation.

LETTERS TO CÉLINE IN THE SUMMER OF 1893

During that summer there were further changes in the family. M. Martin was taken to the château at La Musse: the country quiet and beauty suited him better than the city. But Léonie did not wish to join him there. At the end of June she had made a retreat at Caen with the firm desire to make another attempt at religious life. Mother Agnès and Sister Thérèse were in favour of it, but Céline felt this desertion very keenly. 'There is no one left on earth, there is a void around me, and for a moment I saw myself as the last survivor of our shipwrecked family. Oh, my life seems so very sad!' This was emphasised by the fact that her cousin Marie Guérin was also trying to enter the Lisieux Carmel.

On Mother Agnès's advice Thérèse increased her correspondence with her sister, who continued to puzzle over her future. She needed help. The long letters she received at La Musse spoke of Thérèse's intense meditation on the word of

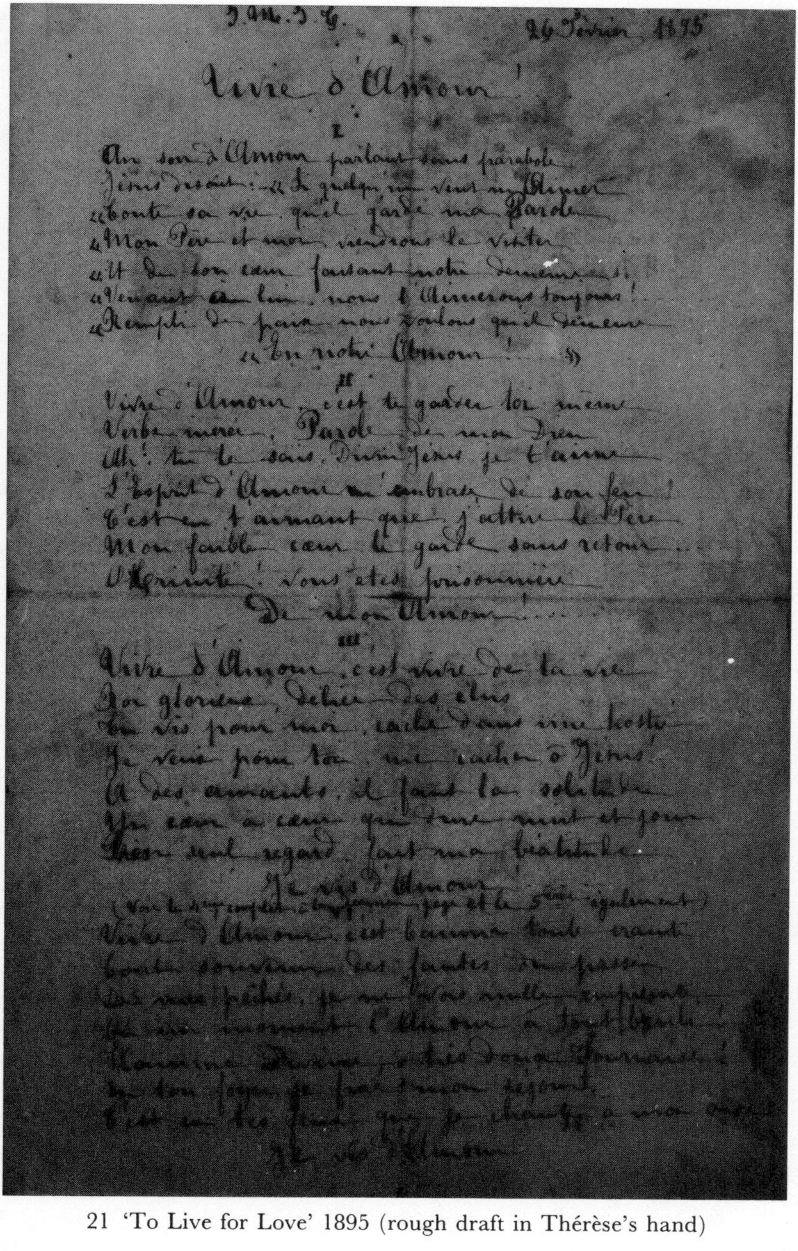
J.M.J.T. 26 Février 1895

Vivre d'Amour!

I

Au soir d'Amour parlant sans parabole
Jésus disait: « Si quelqu'un veut m'aimer
« Toute sa vie qu'il garde ma Parole
« Mon Père et moi viendrons le visiter
« Et de son cœur faisant notre demeure
« Venant à lui, nous l'aimerons toujours!
« Rempli de paix nous voulons qu'il demeure
« En notre Amour! »

II

Vivre d'Amour, c'est te garder toi-même
Verbe incréé, Parole de mon Dieu
Ah! tu le sais, Divin Jésus je t'aime
L'Esprit d'Amour m'embrase de son feu
C'est en t'aimant que j'attire le Père
Mon faible cœur le garde sans retour...
O Trinité! vous êtes prisonnière
De mon Amour!...

III

Vivre d'Amour, c'est vivre de ta vie
Roi glorieux, délice des élus
Tu vis pour moi, caché dans une hostie
Je veux pour toi me cacher ô Jésus!
À des amants, il faut la solitude
Un cœur à cœur qui dure nuit et jour
Ton seul regard fait ma béatitude.
Je vis d'Amour!...

([illegible])
Vivre d'Amour, c'est bannir toute crainte
Tout souvenir des fautes du passé.
De mes péchés je ne vois nulle empreinte,
En un instant l'Amour a tout brûlé!
Flamme Divine, ô très douce Fournaise!
En ton foyer je fixe mon séjour.
C'est en tes feux que je chante à mon aise
Je vis d'Amour!...

21 'To Live for Love' 1895 (rough draft in Thérèse's hand)

God. Verses of Scripture flowed from her pen and she supported her sister by sharing her most intimate spiritual development with her. *I wish to tell you what is happening in my soul.* Céline replied: 'Your letter is food for my soul.'[1]

One example suffices to show the working of the Holy Spirit in this young nun's heart:

> *O Céline, how easy it is to please Jesus, to delight his heart. All we have to do is to love him without looking at ourselves, not examining our faults too closely. Your Thérèse does not find herself on the heights, but Jesus is teaching her to draw profit from all, from the good and from the evil she finds within herself. He is teaching her to play love's bank or rather he plays for her, not telling her just how he goes about it – for that is his business and not Thérèse's; her part is to abandon herself, give herself over, keeping nothing for herself, not even the joy of knowing how his bank is paying . . . Directors make souls advance in the way of perfection by making them do a great many acts of virtue, and they are right in doing so, but my director, who is Jesus, does not teach me to count my acts; he teaches me to do everything for love, to refuse him nothing, to be happy when he gives me a chance to prove to him that I love him – but this is all done in peace, in* ABANDONMENT. *Jesus does everything, I do nothing.*

For the first time she speaks of abandonment. But what flexibility and what detachment there is in her! For at the same time she was making herself go back to her childhood 'beads for good deeds'[2] to help Sister Marthe who needed these methods. Thérèse admitted being caught in *nets which did little to help her*, but sisterly charity came first.

She continues her confidences: *Céline, God no longer asks anything of me – in the beginning* (during her postulancy and noviceship) *he asked me for an infinite number of things. For a while I thought that now, since Jesus was asking nothing of me, I must go gently in peace and love, doing only what he used to ask me. But light has been given me. St Teresa says we must feed the fire of love.* We feed this fire of love by searching for all the little occasions

---

[1] The prioress could read letters written and received by the nuns. During Mother Agnès's term as prioress Thérèse expressed herself without any restraint.

[2] Movable beads used to count short ejaculatory prayers, acts of self-denial, and so on (tr.).

to *please Jesus . . . for example, a smile, a friendly word, when I would have preferred to say nothing or look bored, etc.*

What matters is the essential and not the appearance, the kernel and not the shell. Jesus strips us so as to show that he is the one who is at work. *And these poor little souls, seeing themselves in such great poverty, are afraid. It seems to them that they are good for nothing since they receive everything from others and have nothing to give.*

Good for nothing. She knew what she was talking about. She who worked at painting, while sturdy peasants vigorously got on with the heavy community work, knew the humiliation of being thought useless: 'Several sisters kept saying that she was doing nothing, that it seemed she had come to Carmel to amuse herself' (Mother Agnès).

NOVICE FOR LIFE (8 SEPTEMBER 1893)

Usually after three years of profession a Carmelite left the novitiate. On 8 September 1893 Sister Thérèse asked to remain there permanently. It is true that, as there were already two of her sisters in the chapter, she would never have been able to have a seat on it by legal right and neither could she have been elected to any important position. She was always to be the youngest, always the last, as she had been at Les Buissonnets and Alençon! Mother Agnès was in favour of this sacrifice[1] which enabled her sister to continue to take care of the two novices she had given her to look after.

Mother Agnès had imposed it as a duty on Sister Marie-Madeleine to meet Sister Thérèse for half an hour each Sunday for a year. Very often, instead of going to the arranged meeting-place, the novice would disappear. Thérèse would finally meet her: *I have been looking for you*; 'I was busy.' Sometimes the fugitive would hide in the attic to escape Thérèse's loving but unfailing perspicacity.

[1] All her life Sister Thérèse would therefore have to ask permissions, follow a special timetable and attend novitiate gatherings; in a word, remain a minor. To remain in the novitiate meant never being a fully-fledged nun: 'Simplicity, docility, dependence and subjection to others are the principal virtues to which the novices must apply themselves' (Point of Exaction, 1883).

Thérèse was also appointed second portress under Sister Saint-Raphaël, the temporary sub-prioress, who was gentle, very slow, but with enough 'idiosyncracies to try an angel!' Thérèse had to be wonderfully patient! Her desire to be humiliated found perfect fulfilment in these lesser offices, where no initiative was required. Her inner adventure remained entirely veiled from the eyes of her companions. *The bitterest pain is that of not being understood.*

Henceforth she could fast like all the other nuns for she had just turned twenty-one (2 January 1894). Only one sign of independence marked this coming of age: she abandoned the sloping handwriting her 'teacher' Pauline had imposed on her since childhood. She now began to write in the way that came naturally to her: upright.

With a view to the prioress's feast day (21 January), she prepared two presents: a tableau, 'The Dream of the Child Jesus', inspired by several of Mother Agnès's 'poetical' compositions, and the main one, her first play, borrowed from a current topic.

JOAN OF ARC YEAR IN FRANCE 1894

All France was talking about Joan of Arc at the time. For twenty years Mgr Dupanloup, Bishop of Orleans, had fought for the canonisation of the girl from Lorraine. In 1869 Pope Pius IX had the preparatory proceedings opened. Joan's trials edited by Quicherat (1841–9), Michelot's book (1841) and countless publications, poems and plays, had aroused a response throughout the country.

On 27 January 1894 Leo XIII authorised the introduction of Joan of Arc's beatification cause. From then she was to be called Venerable and could be honoured and prayed to publicly. The following 8 May great national celebrations took place in the whole of France. Republicans, royalists, Catholics and anti-clericals all acclaimed the national heroine. At Lisieux Céline, her Guérin cousin and friends made twelve white banners to decorate Saint-Pierre's Cathedral, the choir of which contained – paradoxically! –

the remains of Pierre Cauchon before whom Joan of Arc was tried.[1] Five thousand people thronged the cathedral that year.

Since her childhood Thérèse had always loved Joan of Arc, her *darling sister*. While reading of her heroic deeds she had even received a grace which left a deep impression on her: *I seemed to feel within me the same burning zeal which had animated her . . . I thought I had been born for glory. God made me understand that my glory would not be visible to mortal eyes, and that it would consist in becoming a great* SAINT! She felt a deep affinity with this young fearless girl who was a martyr at nineteen. Since kissing the sand of the Colosseum in Rome she had often thought of martyrdom. In September 1891 the Congress of Masonic Lodges had stirred up the anti-clerical strife. Was there to be another time of persecution? That same year of 1894 saw the celebration of the centenary of the martyrdom of the sixteen Compiègne Carmelites who were guillotined during the Revolution (17 July 1794).[2]

As Sister Thérèse helped Sister Thérèse of Saint-Augustin to sew some banners for the Compiègne Carmel she said with a sigh: *What happiness, if the same fate, the same grace were ours!*

For her first 'theatrical' attempt Sister Thérèse had big ideas. There were to be two plays on Joan of Arc and she planned to devote two recreations to them: one on Joan's vocation, the other on her suffering, death and triumph. To this end she made a serious study of Henri Wallon's recently published book (1877), which contained extracts from the trials. As author, producer and actress Sister Thérèse did not spare herself. While keeping to the story, she attributed Carmelite sentiments to her heroine. In her first play, *The Mission of Joan of Arc or the Shepherdess of Domrémy listening to her voices*, she emphasises the fright suffered by a child attracted to solitude and prayer, when the Angel Michael wants to give her a sword. After long resistance she finally accepts it. The messenger's command recurs as a refrain: *You must set out!*

Who must set out? Joan for Chinon, or Thérèse for Indo-

---

[1] Pierre Cauchon was Bishop of Bayeux-Lisieux (1432–42). His coffin was discovered in 1931 in the chapel of Saint-Pierre's Cathedral, where Thérèse as a girl went to mass during the week.
[2] Mgr de Teil, Postulator for the Cause for the Beatification of the Carmelites of Compiègne, gave a talk in the parlour in 1896. See also p.210.

China? Or on a still more formidable adventure: sanctity on the waves of confidence and love?

The day the play was presented the community little suspected this identification of the actress with the heroine from Lorraine. The nuns were happy to applaud Thérèse who had taken her role so seriously.

This lengthy work stimulated Sister Thérèse and encouraged her to develop this form of expression which was entirely new to her. In the spring of 1894, asked by sisters who were now discovering her talents, she began to write numerous poems.[1] Four in April and May. For Céline's twenty-first birthday she even ventured to write, spontaneously, a hundred-and-twelve-line poem, 'Saint Cecilia'. The saint of abandonment would help her sister who was uncertain about her future to *live in perfect abandonment, that sweet fruit of love.*

A PERSISTENT SORE THROAT

For some time dust from sweeping and the steam from the washing-up or the clothes-wash had often made Sister Thérèse cough. Despite several applications of silver nitrate her sore throats would not go away and she sometimes had chest pains. During the summer the trouble persisted, and this caused some concern in her family. At the Carmel they wanted Francis La Néele to examine his cousin, but Mother Agnès did not dare to send for him. Dr de Cornière, a great friend of Mother Marie de Gonzague, was the official doctor for the community. In spite of her ability, Mother Agnès was having difficulty asserting her full authority as the new prioress: 'Yes it was Mother Marie de Gonzague who worked for my election, but she would only be hurt if I exercised too much authority. How I suffered and wept during those three years!'

Her youngest sister often had to bear the brunt of this rivalry. Francis had to be content with giving her some medicine.

[1] All Thérèse's poems were written to be sung.

FATHER'S DEATH (29 JULY 1894)

But for the moment serious cause for anxiety was reaching them from elsewhere. M. Martin's health was deteriorating. Auguste, his manservant, was becoming more and more addicted to drink – as an additional worry for Céline – and the Guérins were contemplating another move for the old man, who was often oblivious of what was going on around him. He went back to their house in the rue Paul-Banaston. On Sunday, 27 May he suffered a violent attack which paralysed his left arm. He received the last sacraments. On 5 June he had a heart attack. Nevertheless he was taken to La Musse on 4 July. The 'Patriarch' died there peacefully on Sunday, 29 July. Céline was at his bedside: 'His eyes were full of recognition and tenderness; understanding shone through his face. In an instant, I found my beloved father again as he had been five years before.'

The burial took place at Lisieux on 2 August. So ended the *terrible martyrdom and the glorious trial* of the head of the family.

At first, his last daughter was silent. But at the end of August Thérèse wrote to her sisters. To Céline: *After a death lasting for five years, what a joy to find him still the same, still looking for ways to give us pleasure just as he used to do.* To Léonie (once again experiencing difficulty at the Visitation in Caen): *Papa's death does not feel like death to me, but like true life. I have found him again after six years' absence. I am conscious of him around me, looking at me, protecting me.*

During these weeks while she was pondering over her father's life and death, Thérèse wrote, again quite spontaneously, the 'Prayer of a Saint's Child': nine verses about a patriarch in the midst of his children. The last four verses were about herself:

> Remember the Holy Father's hand
> in the Vatican touched your brow,
> mystery you didn't understand
> of the divine seal placed upon you . . .
> Now your children pray with might and main
> blessing your cross and bitter pain!
> On your brow most glorious

shine in heaven's brightness
nine flowering lilies!!!

In all truth she could now sign this poem 'the Orphan of
Berezina', the name her father had given her so long ago.
One day, all of a sudden, she understood the meaning of the
vision she had had at Les Buissonnets.[1] While recalling this
mysterious event with Sister Marie of the Sacred Heart,
suddenly they both understood: *As Jesus' adorable face was veiled
during his passion, in the same way was the face of his faithful servant
veiled during the days of his sufferings, so that he would be able to
shine in the heavenly home with his Lord, the eternal Word!* Fifteen
years had to pass before she understood the meaning of her
childhood vision. *Why had God given me that light? . . . He adapts
the trials to the strength he gives us. At that time I could never have
been able to bear even the thought of the bitter pains which the future
had in store for me.*

A GREAT DESIRE AT LAST FULFILLED! (14 SEPTEMBER 1894)

Her father's death had freed Céline from the secret she had
been keeping with difficulty for nearly two years. She would
have to make her choice between entering an active religious
life at Bethany in Canada, or a contemplative life at the
Carmel in Lisieux. Her three sisters raised a general outcry
when she told them of her perplexity. They were all united
against Fr Pichon's plan. Thérèse wept so much that she had
headaches as a result. 'She felt very deeply about it' and
wrote a letter of protest to her director. She *did not bear* him
any ill will but, in her opinion, there was no reason for uncertainty about Céline's vocation: her place was in Carmel.
Thérèse swept aside her sister's scruples. Let her not fear
about yielding to sisterly affection: *I have suffered so much for
you that I hope I am not an obstacle to your vocation. Has not our
affection been purified like gold in the furnace?* Céline opted for the
path which she had been thinking about for a long time.
Fresh battles for Carmel ensued! On 8 August Céline wrote
to M. Delatroëtte asking that she might be admitted, even as
a lay-sister. The reply was reasonable. He feared that 'the

[1] See 'Prophetic Vision' (p. 38).

entry of a fourth sister might be contrary to the spirit and
even to the letter of the Rule'. Mother Marie de Gonzague
gave her full weight in favour of the admission. But Sister
Aimée of Jesus categorically opposed the strengthening of the
'Martin clan', and above all the entrance of an 'artist, who
would be useless to the community'. From within the family
circle Céline had to face 'unceasing' opposition from Jeanne
and Francis; she even came up against Uncle Isidore's
hesitancy.

Suddenly all difficulties disappeared. Fr Pichon gave in: 'I
have no doubts. I no longer hesitate. God's will is clear
to me.' Canon Delatroëtte also struck his colours and Mgr
Hugonin gave his consent. The entrance of the postulant
Céline Martin was set for Friday, 14 September 1894, the
feast of the Exaltation of the Holy Cross. Never since St
Teresa of Avila had a Carmel received four sisters from the
same family, for the Spanish Reformer had written (22 July
1579): 'No monastery is to have three sisters living together.'
She would not have admitted her.

There remained Sister Aimée of Jesus' opposition. During
mass Thérèse asked Jesus for a sign. If her father had gone
straight to heaven let Sister Aimée agree to Céline's entry.
As she was coming out of the chapel this sister took her along
to the prioress: to tell her that she had nothing against the
entrance of a fourth Martin sister. Thérèse gave thanks; her
prayer had been so speedily answered.

And so one of her greatest desires, the one which had
seemed to her the most unlikely to be granted, was fulfilled
beyond all hope. Once again she had just experienced that
the Father only puts desires into his children's hearts so that
he might fulfil them. She proved the truth of St John of the
Cross's words: 'The more God wishes to give us, the more he
makes us desire.'

FOREBODINGS

Her father's death, uncertainties concerning Céline, worry
about the novitiate, declining health – all affected Thérèse
and contributed to a sense of foreboding. She wrote letters
to Céline containing mysteriously prophetic sentences: *Fear*

nothing, here more than anywhere you will find the cross and MARTYRDOM*! We shall be suffering together, like the Christians long ago, who kept together to give themselves courage in the hour of trial.* Why did she add: *And then Jesus will come, he will take one of us . . . If I die before you, do not think that I will be far from your soul.* Fearing to alarm her sister, she adds: *But above all, do not be alarmed, I am not ill.*

She must have written to Fr Pichon along similar lines, for he wrote to her on 19 March: 'Do not be in too much of a hurry to reach the Eternal face to face', and, a little later: 'Is it true that you are so intent on going to heaven? . . . If Jesus comes for you, you will remain my little girl in heaven.' And why that last verse of a poem?

> Soon to praise you I'll fly away,
> when that day without nightfall dawns on my soul,
> then I'll sing on the angels' lyre
> the Eternal Today!

Her family was alarmed: 'Sister Thérèse of the Child Jesus was not getting any worse, but there were still times when her sore throat flared up: each morning, and about 8.30 in the evening, and then her voice would become husky. We are doing our best to look after her' (Mother Agnès to Céline). The results of this care were hardly encouraging. Four months later Marie Guérin was still concerned:

> My little Thérèse must take care of herself. Yesterday I found her voice very changed and I consulted Francis about it . . . It is absolutely necessary that she look after herself *properly*. For the moment it is nothing serious, but at some time or other it could become so, and then there would be no cure. She must look after herself constantly, follow the doctor's orders carefully. Francis specialises in these diseases.

But she did not specify what kind of disease.

AN EXPANDING NOVITIATE

Concern about her health did not prevent Sister Thérèse from being more and more involved in the novitiate, which had now doubled in size. On 16 June Marie-Louise Castel, aged twenty, a lively 'Parisian', entered the Lisieux Carmel.[1] She had already spent two years in the rue de Messine Carmel in Paris, and it was not easy for her to fit into this new community. Mother Agnès entrusted her to Sister Thérèse. 'The Angel' had much to do, for Sister Marie-Agnès of the Holy Face[2] had a lot to learn. After one month Thérèse was able to write of her 'daughter': *I think she will stay. She has not had our upbringing, and this is a great misfortune for her. Her training is the reason for her unattractive manners, but deep down she is good. She is very fond of me, but I handle her only 'with white silk gloves'.*

Now Sister Thérèse was no longer the youngest in the Carmel. The new novice was her younger sister. An ever deepening friendship slowly brought them closer together.

On 14 September a fourth postulant, who was very dear to her, arrived: Céline had come at last! When the first excitement was past – they were together again after six years' separation – the older sister had to face severe difficulties. She was a strong young woman of twenty-five with an independent outspoken temperament. After having cared for her father, managed a house and refused two proposals of marriage, it was not easy for her to conform to all the minute details of Carmelite life. A modern young girl, she had studied painting under Krug and was enthusiastic about a recent technique, photography. Her sister the prioress had given her permission to bring into the enclosure her bulky equipment, a 13/18 Darlot lens camera, with all the developing materials. Feast days, professions and recreations would henceforth be captured on glass plates by Sister Marie of the Holy Face (her first name in religion, later changed to that of Geneviève of Sainte-Thérèse). Introduced into the religious life by her 'little' sister, she discovered with amazement that the former, in six years, had covered a considerable distance. Where was the time when the two sisters used to exchange lofty spiritual outpourings in their letters? Here, she had to lower her eyes when moving from one place to another, walk without

---

[1] She was born at Saint-Pierre-sur-Dines (Calvados), but spent most of her youth in Paris.

[2] She was to take the name of Marie of the Trinity at her profession, 30 April 1896.

22 The novitiate 28 April 1895: From left to right, Marie of the Trinity, Marthe, Thérèse, Marie-Madeleine, Mother Marie de Gonzague, Céline

running, be silent, tolerate without answering back any ungracious remark, obey. 'I will never make it!' groaned the novice, whose good will could not overcome her difficult temperament. Thérèse was there. She cheered her up, directed her steps, taught her how to live with herself without becoming discouraged.

Thus the novices went forward, step by step. On 20 November Sister Marie-Madeleine made her profession, and on 18 December Sister Marie-Agnès, the young 'Parisian', received the habit. For each one the senior novice wrote some appropriate verses, in which can be seen the keen understanding she had already acquired of her companions.

THE GREAT DISCOVERY: 'A TOTALLY NEW LITTLE WAY' (END OF 1894 TO BEGINNING OF 1895)

At the end of the year 1894 Sister Thérèse of the Child Jesus asked herself some questions. She had now been a Carmelite for more than six years. She had suffered much, she had struggled much, without renouncing her desire to become a saint. But when she compared herself to the 'great saints' whose lives were read in the refectory or at the office of matins she was profoundly aware of the abyss which separated her from them. Paul, Augustine, Teresa of Avila, by their mortifications, their virtues, their various gifts, were giants – inaccessible mountains. She was only an *obscure grain of sand.* Did she not often fall into imperfections? Did she not often sleep during prayer? Faced with this evidence how could she not be discouraged? Holiness, contrary to what she had thought during her novitiate, appeared really as *impossible.* After this inevitable experience, how many consecrated men and women resign themselves to mediocrity! But Sister Thérèse, keeping to the resolution she had made at her first communion, *never became discouraged.* John of the Cross had taught her that God can never inspire desires that cannot be fulfilled. *Then,* she reasoned, *I can, despite my littleness, aspire to sanctity.* But what was she to do to grow to the height of the giants? She had now experienced the vanity of self-willed efforts and knew she could not do it by sheer brute force. She had to *put up with herself such as she was, with all her imperfections.* Then what? She had to keep looking. Fr Prou had pointed out a little way that was very direct, very short and totally new. No help was forthcoming from Fr Pichon who no longer wrote to her, nor did she find any from within the Carmel, where fear held the nuns back from going along ways they thought dangerous.

Thérèse thought it over. She prayed. At the end of the nineteenth century inventions were increasing: electricity, telephone, cars, photography, various machines – during her trip to Italy she had enjoyed going up in lifts. In a moment one was at the top of the building! Could there not be a similar means to reach sanctity? Time was slipping by. If she died young, what would she have achieved by her life?

In her luggage Céline had brought along some notebooks in which she had copied passages of Scripture from Bibles in the Guérins' home. Thérèse, who did not have the Old Testament, was very soon borrowing them from her and cast her eyes over them 'enthusiastically'. One day she came upon a text in Céline's notebook: 'If anyone is a *very little one* let him come to me' (Prov. 9:4). This struck her instantly. She was that *very little one*. Now here was no hesitation. *Then I have succeeded.* Realising that she was about to find the solution to the vital problem that had been obsessing her, she wondered what God would do to the very little one who came to him with confidence. A passage from Isaiah gave her the answer: 'As a mother comforts her child, so will I comfort you, you shall be carried at my breast and fondled in my lap!' (Isa. 66:12–13).

There was light at last! Thérèse was carried away with joy. Here was the 'lift' she had been seeking! The arms of Jesus would carry her to the heights of sanctity. She drew another inference from this wonderful truth. To be carried in God's arms, one must not only remain little, but become even more so! The inversion is total, in complete conformity with the evangelical paradox. A deep prayer of thanksgiving sprang up from her heart: *O my God, you have surpassed all I have hoped for, and I want to sing of your mercies.*

These two biblical texts came just in time to enable her to pass through an irreversible stage. She was jubilant in the assurance. Yes, Fr Prou had been right. It was necessary to venture forth boldly, like Peter on Lake Tiberias, *on the waves of confidence and love.* Thérèse's littleness, her powerlessness, had become the very cause of her joy, for they are the ground where merciful love can manifest itself.

From that day on, she would often sign her letters *tiny little Thérèse*, with an obvious reference to this 'eureka' which was to accelerate her 'giant's course'. There were those who would see in this signature only an allusion to her position in the family or, worse, a stylistic affectation. For her the expressions *very little, to remain little*, would henceforth refer to this discovery made at the end of the year 1894. What is impossible for humans is not to God. It is enough to abandon oneself totally to his fatherly mercy. More and more, Sister Thérèse of the Child Jesus proved the truth of this *way of confidence and love* in her everyday life. Nothing, ever again, would be as before.

MUCH WRITING

Work was not wanting. Tasks she had not been in the habit of doing were more frequently assigned to her. She had to write a lot and to compose. Up to this time she had to her credit some fifteen poems and a recreational play. Now she had to make up a play for Christmas, and another for the prioress's feast. For these time-consuming tasks, she had only a short hour from midday till one o'clock and another from eight to nine in the evening. But her responsibilities in the novitiate, and unexpected happenings in community life (she was known to be so available) took up these short moments: 'She devoted her free time to poems and gave it to the other nuns to such an extent that she did not find any left for herself.' She did however admit one desire: *If I had the time, I would like to make a commentary on the Song of Songs. I have found in this book such profound things on the union of the soul with its beloved!* Noble daring in so young a Carmelite! To wish to undertake a task similar to that made illustrious by her Spanish patroness and St John of the Cross! For want of time, she had to be content with quoting a few verses, and making only a hasty commentary on them.[1]

For Christmas she wrote *The Angels at the Crib*. The 'theatrical' arrangement is very light: five angels come around the new-born infant, one after another singing their verses. Following the Angel of the Child Jesus and the Angels of the Eucharist, of the Holy Face and of the Resurrection, comes the Angel of the Last Judgment. In the name of divine justice he threatens sinners with his avenging thunderbolts. Only then does the Child Jesus himself break his silence to stop him.

Since her great discovery Thérèse saw all God's perfections only through mercy. *Even justice seemed* to her *to be clothed with love*. This was what she was trying to convey, in these simple verses, to some of the sisters who spoke of nothing but God's justice. *You want God's Justice?* she had said one day to the sub-prioress, Sister Fébronie of the Holy Infancy, *You will get God's justice. The soul receives exactly what it expects of God . . . This justice, which has terrified so many souls, is the reason for my joy and my confidence.*

During the final scene of the Christmas play all the kneeling angels (including the converted Angel of Destruction!) envy

---

[1] She did this in 35 of her letters, 12 poems, 5 plays. She does not seem to have had a complete text at hand, but knew the Song of Songs through the liturgy, St John of the Cross, and so on.

men and women who are called to become gods: *Ah, if they were able to become children themselves!* But did the Carmelites grasp the spiritual depths of these poor verses?

More important still, and theatrically much more spectacular, was the recreational play put on a month later: the second part of the life of the young girl from Lorraine, *Joan of Arc fulfilling her Mission*. The producer, who had no less than sixteen characters on stage, went to great pains. There were rehearsals, costumes and props to be made. The novitiate was called into action.

Fiction almost become reality. The spirit-lamps, intended to represent the stake, set fire to the scenery. Joan-Thérèse narrowly missed being burnt. The prioress ordered her not to move while the fire was being extinguished and she obeyed. Later she would say that she had been ready to die. Despite the outbreak of fire which was quickly brought under control, the play was a complete success. Five photographs taken by Céline show a twenty-two-year-old Thérèse wearing a brown wig, with banner and sword in hand, intensely living the part. She had, as it were, become the heroine whose part she was playing. There are clichés in the text of her play which show that she was really identifying herself with the young imprisoned girl. Joan accepts her agony, only because it resembles that of Jesus. The text from Wisdom, on the meaning of the early death of the just, enlightens the prisoner: 'Having lived for the short time, he had fulfilled the course of a long life, for his soul was pleasing to God . . .'

Who was in fact speaking? Joan of Arc or Sister Thérèse of the Child Jesus?

> Lord, I accept martyrdom for love of you,
> I no longer cringe from death or fire.
> O Jesus how my soul craves for you,
> to see you, my God, is my one desire . . .
> All I want is to die for your love,
> I want to die to begin to live,
> to die to be with Jesus above.

The actress who had written these lines and said them in front of her community on that 21 January 1895 literally meant every word she said.

9

The Blossoming
(January 1895 to April 1896)

*I no longer have any great desires
except to love till I die of loving.*

WRITING HER MEMOIRS — AT TWENTY-TWO

One evening in the winter of 1894–5 the Martin sisters were
chatting together at recreation near the fire. With her usual
gift for story-telling Thérèse was recalling some memories of
Les Buissonnets. Suddenly her godmother spoke to the
prioress: 'Is it possible that you let her write little poems for
one or other of the sisters and that she writes nothing about
her childhood for us? You will see, she is an angel, she will
not stay long on earth, and we will have lost all these details
which are so interesting to us.' Mother Agnès hesitated. It
was not customary to write one's life in Carmel, and her little
sister was not short of work! Marie of the Sacred Heart
persisted: Thérèse laughed; they were making fun of her, she
was not gifted for such a task. Then Mother Agnès spoke
seriously: 'I order you to write for me all your childhood
memories.' *What do you want me to write that you do not know
already?* But she had only to obey.

The first difficulty was to find the time, when her days
were already so short. At the end of January 1895 Sister
Thérèse set to work, generally in the evening after compline,
and on feast days. She acquired a small school exercise
book of about thirty pages, costing 10 centimes. In her cell
on the first floor, which was badly lit by the lamp whose
wick she pushed up with a pin, seated on her little stool,
she rested her book on a writing-desk she had found in the
attic.

Before beginning she prayed to the Virgin of the Smile whose statue had been placed in the room adjoining her cell. Then she opened her Gospel at random. She came upon this passage: 'Jesus went up on the mountain, called to him those *whom he pleased*, and they came to him' (Mark 3:13). These lines seemed to her to fit her own story perfectly:

> *This was indeed the mystery of my vocation, of my whole life, and above all the mystery of the privileges Jesus has lavished on my soul. He does not call those who are worthy, but those whom he pleases, or as St Paul says: 'God has pity on whom he wills and shows mercy to whom he wishes to show mercy. Therefore it does not depend on the exertion of the one who wills, or of the one who runs, but on God's mercy' (Rom. 9:15–16).*

And so, under these precarious conditions, without a plan, just as the pen and inspiration flowed, without erasure or rough draft, Sister Thérèse would make, during the long year of 1895, a second reading of her life in the light of the word of God and the discovery of her *little way:*

> *I find myself at a period in my life when I can look back on the past; my soul has matured in the crucible of outer and inner trials. And now, like a flower strengthened by the storm, I can raise my head, and I see that the words of Psalm 23 have been realised in me: 'The Lord is my shepherd, I shall want for nothing'.*

Mother Agnès's command could not have come at a more opportune moment. Having just discovered the depths of mercy Sister Thérèse now understood better the meaning of her whole life. Through the many different sufferings that she recounts she states that love never abandoned her. Not when her mother had died nor when her sisters left home, not during her illness, her emotional difficulties or her scruples, not during her father's agony, not when she met the thorns of her early days in Carmel, never in any circumstances had God forsaken her. Throughout her six little exercise books – for the first was quickly filled – she would therefore sing of only one reality, *the mercies of the Lord!* These pages voice her magnificat. She is not telling the story of her life in the strict sense, but *the story of her soul, of the graces God has given her.* Her conversion of Christmas 1886 had not been a mirage but the beginning of this *giant's course* which was not yet finished.

23 Thérèse as Joan of Arc (January 1895)

Hence the light tone of these memoirs, their gentle humour, for what had formerly seemed dramatic to her was now lit up by the light of that merciful love, by which she knew she was loved gratuitously. It was a love that seemed to her madness:

> *What happiness to suffer for him who loves us even to* FOLLY, *and to pass for* FOOLS *in the eyes of the world . . . Our beloved was* MAD *to come down on earth looking for sinners to make them his*

friends . . . What happiness that he became man so that we might love him, if he had not done so we would not have dared.

This *exercise book of obedience* would become a companion during the beautiful year of 1895. Céline was the first reader as her sister filled each little book. One day, she said to her 'enthusiastically': 'It will be printed! You will see that it will be useful later!' Thérèse, finding this remark ridiculous, just laughed heartily: *I am not writing to produce a literary work, but through obedience.*

TO LIVE FOR LOVE (26 FEBRUARY 1895)

During this same time she wrote – on request – about twelve poems and four plays for recreation. She had become 'the community poet', and reached the 'peak of her glory' after the success of her second *Joan of Arc*. But the literary genre mattered little to her. Poems, letters, plays or memoirs were for Mother Agnès. Without *worrying about style*, she just expressed fully what was in her heart: her desires, her passionate love for Jesus.

If we are to believe Sister Thérèse of Saint-Augustin, who thought she was one of Thérèse's close friends, that spring she received this confidence: *I will die soon.* During Exposition of the Blessed Sacrament (called the Forty Hours), Thérèse composed spontaneously fifteen verses: 'To Live for Love'. In Céline's opinion it was 'the greatest of her poems'. On the evening of Shrove Tuesday she wrote them out from memory. The last verse reveals what she was living!

> To die of love is what I hope for,
> on fire with his love I want to be,
> to see him, be one with him forever,
> that is my heaven – that's my destiny:
> by love to live.

I OFFER MYSELF AS A SACRIFICIAL VICTIM TO MERCIFUL LOVE (9–11 JUNE 1895)

On the morning of Sunday, 9 June the feast of the Holy Trinity, during the community mass an unexpected inspiration welled up within Sister Thérèse. She must offer herself as a sacrificial victim to merciful love. This strong conviction forced itself upon her. As soon as she came out of the chapel she dragged an astonished Céline along after Mother Agnès, who was going towards the turn. Her face flushed, excited and somewhat embarrassed, she stammered out that she wished, together with her novice, to offer herself as a victim to love. Preoccupied with other matters, and not attaching any importance to it, the prioress granted the permission. Delighted, she drew Céline aside. 'Her face glowing', she briefly explained her plan. *I was thinking of those souls who offer themselves as victims to God's justice in order to divert and bring down on themselves the punishments reserved for the guilty ones.*

The year before, the astonishing story of Mother Agnès of Jesus (of Langeac) who had offered herself as a victim to God's justice, had been read in the refectory. Thérèse also knew that in her own Carmel Sister Marie of the Cross had offered herself as a victim, and had died in 1882 after thirty-three years of suffering. And more recently still her dear Mother Geneviève had followed this road. With no uncertainty the young Thérèse kept her distance from this spirituality. *This offering seemed great and generous to me, but I was far from feeling myself drawn to making it.*

She wished to offer herself, not to justice but to merciful love. She therefore drew up her act of offering, and on Tuesday, 11 June, kneeling with Céline in front of the statue of the Virgin of the Smile, she made it in her own and her sister's name.

> *O my God! Most blessed Trinity, I desire to LOVE you and make you loved, to work for the glory of holy Church by saving souls on earth and liberating those suffering in purgatory. I desire to accomplish your will perfectly and to reach the degree of glory you have prepared for me in your heavenly kingdom. I desire, in a word, to be a saint, but I feel my helplessness and I beg you, O my God, to be yourself my sanctity!*

This act of oblation followed the interior movement which had prompted the discovery of the way of confidence. It was merely the symbolic expression of it. Fire has replaced the lift, the 'holocaust' being the total sacrifice of the victim consumed by the fire of love.

In order to live in one single act of perfect love, I OFFER MYSELF
AS A SACRIFICIAL VICTIM TO YOUR MERCIFUL LOVE, *asking you
to consume me incessantly, allowing the waves of infinite tenderness
within you to overflow into my soul, and that thus I may become a
martyr of your love, O my God. May this martyrdom, after having
prepared me to appear before you, finally cause me to die and may
my soul take its flight without any delay into the eternal embrace of
your merciful love. I want, O my beloved, at each beat of my heart
to renew this offering to you an infinite number of times, until
shadows having disappeared, I may be able to tell you of my love
eternally face to face!*

It marked a new and decisive step in this hidden life. Céline
did not understand too clearly what was happening. But
Thérèse knew. She had just gone right to the end of 'the way'
she had discovered. To him, who had given his life for her,
she could only want to give hers in return, totally. *For love is
to give all and to give oneself . . . Love for love.*

Some days later (possibly Friday, 14 June) when she was
beginning to make the way of the cross privately in the choir,
she was *seized with such a violent love for God* that she thought
she had been totally plunged into fire. *I was on fire with love,
and I felt that one moment, one second more, and I would not have
been able to bear this burning without dying.* For her, it was the
confirmation of the acceptance of her offering.

She lapsed back immediately into her usual state of aridity.
She confided this grace to Mother Agnès but the prioress
paid scant attention to it. Intentionally? This 'mysticism'
made her somewhat uneasy. For her sister was now advo-
cating that this decisive offering did not affect her alone. *O
my God! Is your disdained love going to remain closed up within your
heart? He wishes to pour it out on us.*

After Céline, she wanted to involve her godmother. So one
day as they were raking grass together in the little field, she
said: *Would you like to offer yourself as a victim to the merciful love
of God?* 'Indeed, no,' replied Sister Marie of the Sacred Heart,
'God would take me at my word and I have a great fear of
suffering.' *I do understand what you are saying, but to offer oneself
to love is an entirely different thing to offering oneself to his justice.
One does not suffer more. It is a matter only of loving God more for*

those who do not love him. Her godchild's eloquence won Marie over and she agreed to take the step.

Sister Thérèse did not hesitate to suggest the act of oblation to the novices, Marie-Agnès, and her cousin Marie Guérin, who was Sister Marie of the Eucharist since 15 August.[1] Faced with the proselyte's zeal, the prioress asked herself if the novitiate was embarking on a dangerous road under Thérèse's influence. Was it prudent to let all these young nuns offer themselves as victims?

Mother Agnès consulted the preacher of the annual retreat. Fr Lemonnier, a missionary, had already given retreats there in October 1893 and 1894. He knew Sister Thérèse whom he called 'the little flower'. Prudently he submitted the act of oblation to his superior. They both sanctioned it but asked the Carmelite to qualify her desires with the adjective 'immense' instead of 'infinite', which seemed to them theologically unsound. Thérèse complied, although she regretted this modification. For her the essential remained, and she was very happy. Her act of oblation was recognised by the Church.

A PRIEST-BROTHER: ABBÉ MAURICE BELLIÈRE (17 OCTOBER 1895)

Shortly after the retreat (which had been interrupted by M. Delatroëtte's death), one wash-day Sister Thérèse was called aside by her prioress. A twenty-one-year-old seminarian, Abbé Maurice Bellière, had just written to the Carmel 'to ask for a sister who would devote herself specially to the salvation of his soul and help him by her prayers and sacrifices when he was a missionary, so that he might save many souls'.

Mother Agnès suggested her young sister for this mission. A great joy came over the latter. Yes, God was fulfilling all her desires one by one. She had always dreamt of having a priest-brother. The deaths of her two little brothers seemed

---

[1] It was a big sacrifice for the Guérins to be separated from this charming twenty-five-year-old girl who was delicate, unruly, a good pianist, with a good soprano voice. They lost a daughter but gained a niece: on 20 July Léonie, who had left the Visitation at Caen for the second time, returned. This third failure baffled all the family. At thirty-two, bordering on depression, what was to become of her?

to have deprived her forever of this hope. And now, at twenty-two, she received from heaven a brother of her own age, a future priest and also a future missionary. *Not for years had I experienced this kind of happiness. I felt this part of my soul renewed; it was as if for the first time someone had struck musical strings left forgotten until then.* She immediately wrote a prayer for Abbé Bellière. She redoubled her ardour and fidelity in her everyday life, offering all her prayers and sacrifices for him. The young priest gave no further sign of life until November, when he sent a simple card announcing that he was leaving for military service.[1]

Little did he suspect that his sister was putting a truly heroic strength into 'all sorts of small and microscopic acts', which would be known only after her death. For example, when sitting Sister Thérèse did not lean back, she did not cross her feet. On hot days she avoided openly wiping her face so as not to attract attention. To combat the cold, she did not rub her chilblain-covered hands, she never bent over when she walked. She complied with each sister who needed her services, and effaced herself as much as possible in the parlour. If someone borrowed a book she was reading she did not ask for it back. She pushed poverty to the point that she did not even keep copies of her own poems. She shunned all curiosity, never looking at the choir clock during prayer-time, and avoided every useless question at recreation, and so on.

These 'nothings' (the witnesses at the processes gave many different examples), she lived throughout the days, weeks, years; at every moment she wanted to forget herself for the beloved:

> To delight you, I wish to remain little
> By forgetting myself, I will win your heart.

These verses, and many others, she wrote with her heart's blood.

THE DIVINE LITTLE CHRISTMAS BEGGAR 1895

Already it was time to prepare for Christmas. Once again the oldest novice was responsible for the celebrations. As she had

[1] 'The knapsack priests' law was passed on 9 July 1889 when Sadi-Carnot was President of the Republic.

another play to write for the prioress's feast she kept this one very simple. The infant Jesus comes to beg for the hearts of the twenty-six Carmelites. *He who begs of you is the eternal word!* In the simple framework of twenty-six verses Thérèse voices a truth that was dear to her. In this helpless baby God, who has emptied himself, begs for human love.

She reserved her strength for the feast of 21 January. *The Flight into Egypt* is a dark tale of robbers who meet the holy family in exile. The chief robber's child is a leper. Plunged into the infant Jesus' bath, he is instantly cured. It is a 'missionary' play, which also has some amusing passages when the robbers, Abramin and Torcol, put their heart and soul into singing some comical verses to the tune of *Estudiantina*, a popular old refrain.

But all this was not to Mother Agnès's liking. She found the play written for her feast tediously long, and cut it short before the end – taking the author to task for not having kept it brief. Thérèse was in tears, and the novices, who had played their parts with conviction, were crestfallen.

The day before at evening prayer Sister Thérèse, on entering the choir, had knelt before Mother Agnès and given her the little book of memoirs.[1] The prioress had put it in a drawer in her cell without opening it. Her sister never asked her if she had read it, or what she thought of it.

On the last page (sheet 85) Thérèse at twenty-three, nine years after her conversion and six months after she had offered herself to love, took stock again of her life. She wrote:

My dearest Mother, you allowed me to offer myself to God in this way, and you know the rivers or rather the oceans of grace which have flooded my soul. Oh! since that happy day it seems that love penetrates and surrounds me, that at each moment this merciful love is renewing me, purifying my soul and not leaving any trace of sin in it, and I have no fear of purgatory.

Indeed the fears about sin had been swept away, and her scruples were gone for good. Henceforth Thérèse knew that all her faults were consumed in *this fire of love* which was more sanctifying than the fire of purgatory. Her offering had freed her forever from all trace of Jansenism, from all the fears

---

[1] Thérèse had sewn together the six school exercise books.

which still bound certain sisters. *Without doubt, one can fall, one can commit infidelities, but love, knowing how to draw benefit from everything, quickly consumes all that could displease Jesus, leaving only a humble and profound peace in the heart.*

For example, sleep, which often overpowered her during silent prayer, no longer troubled her, neither did Abbé Youf's reproaches: *I should, instead of rejoicing at my aridity, attribute it to my want of fervour and fidelity. I should be desolate for having slept (for seven years) during prayer-time and thanksgiving: well, I am not desolate. I remember that little children are just as pleasing to their parents when they are asleep as when they are awake.*

She concludes: *Now I no longer have any desire* (her father was in heaven, Céline in Carmel, she had a priest-brother), *except that of loving Jesus to folly . . . Now my whole work consists in loving!* (St John of the Cross).

As she finished this *exercise book of obedience*, she asked herself about her future: *How will this 'story of a little white flower' end? Will she die soon? Will she go to the Saigon Carmel?*[1] *I do not know, but what I am certain of is that God's mercy will always accompany her . . . Abandonment alone guides me.*

On sheet 86 she carefully painted Jesus' and Thérèse's coats of arms and printed beautifully underneath the days of grace which the Lord had given his *little spouse.* On the preceding page a detailed explanation of these coats of arms can be read. A sentence borrowed from St John of the Cross links them together: *Love is repaid by love alone.*

Love is the only word she has beneath her pen, on her lips and in her heart.[2]

CÉLINE'S DIFFICULT PROFESSION (FEBRUARY TO MARCH 1896)

Canon Maupas, parish priest of Saint-Jacques, became superior of the Carmel and took over his duties in January. The time was drawing near for Céline and Marie of the Trinity to make their profession, and for Marie of the Eucharist to receive the habit. Normally all these ceremonies

---

[1] See p. 117.
[2] Her exercise book ends with the word 'love'. It appears 99 times in 86 pages.

24 The community doing the washing (19 April 1885).
Thérèse is fourth from the left

should have taken place under the prioress in office, Mother
Agnès of Jesus, whose term expired on 20 February 1896. An
unexpected obstacle arose: Mother Marie de Gonzague, the
novice mistress, against the new superior's advice, wished to
put off this double profession. Were her reasons obvious? The
elections were coming up. If she were elected, would she not
receive these two young sisters' commitment? And there was
an even more sensitive issue: she was considering the possibility of Sister Geneviève's departure for the Saigon Carmel.
The indirect advantage would be to lessen the influence of
the four Martins and their cousin. Now they represented one-
fifth of the community, which was in danger of being split in
two with one group supporting Mother Marie de Gonzague,
and another the Martins.

One grey day in January 1896 about fifteen Carmelites
were in the laundry doing the washing and a discussion arose
about Sister Geneviève's profession. Sister Aimée of Jesus,
one of those most opposed to the 'Martin clan', declared:

'Mother Marie de Gonzague has every right to test her, why be surprised about it?' A firm voice rose up from the group: *There are some trials which one does not have the right to impose.* Very moved, Sister Thérèse had spoken.

For her it was not a matter of challenging authority, but truth must prevail and duty demanded that she told the novice mistress she was wrong.

Several days later Sister Geneviève came before the chapter. Interpreting the custom in her own way, Mother Marie de Gonzague excluded the prioress from voting, and Mother Agnès awaited the result behind the door. The three Martin sisters only entered the chapter room to hear: 'Sister Geneviève has been accepted.' But Sister Marie of the Trinity's profession was deferred. A sort of compromise had taken place. The elections had been postponed for a month. Mother Agnès would receive her sister for profession and her cousin for clothing, but Mother Marie de Gonzague, if she was elected, would receive Sister Marie of the Trinity's commitment.

It is easy to understand why Sister Thérèse, who was very anxious about the future of these three young sisters, increased her attention towards Céline who had become embittered by these intrigues. Sister Thérèse sent her a long allegorical letter alluding to her misfortunes, gave her an illuminated sheet of parchment, a relic of the saintly Mother Geneviève and a holy picture to soften these unpleasant happenings and help her overcome them in peace.

After the simple profession ceremony on 24 February Sister Geneviève of Sainte-Thérèse took the black veil on 17 March, while her cousin, Sister Marie of the Eucharist, received the habit. In *Le Normand* that day, Uncle Isidore feelingly described the double ceremony presided over by Mgr Hugonin. Several photographs taken inside the enclosure preserve the memory of this event.

With the exception of Léonie, all the girls were therefore 'pulled out from beneath the cart', to borrow an expression M. Martin had used in the past.

MOTHER MARIE DE GONZAGUE'S ELECTION (21 MARCH 1896)

On Saturday, 21 March, the eve of Passion Sunday, a silent air of expectancy pervaded the Lisieux Carmel. They were preparing for the election of the prioress.

Since March 1893 three nuns had left the community: one for heaven, one for the Saigon Carmel and one for the Bon Sauveur at Caen (for mental illness). Three young ones had entered. That day, out of twenty-four nuns, sixteen chapter sisters assembled in the choir. The others prayed. Time dragged on – it took no less than seven ballots to decide between Mother Marie de Gonzague and Mother Agnès. The senior, aged sixty-two, was finally elected by a narrow margin. Sister Marie of the Angels remained sub-prioress, and Mother Agnès became a council sister with Sister Saint-Raphaël. At last the bell rang to summon the eight waiting sisters. Sister Thérèse, on entering the choir, saw Mother Marie de Gonzague in the prioress's stall. She was 'stunned with surprise' but quickly recovered herself.

The re-elected prioress, very affected by what had just happened, took care not to follow the custom of alternation. The law allowed her to hold both the office of prioress and of novice mistress, and she availed herself of it. Mother Agnès would not take charge of the novitiate. But Mother Marie de Gonzague chose an assistant: Sister Thérèse of the Child Jesus, who accepted under obedience this most delicate situation, a difficult mission indeed.

A NOVICE 'MISTRESS OF NOVICES' (MARCH 1896)

In this new period of her Carmelite life, it was now or never for her to live her way of abandonment. She had to exercise serious responsibility without having any status. She still belonged to the novitiate, and the novices were well aware of this fact. How was she to change these five women (four of whom were older than her) into true contemplatives? The task was completely beyond her. Her sister Céline and her cousin Marie showed a certain reserve, despite their good will, in accepting her smiling but firm authority. They found her 'strict'. Sister Marie-Madeleine, who had had such an unhappy childhood, remained withdrawn. What could they say about the changing moods of the prioress, who might undo tomorrow what she had done today with regard to her assistant, whose canonical authority was non-existent. Sister Thérèse had only one hope: the action of the Holy Spirit in herself and in her *lambs*.

Realising it was impossible for her to do anything herself, she prayed: *Lord, I am too little to nourish your children; if you wish to give them through me what is suitable for each one, fill my small hand, and without leaving your arms or turning away my head, I will give your treasures to the soul who will come and ask me for nourishment.* It was the only attitude which would bring her peace and enable her to carry out her delicate task to the end. *All my strength comes from prayer and sacrifice.*

Each day at 2.30 p.m. she met the novices for half an hour, explained the customs, the Rule, answered questions and corrected faults. The meeting was lively and no one was bored, for the young 'mistress' could tell stories and make up parables to get her message across. Céline and Marie of the Trinity collected these teaching devices in their notes: the kaleidoscope, which called to mind the love of the Trinity; the love bank where one must play for high stakes; the ordinary looking little pears representing the unknown sisters we brush past; the hen and her chicks a symbol of the Father's love; the rich lady and her little brother; the shell into which Marie shed her tears, and so on. Thérèse used everything. Marie of the Trinity told her some facts about magnetism which she had seen and the following day her mistress said to her: *I would like to be magnetised by Jesus! Yes, I want him to take hold of my faculties in such a way that I can only perform actions which are wholly divine and directed by the Holy Spirit.*

She had not received any instruction, but her intuitive teaching method, based on love of others, was incredible. She knew that her companions could speak freely to her: *Everything is permitted to the novices.* And they did not hesitate sometimes to serve her with *well-vinegared salads.* But Thérèse said she preferred *vinegar to sugar.*

They found her 'strict'. She knew this, but did not change. She loved her flock too much to be weak. *If I'm not loved, that's just too bad! I tell the whole truth and if anyone does not want to know it, let her not come looking for me.*

But above all, she taught the *little way* which had been so successful for her: the way of confidence and love towards the Father. On this subject, which is at the heart of the Gospel message, she showed herself a true mistress of the spiritual life. She always knew how to go to the essential, and she 'detested old wives' devotions which were sometimes introduced into communities' (Mother Agnès).

She had the ability to adapt herself to each pupil. Fr Pichon had been right: 'There are many more differences between souls than there are between faces.' It is impossible to behave the same way with everyone. *There are some I have to take by the scruff of the neck, and others by the tip of their wings,* she confided to Mother Agnès. Young Marie of the Trinity needed some relaxation: let her then go up to the attic and whip a top there. But Céline must not go out of her way to avoid Mother Hermance of the Heart of Jesus, a neurasthenic, who was sure to ask for a service if she saw her passing by. And woe betide those who called Mother Marie de Gonzague 'the wolf'!

In that little group (whose average age was twenty-five and a half), she was both sister and mother. Youth attracts youth. There were outbursts of laughter at recreation when Thérèse did her humorous imitations, or when the whole troop gave chase to a thief who had entered the enclosure.

This work of training even in a subordinate capacity taught her much about human nature. Her wisdom was the fruit of her experience. And so the attraction shown by certain sisters (one of whom was Mother Agnès) for supererogatory mortifications and instruments of penance then in use, did not have her approval. At the beginning of her religious life her generosity might have led her along this way. In April 1896 she would even wear a little iron cross. But she abandoned it. She had noticed that the nuns most given to the severest austerities were not the most perfect, and that there was even an element of self-love in excessive bodily penances. These were worthless when weighed against charity. She did not judge others. But this was not her 'way'. She drew the novices' attention to this point, as she did to so many others. She often quoted this verse from St John: 'In my Father's kingdom there are many mansions' (John 14:2).

Such wisdom was later to prompt certain sisters to say:

'She would have made a good prioress if she had lived.' Her spiritual instinct was such that the novices sometimes believed she had the ability to read souls. Thérèse protested, but had to admit that the Holy Spirit often helped her to guess right.

Besides this important office Sister Thérèse worked in the sacristy under Sister Marie of the Angels and at painting, and helped Sister Marie of Saint-Joseph in the linen room. This thirty-eight-year-old nun (orphaned when she was nine) was feared by the whole community. Her violent outbursts of anger isolated her and no one wanted to work with her. Thérèse volunteered.

In that office she was to discover the true meaning of sisterly charity. Until then she had not fully understood that we must love *as* Jesus loved his disciples. No one must be excluded from this love, not even Sister Marie of Saint-Joseph, whom she tried to pull out of her isolation by her smile and her friendly little notes.

The winter of 1895–6 had been long and hard, and Lent began at the end of it. Thérèse obtained permission to keep the fast in all its austerity. She had never felt so well and strong.

A STREAM BUBBLING UP TO MY LIPS (3–4 APRIL 1896)

On Holy Thursday night, 3 April, Thérèse had stayed to keep watch in the choir till midnight. She had scarcely been in bed when she felt something like a stream which came *bubbling up* to her lips. She put away her handkerchief. Her lamp had been extinguished and she made no attempt to check what she had brought up. If it was blood, perhaps she was going to die on that Good Friday which was just beginning. She had no fear. She was happy, for she had always wanted to be like Jesus. She fell asleep. At 5.45 a.m. the matraque woke her.[1] The half-opened shutter revealed that her handkerchief was full of blood. Her spouse was announcing himself. He was not far off. How could she fear him to whom she had given her life?

---

[1] A wooden instrument with a metal hand-rattle which was shaken under the cloisters and in the corridors to signal the rising time.

After the office, as on every Good Friday, the prioress gave a talk to the community on sisterly charity. The Carmelites asked pardon of each other. When it was Thérèse's turn, she embraced Mother Marie de Gonzague and told her what had happened that night. *I am not in pain, Mother, please do not give me anything special.* The prioress, undoubtedly not realising the true state of the nun on her knees, agreed. Sister Thérèse fasted and cleaned the glass panes of the cloister doors, standing on a step-ladder in the draught. *Never had the austerities of Carmel seemed so delightful to me, the hope of going to heaven transported me with joy.*

Sister Marie of the Trinity, the assistant infirmarian, had been let into the secret. She protested strongly. She wept: in that state her mistress could leave this work to the others! It was in vain. And especially since Mother Agnès knew nothing of it.

Night returned, and so did the haemoptysis as on the preceding day. This time there was no room for doubt. The few lines Sister Thérèse had just written for Sister Marie of Saint-Joseph express her desire:

> Love, glowing coal,
> burn into my soul,
> come when I call,
> come and consume me.
>
> Your fires press,
> I long without cease,
> O divine furnace,
> to be lost in thee.

She was going to be heard. Her faith was living, clear, and she thought only of the joy of heaven.

But this second warning worried the prioress and infirmarians even more. Dr La Néele finally examined his cousin. When questioned closely she admitted she had been very hungry every evening during Lent. A swollen gland in her neck testified to her weakness. Putting his head through the small opening of the grille in the oratory (where the sick nuns received communion), Francis 'examined her' through her rough homespun habit. He thought the bleeding could have come from a burst blood-vessel in the throat. Medication was prescribed: creosote by the spoon, throat sprays and rubbing with camphorated oil. Thérèse was not under any illusions about the efficacy of this treatment. Her joy remained. Soon she would see him whom her heart loved.

10

Spiritual Darkness, her Vocation Found at Last!
(April 1986 to April 1897)

It is a wall which reaches right up to the heavens.
Everything has disappeared!

I have found my vocation at last. My vocation is love!

THE NIGHT OF NOTHINGNESS (APRIL 1896)

Suddenly this joy disappeared without any warning and an unexpected suffering came down on Thérèse. In that Paschaltide – the time of light – she entered into the densest inner spiritual darkness. She who was thinking of going very quickly to heaven (for heaven is Jesus himself, she had written), found herself without any sense of faith. She went forward in *darkness*, in the *spiritual night*, in a *tunnel*. She was confronted by a *wall* which reached right up to the heavens. She had been joyful at the thought of *dying of love*. Now horrible inner voices suggested to her that all her great desires, the *little way*, her offering, her whole spiritual life, had been illusions. There was only one obvious fact. She was going to die young, for nothing.

It seems that the darkness, borrowing the voice of sinners, says mockingly to me: 'You are dreaming about the light, about a country fragrant with sweetest perfumes; you are dreaming about the eternal possession of the creator of all these marvels; you believe that one day you will walk out of this fog which surrounds you! Dream on, dream on; rejoice in death which will not give you what you hope for, but even deeper night, the night of nothingness.'

She gave this written confidence, with its Nietzschean tone, to Mother Marie de Gonzague, but not until fifteen months later. She confided her affliction verbally only to her and the chaplain. One day she said to Mother Agnès: *The worst kind of materialistic arguments come into my mind. Later, science, by making ever-increasing new progress, will explain everything naturally. It will have the absolute answer for all that exists and which is still a problem, because there are still many things to discover, etc. etc.* Perhaps some of these questions had been discussed in the writings of Diana Vaughan which she discovered at this time. Her reading of Arminjon's book could have taught her many things about the claims made by materialistic science. But what did she know about the tide of unbelief running through the end of the nineteenth century? She would not have heard of Karl Marx who died in 1883, or Nietzsche who had published *Beyond Good and Evil* in the same year as her conversion (1886), and *The Antichrist* just when she was entering Carmel (1888). In the year of her profession (1890), Renan wrote *The Future of Science*; when he was studying in Paris Isidore Guérin might have attended some of his lectures. In 1891 her uncle had become a journalist. In *Le Normand*, he fought the irreligious over the issue of secular education laws, anti-clerical decrees, and Catholic doubts about supporting the Republic. He slammed his former clerk, Henri Chéron[1] who, in the rival newspaper, *Le Progrès Lexovien*, denounced the obscurantism of the Catholic Church.

Without reading newspapers regularly, Sister Thérèse knew of her monarchist anti-Dreyfus uncle's battles. Behind her grille she remained alive to her times. But her battle was not in the same field. Just as she had not been 'against' Pranzini and Loyson, she was not 'against' the materialists and the anarchists. She prayed for them; she gave her life for them.

Outwardly none of these violent struggles showed. The

---

[1] Henri Chéron (13 May 1867 to 16 April 1936), Mayor of Lisieux 1894–1908 and 1932–6; Senator for Calvados, 1913, after being deputy, 1906; Under-Secretary of State for War during the First World War, and Minister of Finance and Justice. He was a member of the Combes ministry. He liked to tell that he had known Thérèse Martin at the Guérins' pharmacy. Despite his anti-clericalism, he showed himself well-disposed towards all the Lisieux undertakings which extolled the cult of his contemporary.

verses which she continued to write, at her sisters' request, reveal the change. More attentive listeners may have detected veiled confidences. For example, as when she paraphrased St John of the Cross:

> Supported without any support,
> in darkness without any light,
> I am being burned up by love.

Or when she sang:

> My heaven is to smile at this God I adore
> when he is hiding and testing my love.

But her sisters would never have dreamt that the writer of these lines was literally living what she wrote: *If you are going by the feelings I express in my little poems written this year, I must appear to you as a soul filled with consolations – and yet.* The hearers only caught the light. Nevertheless these lines clearly imply shadows.

In the midst of her darkness a brief ray of light was to shine and strengthen her. On the night of 10 May she dreamt that a Carmelite whom she had only heard spoken of rarely (Anne de Lobera, Teresa of Avila's companion and foundress of Carmel in France), covered her with caresses. In answer to her questions the Spanish nun told her that she would die *soon* and that God was *very pleased* with her. These two words filled Thérèse with joy. She realised furthermore that in heaven (that heaven she doubted), she was loved! But after this dream, which affected her deeply (usually her dreams had no bearing on the spiritual life), the darkness increased. Certainly in the course of her eight years in religious life she had known times of aridity, but never with such intensity. When would she come out of this fog?

A SECOND BROTHER: ABBÉ ADOLPHE ROULLAND (MAY 1896)

One day at the end of May, just before going to the refectory, Mother Marie de Gonzague summoned Sister Thérèse into her office. The young sister's heart was beating rapidly: the mother prioress had never called her in this way before. It was about entrusting her with a twenty-six-year-old

25 Nine priests who played a part in Thérèse's life
top row l. to r. Abbé Domin, chaplain to the Benedictines of Lisieux,
Abbé Révérony, Vicar General of Bayeux, Mgr Hugonin, Bishop of
Bayeux and Lisieux
middle row l. to r. Canon Delatroëtte, ecclesiastical superior of the
Carmel, Fr Almire Pichon SJ, Fr Alexis Prou, who preached the retreat
of October 1891
bottom row l. to r. Abbé Youf, chaplain to the Carmel, Fathers Bellière
and Roulland, spiritual brothers of Thérèse

missionary, the Abbé Adolphe Roulland of the Foreign
Missions Society in Paris, who was to be ordained priest on
28 June before setting out for China.

A great missionary zeal linked with the colonial expansion
was inspiring countless young French Catholics. Vocations
were plentiful.

Sister Thérèse declined. She said she already had one spiritual brother for whom she was offering up all her prayers and sacrifices. And there were many of the sisters more worthy than she in the community. But the prioress dismissed all her objections one by one. Let her obey!

In her heart Sister Thérèse really experienced great joy. The Lord was continuing to fulfil all her desires. She had lost two brothers; she received two missionaries as brothers! She would have to redouble her fervour. She wished to be a *daughter of the Church* like her Mother Teresa of Avila: *a Carmelite's zeal must embrace the world.*

The new priest came to celebrate one of his first masses at the Lisieux Carmel on 3 July. His sister gave him an altar pall which she had painted for him. They spoke together in the parlour. The missionary was soon to set sail for China and join the eastern Su-Chuen province. In the place where she worked Thérèse pinned up a map of the region to follow her new brother's journey. She wrote to him at Marseilles: *Good-bye, Brother – distance can never separate our souls, even death will only make our union closer. If I go to heaven soon[1] I shall ask Jesus' permission to visit you in Su-Chuen and we shall continue our apostolate together.* She gave him a collection of her poems, adding to it 'To Our Lady of Victories', which she had written about their future apostolic collaboration.

As far as the community was concerned Fr Roulland was 'Our Mother's missionary'. The prioress had asked Sister Thérèse to be secret about this task entrusted to her and her unusual correspondence. But she allowed the brother and sister to exchange photographs.

The prioress also spoke confidentially to Sister Thérèse about other matters. Mother Marie de Gonzague had not got over the little drama of the March elections. She felt that the community was divided and she no longer had the loyalty of some of the sisters. She regarded them all as 'traitors'. Only her assistant in the novitiate seemed to her worthy of complete trust.

For the occasion of her feast, 21 June, the energetic novitiate, inspired by its young mistress, prepared a play 'to put everything upside down', as Sister Marie of the Eucharist wrote to her parents. For the seventh time Thérèse had to

[1] This was the word Anne de Lobera had used in the dream of 10 May.

write a play. She based her subject on a burning issue of the day and called it *The Triumph of Humility*, a play about devils.

THE DIANA VAUGHAN AFFAIR

For some time Catholic opinion had been disturbed by 'the Diana Vaughan affair'. A young woman who belonged to a Freemason sect had published in 1895 *The Memoirs of an Independent, Fully-Initiated, ex-Palatine: unveiling the mysteries and satanic practices of the Luciferian triangles*. In it she relates her extraordinary adventures into the satanic world and her conversion, due to Joan of Arc's influence. Henceforth she was devoting her energies to burning, combating and denouncing what she had adored. After this, she thought of entering a monastery.

At the end of the nineteenth century the battle between Catholics and Freemasons was raging. Pope Leo XIII, in his encyclical *Humanum Genus* (1884), had strongly denounced freemasonry: its errors breathed satanic hate. Satan was doing well. In 1892 a certain Dr Bataille had published *The Devil in the Nineteenth Century*. Many Catholics were enthusiastic about these revelations; however there were a few rare exceptions. For example, Léon Bloy from his solitude thundered against these naive people who were avid for the extraordinary. But who would listen to the diatribes of the 'Old Man of the Mountain'?

The Diana Vaughan affair stirred up Catholic opinion even more, because an air of mystery and 'suspense' surrounded the convert. *La Croix* published fiery articles by reverend fathers in favour of Diana. At Lisieux Uncle Guérin's *Le Normand* joined the crusade.[1] The writings of the former Luciferian made their way into the enclosure of the Carmel, possibly through the influence of Fr Mustel, editor of *Revue Catholique de Coutances*, and an out-and-out supporter of Diana Vaughan. In this way Thérèse read *The Eucharistic Novena of Reparation*, published by the convert in 1895. Thérèse was moved, like Leo XIII, by the spiritual loftiness of this young

---

[1] *Is it not for our Lord's glory that my uncle's arm does not grow weary of writing these wonderful pages which must save souls and make demons tremble?* (letter to her uncle).

woman who loved Joan of Arc so much and had offered
herself as a victim to divine justice on 13 June 1895. It was
a strange coincidence! The Carmelite, who had offered herself
to merciful love, copied out certain passages from this novena.
Diana thought of entering a monastery one day. Would it be
the Lisieux Carmel? At the suggestion of Mother Agnès, who
was very excited about the story, Thérèse tried to write a
poem for the convert. It was in vain. No inspiration was
forthcoming so she had to be content with writing her a letter
and sending the photograph of herself as Joan of Arc in her
prison. Diana Vaughan answered her letter.

The Carmel had its part to play in this battle against Satan,
above all at the time when divisions within the community
were threatening to weaken it. In her work for that family
feast of 21 June, Thérèse wanted both to distract her sisters
and make them reflect.

The entertainment raised smiles. The author put on stage
Lucifer and his band of devils, Beelzebub, Asmodaeus, Ashta-
roth, Astarte, names taken from Diana Vaughan's book. The
novices, behind screens (for you cannot see hell), enjoyed
themselves immensely rattling chains and making thunder.

The reflection came from the theme of the play. Carmelites
must shun curiosity and agitation. Humility is the only
weapon that can overcome devils. Thérèse, playing her own
role of novice mistress, drew the conclusion herself:

*We now know the way to conquer the demon, and so, henceforth let
us have but one desire: to practise humility. It is our weapon, our
shield. With this all-powerful strength we, like new Joans of Arc,
will know how to drive the stranger out of the kingdom, that is, to
prevent proud Satan from entering into our monasteries.*

The final verse directs the community towards the *little
way*:

> O fervent Carmelites your will
> is to win hearts for your spouse Jesus.
> So for him you must stay little,
> humility all hell confuses.

But while she was acting her play, the author could not
have known that the powers of evil were much more subtle
than she supposed.

Eight days later Sister Thérèse of the Child Jesus wrote a long letter in the form of a parable to her prioress: 'Legend of a Very Little Lamb'. That 'lamb' was Thérèse, to whom Mother Marie de Gonzague had confided her troubles as to an *equal*, and with whom she had sometimes wept.

Making Jesus speak, Thérèse tries to console her prioress so that she might see her *trial* as a purification. Tactfully the young nun tries to point out the spiritual attitude she must have, the one which will bring her peace. She dares to speak to her senior who was then sixty-two years old. The latter seems to have accepted the discerning advice. Here again the young sister had put on her *silk gloves*. Truth liberates.

As for her health, she made light of it. When Léonie was anxious Thérèse told her that she was not coughing any more. She had even been *introduced to the famous Dr de Cornière* who had declared that she *looked well!* This did not prevent her from thinking about the 'soon' of her dream. Her gaiety remained. No gloomy atmosphere pervaded the sacristy where she worked with her cousin: *We must be very careful not to say any unnecessary words, for an amusing little refrain always comes to mind after each necessary sentence, and we must keep it for recreation.*[1]

She smiled and joked but was also undergoing a profound development. During those summer months of 1896 she meditated on the texts of the prophet Isaiah and St Paul. On 6 August, the feast of the Transfiguration, Thérèse consecrated herself to the Holy Face together with her Sisters Geneviève and Marie of the Trinity, using a lyrical prayer she had written: *O adorable face of Jesus! O face more beautiful than lilies. Beloved spouse of our souls. O dearest face of Jesus*, etc. We find the same intensity in her poem of 15 August, *Jesus alone*, later changed to *My only love*:

> My only peace, my only good,
> my only love is you, my Lord.
> . . . you are a beggar for my love.
> You want my heart, Jesus, I give.

---

[1] Perhaps this is referring to the humorous verses about Carmelite life, 'Le Ciel en est le prix', composed by Marie of the Eucharist but copied out by Thérèse.

AT LAST I HAVE FOUND MY VOCATION (SEPTEMBER 1896)

It was with these sentiments that Sister Thérèse of the Child Jesus of the Holy Face began her annual private retreat on the evening of 7 September. She did not go to recreation and profited from a few additional hours of personal prayer. The following day in her solitude, on the feast of the Nativity of the Blessed Virgin, she commemorated the sixth anniversary of her profession. She took advantage of it to write directly to Jesus everything that had happened to her in these past weeks. As she was speaking to him, her pen ran along more lightly.

She began by reminding him of the grace received through her dream of 10 May which had broken into her darkness. *Oh my beloved! this grace was only the prelude to the greater graces you wished to bestow upon me* (in private Thérèse used the familiar 'tu' when addressing Jesus); *allow me, my only love, to recall them to you today – today, the sixth anniversary of* OUR UNION. *Oh, forgive me Jesus, if I am unreasonable in wishing to repeat my desires and hopes which border on the infinite, forgive me and heal my soul by giving it what it longs for!!!*

Thérèse knew that, sitting in her cell with her small writing-desk on her lap, she was writing foolish things. She was no longer satisfied with her vocation to be a *Carmelite, a spouse, a mother.* She felt immense seemingly contradictory desires welling up within her. She aspired to other, essentially masculine vocations: she would like to be *a warrior, a priest,*[1] *a deacon, an apostle, a doctor of the Church, a martyr.* And she wanted to experience each of these vocations in all its fullness, in space and time. To preach the Gospel in the five continents of the world, to be a missionary from the dawn of creation till the end of time, to be martyred in every possible way; these desires which tortured her were *greater than the universe!*

Yet realistically she asks herself: *O my Jesus! What is your answer to all my foolishness? Is there a soul more* LITTLE, *more powerless than mine?*

---

[1] She had often expressed this desire for priesthood and it became a reality when a certain occasion arose. One day when she was sacristan, she found a particle of a host on the paten. She motioned to Marie of the Trinity to accompany her to the sacristy: 'Follow me, I am carrying Jesus!' She also would have liked to preach.

The answer, as always, had to be found in the word of God which she meditated on night and day. She opened her New Testament at random, at St Paul's first letter to the Corinthians. She should have been discouraged by what she read there: 'All cannot be apostles, prophets, doctors . . . the eye cannot be the hand' (1 Cor. 12:29, 21). That was common sense. Not to be put off, she continued her search. Chapter 13 gave her a light: 'Charity is the excellent way which leads most surely to God.' She had found her answer!

> *At last my mind was at rest . . .* CHARITY *gave me the key to my vocation. I understood that the Church had a body made up of different members, the most necessary and most noble of all could not be lacking, and so I understood that the Church had a heart,*[1] *and that this heart was* BURNING WITH LOVE. *I understood that it was* LOVE ALONE *that made the Church's members act, and that if love ever became extinct, apostles would not preach the Gospel, martyrs would refuse to shed their blood. I understood that* LOVE CONTAINED ALL VOCATIONS, THAT LOVE WAS EVERYTHING, THAT IT EMBRACED ALL TIME AND ALL PLACES. IN A WORD, THAT IT IS ETERNAL!
>
> *Then, in the excess of my ecstatic joy, I cried out: O Jesus, my love, at last I have found my vocation.* MY VOCATION IS LOVE!
>
> *Yes, I have found my place in the Church and it is you, O my God, who have given me this place – in the heart of the Church, my mother, I shall be* LOVE. *Thus I shall be everything – and thus my dream will be fulfilled!!!*

The Carmelite, after making this discovery which fulfilled all her desires, continues her dialogue with Jesus and changes the symbol. This universal vocation which she had found at last (she was nearly twenty-four), far from tearing her away from her everyday life would establish her in her hidden life. To do everything out of love would transform her completely. Little, weak, poor, *like a small bird*, asleep or distracted at prayer-time, still very imperfect, her strength would come from abandoning herself completely to love, from daring to believe with a reckless, bold abandon that her life offered to the divine sun (or the divine eagle), Jesus, could save the

[1] Let us note that the heart is not mentioned explicitly in Paul's text. Thérèse includes it as a logical consequence.

world. By daring to believe, unconditionally, in this love, she would be an apostle, doctor, warrior, priest, martyr. Spectacular feats were denied her, but she could *throw flowers*, that is, offer up all the little occasions to love which life presented each day.

To throw flowers had been a familiar gesture of Thérèse since her childhood, and she had continued it with her novices, on summer evenings, when they threw rose petals at the crucifix in the cloister. The ones that touched the crucified Jesus acquired an infinite value for the Church and for the world. It meant, in plain language, that the 'nothings' of Thérèse's life, united to Christ, became treasures of grace for all. Thus she expressed, in her flowery language, the unfathomable mystery of the communion of saints. Her life was a rose whose petals had fallen for the life of the world.

Sister Thérèse, her heart full of thanksgiving, ends her ardent letter with a prayer and an appeal: *O Jesus, why can't I tell all* LITTLE SOULS *how unspeakable is your condescension? I feel that if it were possible for you to find a soul weaker and littler than mine, you would be pleased to grant it still greater favours, provided it abandon itself with complete confidence to your infinite mercy . . . I beg you to choose a legion of* LITTLE *victims worthy of your* LOVE

As Sister Marie of the Sacred Heart had asked her sister, before she went into retreat, to write her something about 'her little doctrine', Thérèse gave her these pages. But she realised that her godmother would perhaps find them *exaggerated*. Was her godchild filled with spiritual consolations? Thérèse therefore took care to write for her, on 13 September, a sort of introduction: *Do not think that I am swimming in consolations, oh, no! my consolation is to have none on this earth.* (Her sister knew nothing of her trial of faith.) *Without showing himself, without making his voice heard . . . Jesus is pleased to show me the only road that leads to that divine furnace, and this road is the abandon of a little child who sleeps without fear in its Father's arms.*

Thérèse then gave these pages to her sister, assuring her that she was not exaggerating anything, and that she was completely calm and at peace.

The first reader of these *pages burning with love* realised that she was in possession of a 'treasure'. Sister Marie of the Sacred Heart replied (one does not speak to Carmelites in retreat): 'Do you want me to tell you? I will. You are

26 Thérèse (extreme right) with members of her family (November 1896).
from left to right: Sister Marie of the Sacred Heart, Mother Agnès,
Céline, her cousin Marie Guérin (kneeling)

possessed by God, literally possessed, just as the wicked are by the devil.' But, on reflection, she herself became very distressed. How far she was, yes, how very far from having such desires! How could she not envy her godchild who was so blessed?

Some fortunate objections gained further details for us. Sister Marie of the Sacred Heart had not understood the parable of the little bird. Either Thérèse had expressed herself badly, or her sister's soul was too great.

She explains again: the treasures of merciful love are offered to *all*. Thérèse is no privileged exception. Quite the contrary. Because she is weak and powerless she is living proof that love chooses the little ones.

> *What pleases God in my little soul is* TO SEE ME LOVE MY LITTLENESS AND MY POVERTY, THE BLIND HOPE I HAVE IN HIS MERCY ... *Understand that to love Jesus, to be his* VICTIM OF LOVE, *the weaker one is, without desires, without virtues, the more fit one is for the operations of that consuming and transforming love ... One must consent always to stay poor and without strength, and that's the difficulty ... It is trust, and nothing but trust that must bring us to love.*

In these three letters Sister Thérèse of the Child Jesus of the Holy Face had written, unknowingly, 'the charter of the little way of childhood' (Conrad de Meester), one of the jewels of spiritual literature.

Thérèse was barely out of her solitude when she followed the preached retreat given by Fr Godefroy Madeleine, prior of the Praemonstratensian abbey at Mondaye (8–15 October). She had already met this rather strict monk and had confided to him her temptations against the faith ... that trial which had not left her. He advised her always to carry the creed on her person and to put her hand on it when she was assailed by doubts. She therefore wrote out the prayer in her blood and put it in the book of the Gospels which never left her. *I believe I have made more acts of faith in the past year than I have in my whole life.* Over the doorway of her cell, above her eyes, she carved: *Jesus is my only love.* Her temptations must have been violent for her to have dared to write on a dividing wall!

The last day of the retreat was the feast of Teresa of Avila,

and like all her sisters Thérèse drew a card from a basket.
The custom was that each one thus received a sentence for
meditation. Hers recalled the Madre's zeal for God's glory
and the salvation of the world. Thérèse was happy with it.
That was indeed her road.

TO INDO-CHINA? (NOVEMBER 1896)

Her missionary desire was intensified through her ever
growing correspondence with her two priest-brothers. From
China Fr Roulland told her about the beginnings of his
apostolate. He had sent her a copy of *L'Ame d'un Missionnaire
(The Soul of a Missionary)*, the life of Fr Nempon. The
missionary had died at twenty-seven in Tonkin when Thérèse
was sixteen. She had also received the important dates of her
brother's life which she had asked for. She discovered with
delight that the missionary's vocation had been 'saved' on 8
September 1890, the day of her profession. *I did not know that
for six years I had had a brother preparing to become a missionary.
Now that this brother is truly his apostle, Jesus reveals this mystery to
me, surely in order to increase still more the desire in my heart to love
him and make him loved.* It was a desire which did not cease
growing in her, and would be expressed more and more
strongly.

As a New Year's wish, she wished martyrdom for her
brother, and asked him in advance for relics: some locks of
his hair! Did she hope for this martyrdom for herself too, as
the Republican laws in France were threatening the existence
of religious congregations? 'Rumours of persecution made us
always live as if we were on a volcano,' Céline was to say.

In November there was still talk of Sister Thérèse going to
Tonkin,[1] for she seemed well restored to health. She was not
absent from any community exercises and even went to the
night office. So as 'to be given a sign of God's will', a novena
to the young martyr Théophane Venard (1829–61), her great

---

[1] The mission had followed the conquest of Tonkin (1882–5) led by Jules
Ferry, called 'the Tonkinese' by the anti-colonialists. His ministry would
end after the evacuation of Lang-Son in 1885. The Hanoi Carmel was
founded on 15 October 1895 from Saigon, which had been founded from
Lisieux in 1861.

friend, was begun. Thérèse had just read his life and letters. His youth, cheerfulness, love for his family; his death, delighted her. She loved him even more than St Louis de Gonzague because his life was so ordinary.

The answer was clearly given. In the middle of the novena Thérèse began to cough again and her health deteriorated. During that winter of 1896 Mother Marie de Gonzague allowed her to have a foot-warmer which she made use of but sparingly. She joked with Sister Marie of the Trinity: *This does not make sense, saints go to heaven with their instruments of penance, and I will go in with my foot-warmer!* She had to have painful vesicatories.[1] Just before seven o'clock Sister Geneviève, the assistant infirmarian, came in to wake her in order 'to trounce' her with a friction glove. One day in December, when she was exhausted by all this treatment and unable to leave her cell, the Guérins sent her some veal with morel. But whenever she was able she got up and went to mass. *It is not too much to suffer to have communion.*

Her care for the other novices kept her vigilant. Sister Marie-Madeleine still ran away from her, 'feeling that the depths of her soul were laid bare'. She advised Sister Marie of the Trinity, whom she sometimes called her 'doll', to change her game with the Child Jesus (this young sister had contrived to play all sorts of games with him): not to play skittles with him any more, but to become Jesus' spinning-top and accept the blows from the cord of his reproaches. She wrote amusing and consoling little notes to Sister Marie of Saint-Joseph.

However, for Christmas, as she did not have the strength (or the time), to write a play as usual, she contented herself with writing *The Child Jesus' Aviary*. The Carmelites, 'in a cage', come to entertain the newborn baby of the crib. But one day:

> All the birds from your aviary
> Will take their flight to heaven.

She was no doubt remembering her aviary at Les Buissonnets during her adolescence, which was now ten years ago.

---

[1] Hot plasters applied to the skin to induce blistering. They left a mark and a burn.

But she was thinking much more of the heaven which remained strangely veiled from her than of her past. On the feast of the Holy Innocents (28 December) she kept the feast of her four brothers and sisters who had died while still young. For several months she had been meditating on the fate of those children who come before God *with empty hands*. And on this subject she had painted a picture with the quotation from the letter to the Romans: 'Happy are those whom God considers just without works, for those who do works see the reward, not as a grace, but as something due. Those who do not have works are therefore justified freely by grace, through the redemption of Jesus Christ who is its author.'

She gained an unexpected humiliation when her poem, 'To my Little Brothers in Heaven', was sung in community that 28 December.[1] Mother Marie de Gonzague, after giving permission for the concert, left the community room, furious, saying in a loud voice that putting Sister Thérèse's poems to music would only nourish her pride. A few minutes later, at the night office, the latter retained her peaceful expression.

I BELIEVE MY COURSE HERE BELOW WILL NOT BE LONG (JANUARY TO MARCH 1897)

Thus began 1897, the year of her twenty-fourth birthday. On 9 January, she confided to her little mother (Agnès): *I hope to go there soon.* On the 27th, to Brother Siméon in Rome, who was eighty-three, she wrote: *I believe that my course here below will not be long.* In February, in a letter to Abbé Bellière, she quoted her poem 'Vivre d'Amour': *I have the hope that my exile will be short.* She added to reassure the seminarian: *If Jesus does what I expect I promise you I will remain your little sister up there.*

All that she wrote in these months took on the colour of a last will and testament. *My whole soul is there*, she said to Mother Agnès when she gave her the poem, 'My Joy' for her feast day on 21 January.

The trial of faith and hope seemed to redouble in intensity. To Sister Thérèse of Saint-Augustin (the nun for whom she

[1] On Holy Innocents day, the novitiate organises the day as it pleases.

felt natural antipathy in *everything*, but whom she loved with all her will), she confided: *I do not believe in eternal life. It seems to me that after this mortal life there is nothing more. I cannot convey to you the darkness into which I am plunged.* 'My Joy' voices the violence of this battle:

> When the blue sky turns black
> and he seems to abandon me
> my joy is to stay in the dark,
> to hide and keep down.

> Jesus my only love,
> his holy will is my joy,
> therefore fearless I live,
> I like night time as much as the day.

> . . . And I redouble my love
> When he hides from my faith.

> . . . What are life or death to me?
> Jesus, my joy is to love you!

For the thirty-sixth anniversary of young Théophane Venard's martyrdom – he was beheaded in Tonkin in 1861 – she wrote a poem spontaneously, and was to say: *My soul is like his.* Like her friend, she fought courageously with missionary zeal:

> My feeble love, my little sufferings
> Blessed by him, will make him loved abroad!

That same day, serving in the refectory, she broke a glass window in the servery with a plate. Céline helped Thérèse, who was in tears, to gather up the pieces of glass: *I had asked to have something big today to offer him in honour of my dear little brother, Théophane. Well! here it is!*

Although very tired, Thérèse nevertheless continued to write a lot. For Sister Saint-Stanislas's golden jubilee as a Carmelite nun (she was the oldest sister in the community), Thérèse wrote her eighth play, *Saint Stanislaus Kostka*. In the life of this young Jesuit novice she had been fascinated by the account of St Barbara, during a vision, bringing him Holy Communion. This had made Thérèse think. Perhaps St Barbara had desired, while on earth, to share in the sublime priestly duties, and the Lord had wanted to fulfil this desire? No doubt it would be the same for her who wanted so much to be a priest. But above all, the young Théophane had been obsessed by one desire, 'to do good after his death'; a desire which was growing in Thérèse.

On Wednesday, 3 March, at the very beginning of the Lenten fast, she began a novena to St Francis Xavier, patron of the universal missions, precisely for this intention: that she too might do good after her death! This novena of grace, as it is called, was said to be unfailing. On 19 March, the feast of St Joseph, she begged him as well, in the hermitage dedicated to him, for this intention. Sister Marie of the Sacred Heart found her there, very ill, and advised her to go and rest in her cell. Later in the day Thérèse wrote to Fr Roulland in China: *I want to save souls and forget myself for them – I want to save them even after my death.* Once again she mentions going to the Hanoi Carmel. Her prioress believed she had a missionary vocation, but the scabbard was not strong enough for the sword. *It is really not convenient to be made up of body and soul. Especially when the former is slowly and surely becoming weaker.*

But Thérèse kept going. *If I die, someone will notice it*, she said to Sister Marie of the Trinity. For the profession of the last of her novices, Sister Marie of the Eucharist, she wrote, 'My Weapons'. In it the sick nun proves herself a warrior.[1] That same evening her cousin, who had a beautiful voice, sang it in front of the community.

> I must struggle on without respite or rest
> . . . I brave the fury of all hell.

She concludes thus the five verses:

> I face the gunfire with a smile
> and in your arms, my spouse,
> I will die singing in battle,
> weapons in my hand.

The community, without knowing it, had just heard Thérèse's testament. These were the last words she would address to her sisters gathered round the fire in the community room.

---

[1] This poem was to make the soldier seminarian, Maurice Bellière, smile when Thérèse sent it to him.

27 Thérèse's last cell (1894–7) before the infirmary

11

Sickness, Passion, Death
(April to 30 September 1897)

*To live for love is not to set up one's tent
here below on the heights of Tabor,
but to climb Calvary with Jesus.*

SERIOUSLY ILL (APRIL 1897)

Until April the nuns who saw Thérèse still walking about, taking part in community exercises, did not suspect that her health was deteriorating. Aware of these deceptive appearances, she said later: *They do not believe I am as sick as I am.*

But family affection made her near relatives more watchful. At the end of April Sister Geneviève wrote to Brother Siméon in Rome: 'The health of your other little Carmelite, Sister Thérèse of the Child Jesus, is in grave danger . . . Everyone expects to see the divine master pick this flower which is so beautiful.' On 4 April we have the first of the 'health reports' Marie Guérin sent to her parents, telling them of digestive troubles, a daily fever, *at three o'clock sharp*, stated Thérèse in a postscript. Dr de Cornière was called in.

As the days went by there was vomiting, acute chest pains and frequent coughing up of blood. 'I fear I am worrying you, dear Father, but really we are very worried,' wrote Marie on 5 June. 'The way her illness is going, she is in a state of great exhaustion and tells us that at times her agonies are such that she feels as if she is going to die.'

Racked by long coughing fits (*I cough and cough! I am just like a train when it gets into the station*), Thérèse progressively gave up all community exercises: recreations, chanted office, common duties. On 18 May she was relieved of all work. During Easter week she had spoken at length with Mother

Agnès who began to write down some of her words. That was the beginning of the 'last conversations' which would continue for six months.

LÉO TAXIL UNMASKED OR THE TRIUMPH OF HUMILIATION
(19 APRIL 1897)

A long-awaited press conference took place on Easter Monday night in the Geographical Society's room in Paris. Miss Diana Vaughan was going to show herself at last and speak to the public. For some time she had been summoned to appear. Some German Jesuits had even questioned her existence. But she had replied that, having betrayed the Freemasons, she feared for her life. That evening a full room awaited her.

But instead of a charming young woman, a small stout man with scant hair and a little goatee beard appeared on the platform: Léo Taxil. In front of a room crowded with Catholic journalists (many priests) and anti-clericals, he flung off the mask. He was Diana Vaughan! The convert had only ever existed in his more than fertile imagination. For twelve years his writings had taken in thousands of credulous readers: Christians, priests, bishops, even the Pope, but also the Freemasons. He had written *The Eucharistic Novena* himself! As for the tales of satanic knighthood, they were the product of his Marseilles[1] brain which had specialised in outrageous practical jokes from its youth. He was very proud of 'the most grandiose hoax of his life!'

Nearly all those present wanted to lay hands on the impostor, who smartly disappeared from the scene, protected by police. The session of slides which was to have illustrated Diana Vaughan's conference did not take place. During Léo Taxil's talk there was only one picture on the wall, a photograph representing Joan of Arc.

On 21 April *Le Normand* published an unobtrusive paragraph on the memorable press conference. The Catholics who had 'believed' in Diana Vaughan were shamefaced. But on the 24th, on the front page, the paper gave a lengthy account

[1] Léo Taxil's real name was Gabriel Jogand-Pagès. He was born in Marseilles on 21 March 1854.

of the meeting. If the Martin sisters at the Lisieux Carmel had read to the end of the article (which was very likely), there must have been amazement: 'What remains to be said about that meeting? Of the pictures he was to have had there by the hundred – there was only one, a photograph representing Joan of Arc's vision of St Catherine, from a play which had been put on in honour of Diana Vaughan in a Carmelite Convent. What convent? Probably Taxil's house!'

Oh, no! For once Léo Taxil had spoken the truth. The photograph had indeed come from a Carmel, that of Lisieux. Catherine and Joan were Céline and Thérèse Martin. They had 'presided' at the meeting on 19 April! Léo Taxil had made use of the print Sister Thérèse of the Child Jesus had sent him.

It was a cruel blow for the Carmelites. For the sick nun still in the night of faith it must have struck very deep. She had written *The Triumph of Humility*: now she touched the depths of humiliation. She remained silent. She tore up the letter she had received from 'Diana Vaughan' and threw it on the manure heap. She was staggered at the sacrilegious low humour that could make fun of the truths by which she lived. So was it all an illusion? Two months after this revelation, she wrote: *Those souls who have no faith, and who, through the abuse of grace, lose this precious treasure*; clearly thinking of this impostor. For he also had to accept living in darkness. And for him, and all like him, she prayed:

> *Lord, your child has understood your divine light, and she begs your forgiveness for her brothers. She agrees to eat the bread of sorrow for as long as you wish, and she does not want to leave this table filled with bitterness where poor sinners are eating before the day you have appointed. But can she not also say in her own name and in the name of her brothers: 'Have pity on us, Lord, for we are poor sinners!' Oh! Lord, send us away justified. May all those who are not enlightened by the bright flame of faith see it shine one day: O Jesus! if the table defiled by them has to be purified by a soul who loves you, I will eat the bread of trial there alone until it please you to bring me into your luminous kingdom.*

Nothing of this terrible deception came through in the letter she wrote the following Sunday to Abbé Bellière. Henceforth abandoning the formal 'Monsieur l'Abbé', she calls him her 'dear little brother'. Let him not be mistaken about his sister: she is not one of those *great souls* that one sometimes meets in contemplative monasteries. In truth she is only a *very small soul*, very imperfect, but she recognises God's gifts. He has done great things in her. She loved to note the date of all the graces she received, and she sent the memorable dates in her own life to the seminarian and asked him, in return, for those of his journey.

She also shared her *little way full of confidence and love* with Fr Roulland in China.

Sometimes when I read spiritual treatises, in which perfection is shown with a thousand obstacles and surrounded by a host of illusions, my poor little mind is very quickly wearied, I close the learned book which wearies my head and leaves my heart parched, and I take up the holy Scriptures. Then everything seems so clear, a single word opens up infinite horizons to my soul, perfection seems easy. I see that it is enough to recognise one's nothingness and abandon oneself, like a child, into the arms of God.

She regarded herself as the zero which, by itself, is of no value but put after a unit becomes useful. The Carmelite can do *absolutely nothing*, she only follows the missionary by *prayer and sacrifice*. She was living what she said. Sister Marie of the Sacred Heart, seeing her making her way slowly in the garden, very tired, strongly advised her to go and rest. *I am walking for a missionary*, replied Thérèse.

WHY I LOVE YOU, MARY (MAY 1897)

Suffering from fever, coughing fits and pain Thérèse, in her cell, continued to sew. She hated to waste her time. She could also write poems to *give pleasure* to her sisters. Mother Henriette, of the Paris Carmel, had heard about this young Carmelite who wrote poetry. 'If it is true that this little sister is a pearl and writes such beautiful poetry, let her then send me one of her poems and I will see that for myself.' She threw out to her a sort of challenge which the sick nun took up. Mother Henriette received 'A Rose Unpetalled', a poem of five verses:

A rose unpetalled gives itself unselfishly
no more to be.
. . . heedlessly trampled underfoot
its scattered petals
artlessly decorate,
as I know well.

The Carmelite in Paris found this poem beautiful but incomplete: it needed a concluding verse. At death, God will gather up these scattered petals to make of them a beautiful rose which will shine for all eternity. For Thérèse this was a total misconstruction of her meaning. She replied: *Let the good mother write this verse as she understands it, I am not at all inspired to do it. My desire is to be unpetalled for ever, to delight God. Full stop, that's all.*

She was still misunderstood. *God alone can understand me.* She had a foreboding that it would soon be impossible for her to express herself in this way, and so she wrote two poems spontaneously. The first, 'To Joan of Arc'; more and more she was thinking about her sister in prison, facing death:

Joan, I find you more brilliant, beautiful
in your dark prison than at your king's coronation.
How came you to shine with the glory of heaven?
It was your betrayal.

Joan was betrayed by her own party, as Thérèse had been by 'Diana Vaughan'.

The second poem, written in May, Mary's month, is her Marian testament. To Sister Geneviève she confided: *I still have something to do before I die. I have always dreamed of expressing in song to the Blessed Virgin all that I think of her.* The countless sermons she had heard during her life[1] had not satisfied her at all. What *improbable things* are said by preachers! They show Mary as *unapproachable*, more Queen than Mother, eclipsing the glory of her children. *How I would have loved to be a priest in order to preach about the Blessed Virgin.* Thérèse would have shown her as someone we can *imitate* and *more Mother than Queen.* In twenty-five verses Thérèse went through the *real and not imagined* life of Mary of Nazareth, according to the chronology of the Gospels which were her only guide. It was

[1] The Carmelite order is a Marian order.

a very simple life, a life of faith. Like us – like Thérèse – Mary knew trial.

Mother, your child wants you to be the example
Of the soul who seeks him in darkness and faith.

It is only in the last verse that the Carmelite refers to her own story:

Soon I shall see you in the beautiful heavens
You, who came and smiled on my life's morning
Come and smile on me again . . . Mother . . .
for it is evening!

She realised now that her unpretentious compositions could *do good*. Adapting them to her correspondents, she copied out some of them to send to her spiritual brothers, who treasured them. The Carmelites also reproduced them. They were sent to the families (the Guérins had priority), and the Carmels (Paris, Saigon). In Rome Brother Siméon lent them to Brother Salutaire who was a 'poet' himself. The latter even tried to obtain a preface from his poetic colleague for a collection of his poems, *Mes Dévotions*. Thérèse did not reply. She was not interested in 'literature'.

If during this period she re-read everything she had written, pencil in hand, it was not from a literary perspective. She could hardly work any more. She perhaps re-read her life in order to struggle against the obsessing temptations which wanted her to forget the love with which she had been filled. One of the aspects of her trial was a spiritual amnesia.

She now saw her second play on Joan of Arc in a totally new light. She herself was that young girl facing death, who was living an inner agony. Unconsciously, she had prophesied. She confided to Mother Agnès: *I have re-read the play on Joan of Arc that I wrote. You will see there all my feelings about death. They are all expressed.*

A LITTLE BLACK EXERCISE BOOK (4 JUNE TO 8 JULY 1897)

Over these days the intimacy between the sick nun and her sister Agnès intensified. Thérèse wanted her to know the truth. In the evening of Sunday, 30 May she told her that she had coughed up blood twice the year before. The 'little mother' was terribly upset. Her sister was going to die and for the past months had hidden something from her. In an exchange of affectionate little notes Thérèse tried to alleviate her older sister's very keen sensitivity. This time, Agnès grasped the situation. 'Your condition is so much worse! When I think that you are going to die!'

This 'treasure' she had with her was going to disappear. She remembered the exercise book of memoirs she had received two years ago and which she had read with amazement. Her sister had so many things to say! Why should she not continue while there was still time?

On the night of 2 June, after matins, the former prioress knocked on Mother Marie de Gonzague's door; it was nearly midnight.

> Mother, it is impossible for me to sleep before confiding a secret to you. When I was prioress Sister Thérèse wrote for me, to please me and under obedience, some memories of her childhood. I re-read them the other day. They are good, but you would not be able to draw a great deal from them to help you with her circular[1] after her death, for there is almost nothing about her religious life. If you commanded her to do it, she could write something more serious, and no doubt you would have something incomparably better than I have.

It was a prudent and shrewd request which obtained full success. The following day Mother Marie de Gonzague ordered the sick nun, who had been vomiting and was suffering pain, to continue writing. Sister Thérèse was surprised. *Write about what?* 'About the novices, about your spiritual brothers,' replied Mother Agnès. Thérèse was given a small exercise book with a black imitation leather cover which she thought far too beautiful for her.

I'm not going to weary my head writing my 'little way'. It's as if I were fishing with a line: I write just what comes at the end of my pen. On 3 or 4 June she began, addressing herself this time to Mother Marie de Gonzague: *My beloved Mother, you have told*

---

[1] After the death of a religious, a letter is sent out to all the Carmels, more or less at length, relating to her life.

me of your desire that I finish with you SINGING THE MERCIES OF
THE LORD *. . . Yes, it is with you, beloved Mother, in answer to your
wish that I am going to try and express the sentiments of my soul, my
gratitude to God, and to you who represent him visibly to me.*

This change of addressee obviously had its importance.
Since Mother Marie de Gonzague's difficult election a year
and a half ago, Thérèse's relationship with her prioress had
changed. She had become her assistant in the novitiate. She
had come a long way spiritually. She was facing death. *Now*
she saw herself as she stood before God, *a poor little nothing.*
With complete liberty, with childlike simplicity, she could
speak to her prioress. It was too bad if she did *not always
remain within the limits prescribed for subjects.* It was Mother
Marie de Gonzague's fault, for she had acted towards her
more as a *mother* than as a *prioress.*

In all truth Thérèse could begin her *assignment* by thanking
her for not having spoilt her at the beginning of her religious
life. Her *firm* and *maternal* training had been very beneficial to
her. Thus moulded by humiliations, she did not have to fear
the praises she received today.

Throughout that beautiful June, whether in her cell, in a
pretty little white armchair, or in her father's invalid chair
(which had been given to the Carmel), Thérèse wrote, often
interrupted by the infirmarians, the sisters passing by and
the novices who wished to speak to her.

*I do not know what I am writing . . . I do not know if I have been
able to write ten lines without being interrupted . . . There goes a
haymaker who is just leaving me after having said very sympatheti-
cally: 'Poor little Sister, it must tire you out writing like that all
day long!' 'Don't worry,' I replied, 'I appear to be writing a lot,
but really I am writing almost nothing.' 'That's good! But just the
same, I am very happy that we are doing the hay, for it will distract
you a little.'*

Her humour and gift of mimicry were not dulled by illness:
*I have tried not to become impatient, to put into practice what I am
writing.* In fact, sisterly charity was a subject very dear to her
heart and she had received abundant light on it.

SEATED AT THE TABLE OF SINNERS

But first she wanted to speak about the fog in which she had been living since Easter 1896. On 9 June, the second anniversary of her offering to merciful love, she described as much of her inner trial as words could express. That day *the ugly serpents were not hissing in (her) ears.* But she felt that what she did say about it was as imperfect as a sketch compared to the model. For thirteen months now she had made acts of faith in order to resist the inner voices which suggested to her that she was heading towards *nothingness.*

Before this period she could not have even conceived that there were really unbelievers. She had been living in the faith she had received in her infancy, like a fish in water. But now, *everything disappeared.* She understood that it was a trial which had to purify her too natural desire for heaven. But above all, she found herself on an equal footing with unbelievers. She was ready to sit down without any condescension *at the table of sinners,* just as Jesus had done. She thought of Pranzini, of Henri Chéron, of Léo Taxil, of René Tostain,[1] and of the immense crowd of others she did not know.

One day she had surprised Marie of the Trinity with an unusual confidence: *If I had not been accepted in Carmel I would have entered a refuge to live there unknown and despised, in the midst of the poor penitents! My happiness would have been to pass for such in the eyes of all; and I would have become the apostle of my companions, telling them what I thought of God's mercy.*

This trial had made her cover a considerable path. Through sharing the experience of unbelievers she discovered that she was like them. Her Carmelite life, praying for others, made pharisaism a danger. She knew now that she had been saved freely and if she had not fallen, it was due to the care of her Father who had removed the stones from her path. Oh! if she could give her life for these sinners so that they too might discover they are passionately loved by the One who revealed himself to Zacchaeus, Mary Magdalene, the Samaritan woman, Augustine – and Thérèse Martin!

She had written it:

I have no merit in not having given myself up to the love of creatures.

[1] See page 116.

I was preserved from it only through God's great mercy! I know that without him, I might have fallen as low as the Magdalene but I also know that Jesus has forgiven me more than St Mary Magdalene, since he forgave me in advance by preventing me from falling ... I have heard it said that one cannot meet a pure soul who loves more than a repentant one; oh, how I should like to give those words the lie!

She did not wish to write about her inner trial at length in the exercise book. She feared she might blaspheme; she was afraid she had said too much already. She confided her sufferings only to Mother Marie de Gonzague, the chaplain, and now Mother Agnès. One day she was tempted to speak of it to her godmother: *Do you have temptations against faith?* When she saw Marie of the Sacred Heart's indignant surprise, she knew that she had to be very prudent about this matter, so as not to 'contaminate' her sisters.

No one suspected what she was going through. She was always seen smiling and cheerful. Each day she continued to write 'just as it came, without rubbing out'. She tells of her joy in now having two brothers, but warns the prioress to be very prudent about this kind of spiritual correspondence after her death. *Without obedience, this correspondence could do more harm than good, if not to the missionary, then at least to the Carmelite whose way of life tends to make her continually fall back on herself.*

She explains at length her manner of dealing with the novices, and above all, the discovery she had recently made about the meaning of real sisterly charity. *I understand now that perfect charity consists in bearing with others' faults, in not being surprised at their weakness, in being edified by the smallest acts of virtue we see them practise.*

THE BUSINESS OF BEING ILL

From 10 June onwards the writer was a little better. On Monday, 7th Sister Geneviève had photographed her. Kneeling in front of the large camera with its black cover, Sister Thérèse posed for nine seconds. She held in her hands the two pictures from her breviary which expressed her name and summarised her vocation: the Child Jesus and the Holy

Face. The exposure did not satisfy the photographer. She repeated it twice. Her sister was exhausted, Céline was impatient. That evening Céline apologised and received this note: *Let us humbly number ourselves among the imperfect, see ourselves as little souls. Yes, it is enough to humble oneself and to bear with one's imperfections meekly. That is true sanctity.*

Thérèse had just related in her exercise book the discovery of the 'little way', approximately two years ago. Before going in she sat in the garden with Mother Agnès. Gazing at a white hen gathering her chicks beneath her wings, Thérèse began to cry from love and gratitude. Her whole life had been thus: God had protected her.

Since 4 June the community had been making a novena to Our Lady of Victories for Sister Thérèse's cure. Had not their prayers been answered in May 1883, at the time of her terrible illness? This time however the sick nun did not believe that the Blessed Virgin would perform a miracle.

That same day at recreation, lying on Sister Geneviève's straw mattress, she bade her farewells to the Martin sisters who wanted to see her and listen to her continually: *Oh, my little sisters, how happy I am! I see that I am going to die soon, I am sure of it now. Do not be surprised if I do not appear to you after my death, and if you do not see anything extraordinary as a sign of my happiness. Remember it is 'my little way' to desire to see nothing.* She had a foreboding that she would not be able to receive communion often now. *If you find me dead one morning, don't worry. God will quite simply have come for me. Yes, it is a great grace to receive the sacraments, but when God does not permit it, it is good just the same. Everything is grace.*

It was a fact that she had always regretted the strict attitude of Mother Marie de Gonzague, who refused to put into effect the decrees of 1891 allowing more frequent communion.[1] These hangovers of timid Jansenism ran counter to her bold confidence. *My way is all confidence and love, I don't understand souls who are afraid of so loving a Friend.* In the infirmary she was to say to the prioress: *After my death I will make you change your mind.*[2]

---

[1] These decrees deprived the prioress of the power to sanction or refuse her nuns' reception of communion, and transferred it to the Carmel's superior.

[2] M. Hodierne, the new chaplain appointed in 1897 introduced daily communion into the Lisieux Carmel.

28 Different faces of Thérèse: from top to bottom
1st row l. January 1889. r. 1894
2nd row l. April 1895. r. March 1896
3rd row July 1896 (both photographs)
4th row l. 1897. r. 30 August 1897

On the last day of the novena she was better. This was a disappointment to her. *I am better. It's over. The hope of death is gone. God wills that I abandon myself like a very little child who does not worry about what is done to her.*

At the end of June there was a last meeting with her family in the parlour: *How shy I was in the parlour with my Uncle! When I came out I scolded a novice very severely, I did not recognise myself. What contrasts there are in my character!* Another day she would say: *I have never feared anyone. I have always gone where I pleased.*

She did not see her family again for they went on holiday to La Musse. Throughout the summer Sister Marie of the Eucharist wrote to give them news. In the glorious month of July, which was beginning, Thérèse became less and less well. She could no longer hold her pen and used a small pencil to write letters and go on with her exercise book.

On Tuesday, 6th she brought up a lot of blood 'like liver'. This marked the beginning of the period of haemoptysis which would continue until 5 August. Dr de Cornière – whom she nicknamed 'Clodion the long-haired' – visited her each day. On the 8th she made her confession to Abbé Youf and asked for the last anointing. 'Overflowing with joy', she joked all through the day: *It's really something to be in one's agony! But, after all, what's that! I have sometimes been in agony over silly things.* She was too successful. When the doctor visited her on the Friday he did not think she was yet ready for the last anointing. Canon Maupas came to see her and put off the ceremony. This was a great disappointment to the dying nun: *I don't know the business.* Next time she would be better prepared. She had only to drink a glass of that condensed milk prescribed by the doctor and for which she had a repugnance. Then perhaps, she would be 'anointed' at last.

TO THE INFIRMARY (8 JULY 1897)

Although the doctor had forbidden all movement, Thérèse was taken from her cell on a mattress down to the infirmary of the Holy Face, on the ground floor at the north-east corner of the cloister. The twelve-by-fifteen-foot window of this room looked out on to the garden. From her iron bed surrounded with brown curtains (she had pinned on them her favourite

29 The infirmary of the Carmel. On the right, the Virgin of the Smile

pictures: Mary, Théophane Venard, her little brothers and sisters), she saw the statue of the Virgin of the Smile which had been brought down with her. Such was henceforth Thérèse's world.

Sister Saint-Stanislas, the official infirmarian, was seventy-three years old. She willingly handed over her duties to her assistant, Sister Geneviève, who slept in the adjoining cell. Mother Agnès was with her the most. She had been given permission to stay with her sister during the office of matins, and continued to write down her words. Through this almost daily diary we see Thérèse living, suffering, joking, loving.

She was ill like others, and weak. *Since I have been ill I think about almost nothing.* How did she pray? *I say nothing to him, I love him.* During the times of extreme physical weakness she groaned.

She knew all the humiliations of a bedridden person, totally dependent on those around them. *How easy it is to be discouraged when you are very ill.* She had to abandon herself, as always, and now more than ever.

In her physical sufferings (fevers, profuse sweatings, suffocation, insomnia, constipation, bed-sores, gangrene of the intestines), and her moral sufferings, her face remained the same and certain sisters did not think that she was really ill. The uncertainties about the disease baffled her, as they did the doctor. For some time she feared she would remain the burden of a poor community. Thérèse bore the brunt of the scenes which Mother Marie de Gonzague's moodiness still caused. The lack of sensitivity on the part of certain sisters (and even Céline) made her suffer. Someone charitably repeated to her what Sister Saint-Vincent-de-Paul had said at recreation: 'I don't know why they are speaking so much about Sister Thérèse of the Child Jesus; she is not doing anything exceptional. One does not see her practising virtue, you cannot even say that she is a good nun.' To which Thérèse replied: *To hear on my death-bed that I am not a good nun, what joy! Nothing could give me greater pleasure.* She submitted to the repeated questions of those around her about her past, about the date of her death. 'Of what then will you die?' *But I will die of love! . . . Why should I be protected more than anyone else from the fear of death?*

And the spiritual sufferings; there was still the inner anguish. *I look at the physical heaven, the other is closed to me more and more.* From 19 August onwards she was deprived of Holy Communion because she could not endure the complicated ceremonial. Once she was on the verge of a nervous breakdown. Another day her suffering was such that she stated that dangerous medicines should not be left near seriously ill patients. *I am surprised that more atheists do not take their own lives. If I had not had faith, I would have taken my life without hesitation.*

And yet she was still cheerful and humorous under these conditions. *I am always cheerful and happy.* Mother Agnès noted her puns, imitations, smiles, mimicry, her pronunciation. Thérèse called Céline *Bobonne, Mlle Lili. You must let me do my little monkey tricks.* For it comforted her visitors. This infirmary became a centre of attraction and radiance. The novices – especially 'the doll', Marie of the Trinity, complained of not having access to it. Sister St John of the Cross and other senior nuns used to come on the quiet to seek her counsel.

Thérèse taught her 'little way' to the dashing soldier Maurice (Bellière), through the written word, *'as to a little girl'*.

Her heart knew the joy of real love and she knew how to express her affection. She asked Mother Agnès for a kiss that made a noise, 'smack'! Still clear-sighted, she knew she had crossed a threshold which she expressed by the word *now*.

How happy I am now for having deprived myself from the beginning of my religious life! I am already enjoying the reward promised to those who fight courageously. I no longer feel the necessity of refusing all human consolations, for my soul is strengthened by him whom I wanted to love above all. I see with joy that in loving him the heart expands and can give to those who are dear to it incomparably more loving affection than if it had concentrated upon one egotistical and unfruitful love.

She wanted to see if all she had written was indeed true. She had wanted to love until she died of love. Love of Jesus, of all her sisters, a universal love. She attained her full maturity when disease was destroying her body. Yet she remained nevertheless a child. Often in fun (she had been put on a milk diet) she called herself *baby*. But when she said to Marie of the Sacred Heart: *I am a baby who is old*, she was no longer joking. She was speaking the truth. She was coming to the end of her *giant's course*.

She admitted she was very tired, at the end. *But I am falling into the arms of God.* She no longer had the strength to continue her memoirs in pencil. The little black exercise book ends on sheet 37 with these lines:

Yes, I feel it; even though I had on my conscience all the sins that can be committed, I would go, my heart broken with sorrow, and throw myself into the arms of Jesus, for I know how much he loves the prodigal child who returns to him. It is not because God, in his PREVENIENT *mercy, has preserved my soul from mortal sin that I go to him with confidence and love –*

She could go no further.

Before finishing sheet 35 she had again cast a final glance over her life:

Your love has gone before me, it has grown with me, and now it is an abyss whose depths I cannot fathom . . . O my Jesus, perhaps it is an illusion, but it seems to me that you cannot fill a soul with more love than the love with which you have filled mine . . . *Here on earth, I cannot conceive a greater immensity of love than the one which it has pleased you to give me freely,* WITHOUT ANY MERIT ON MY PART.

Thus Thérèse finished singing the mercies of the Lord in her regard.

PUBLISHING HER MANUSCRIPTS

In July Mother Agnès mentioned to Thérèse one of her projects. What if they were to publish what she had written for her circular? She added quickly: 'What you have written could very well go one day to the Holy Father.' Thérèse laughed: *Et nunc et semper!*[1]

But seriously she foresaw this possibility and made some recommendations to Mother Agnès:

Really tell them, Mother, that if I had committed all possible crimes I would always have the same confidence. I feel that this whole multitude of offences would be like a drop of water thrown into a fiery furnace. You will then tell the story about the converted sinner who died of love.[2] *Souls will understand immediately, for it's such a striking example of what I'm trying to say.*

The anxious Mother Agnès foresaw all kinds of difficulties for this publication. *Well, like Joan of Arc, I say, 'The will of God will be done despite men's jealousy.'* With a smile she appointed her sister her 'historian'. Let her add or cut passages as she pleased. She trusted her. She had a mysterious feeling that this *exercise book of her life* would be able to do good.

A short time later Mother Agnès asked her sister to re-write a passage of the manuscript which she thought was incomplete. Following this she found Thérèse in tears: *What*

---

[1] An example of Thérèse's puns: In the French there is a play on words, Holy Father, Saint-Père. Thérèse replies: 'Now and for ever', using the Latin phrase (tr.).

[2] The story of Paesie told in *The Lives of the Desert Fathers*; she died the same day as her conversion and the Father saw her soul enter Paradise.

I am re-reading in this exercise book is indeed my soul! Mother, these pages will do much good. They will then understand God's gentleness much better. She added: *Oh! I know everyone will love me – a very important work. But take care! There will be something there for all tastes, except for those living in extraordinary ways.*

MY HEAVEN WILL BE SPENT ON EARTH

Leaving a book could not satisfy Thérèse, especially as she was completely indifferent to its future. It mattered little to her if Mother Marie de Gonzague decided to burn her manuscript. She was obsessed with the desire *not to remain inactive in heaven.* She was struck by the persistence of this desire. She reasoned: *God would not give me this desire to do good on earth after my death if he did not want to realise it; he would give me rather the desire to rest in him.* It was impossible for her to imagine heaven as a place of rest. *A soul on fire with love cannot remain inactive . . . If you knew what projects I have in mind, what I will do with things when I am in heaven. I will begin my mission* (to Marie of the Sacred Heart). She explained: *My mission is about to begin, my mission to make God loved as I love him, to give my* LITTLE WAY *to souls. If God grants my desires, my heaven will be spent on earth until the end of time. Yes, I will spend my heaven doing good upon earth . . . I will return! I will come down!*

Her boldness knew no limits: *God will have to do my will in heaven, because I have never done my own will on earth.* She confided to Sister Marie of the Trinity that the presentiment she had of the future made her dizzy. Laughing, she said: *Anyone else but you would take me for a fool, or else someone terribly proud!* But she remained completely poor, *with empty hands. All that I have, all that I gain, is for the Church and for souls. Even if I lived to be eighty, I would still be as poor.*

The feast of Our Lady of Mount Carmel, 16 July, was full of joy. Abbé Troude,[1] newly ordained, brought her communion. Her cousin Marie sang – without crying – a communion verse written by Thérèse, who was surprised she

---

[1] Sister Marie Philomène's nephew, and fellow student of Abbé Bellière. He was a contemporary of Thérèse and died at the age of twenty-seven (30 January 1873 to March 1900).

could still write verses. She was still very much alive; she took advantage of it to write her farewell letters.

To Fr Roulland: *'Oh my Brother, I feel I shall be more useful to you in heaven than on earth, and so it is with joy that I announce my approaching entrance into that blissful city.*

To the Guérins: *Goodbye, dear Uncle and Aunt, only in heaven shall I put into words my affection for you. While I am dragging on, my pencil cannot convey it to you.*

To Léonie: *Goodbye, dearest sister, I want the thought of my entry into heaven to fill you with joy, for there I will be able to love you still more.* She had told Sister Marie of the Sacred Heart that she was convinced her sister would finally enter and stay at the Visitation in Caen.

There was one exception: Abbé Bellière received letters until her strength was exhausted. There were three more to him, written in pencil in shaky handwriting. The young seminarian spent his holidays at Langrune in Calvados. He was dismayed at the prospect of losing his sister. She knew he needed her. She firmly strengthened him.

More than ever I realise the degree to which your soul is sister to mine, since it is called up to God by THE LIFT *of love and not by the rough stairway of fear . . . You must know me very imperfectly if you fear that a detailed account of your faults would lessen my affection for your soul . . . You are barred from going to heaven by any other way than your poor little sister's.*

On Friday, 30 July, unlike the preceding days, the haemoptysis continued all day. She was suffocating and was given ether to help her breathe. Dr de Cornière thought she would not last the night. At six o'clock in the evening Canon Maupas finally anointed her and administered communion as the last sacrament. In the next room the sacristans prepared the candles, holy water and a palliasse for her burial. Through the door, which had been unfortunately left half open, Sister Thérèse saw all these things. *You see that candle over there, when the divine thief comes to take me it will be put in my hand, but you must not give me the candlestick, it is too ugly.* Her dark humour did not make her afraid.

Once again the illness disappointed her. The next day, she was 'better'. *But of what will I die?* As they were debating around her bed about the days she still had to live, she

18 Juillet 1897

Jésus †

Mon pauvre et cher petit Frère

Votre douleur me touche profondément, mais voyez comme Jésus est bon! Il permet que je puisse encore vous écrire pour essayer de vous consoler et sans doute ce n'est pas la dernière fois. Ce doux Sauveur entend vos plaintes et vos prières c'est pour cela qu'il me laisse encore sur la terre. Ne croyez pas que je m'en afflige, oh non mon cher petit frère, au contraire, car je vois dans cette conduite de Jésus combien Il vous aime!.....
Je me suis sans doute bien mal expliquée dans mon dernier petit mot puisque vous me dites, mon très cher petit frère "de ne pas vous demander cette joie que je ressens à l'approche du bonheur" Ah si pour quelques instants vous pouviez lire dans mon âme, que vous seriez surpris! La pensée du bonheur céleste, non seulement ne me cause aucune joie, mais encore je me demande parfois comment il me sera possible d'être heureuse sans souffrir. Jésus sans doute changera ma nature, autrement je regretterais la souffrance et la vallée des larmes. Jamais je n'ai demandé au bon Dieu de mourir jeune

30 Letter to Abbé Bellière (18 July 1897)

interrupted: *It's still the patient who knows best! And I feel I still have a long time to go.*

In fact, contrary to all expectations, her condition remained stable from the 6 to 15 August. Dr de Cornière went on holiday.

HOW LITTLE I HAVE LIVED (6–15 AUGUST 1897)

In the long moments of solitude, inactivity, in the silence of the infirmary her whole life came back to her: childhood, her struggles, nine years of Carmelite life. *Alas, how little I've lived!* she said in July. *Life has always appeared short to me. My childhood days seem like yesterday.* But she was living in the present moment. *Just for today.*

She had a horror of 'pretence'. It did not matter what the doctor or the Carmelites thought of her. Mother Agnès suggested that she said something edifying to Dr de Cornière but she refused. Even her sister did not really understand her. 'I was telling her that she must have had to struggle a lot in order to have become perfect.' *Oh, it's not that!*

Throughout those two hundred days of illness she kept her eyes on Jesus. Her crucifix did not leave her. She often kissed it *on the face*, and not on the feet as was customary. *Our Lord died on the cross, in agony, and yet that was the most beautiful death of love. This is the only one that has been seen . . . To die of love is not to die in transports* (as her sisters imagined). *I frankly admit, it seems to me that this is what I am experiencing.*

This discreet comparison of her passion to that of Jesus occurs in the last conversations. When she had a pain in her shoulder she thought of the carrying of the cross. When her three sisters, who had fallen asleep beside her bed, awoke, she pointed her finger: *Peter, James and John!*

Deprived of communion? What did it matter! She herself had become a victim for sacrifice. *I often think of the words of St Ignatius of Antioch: I too must be ground down through suffering in order to become the wheat of God.*

GREAT SUFFERINGS (15–27 AUGUST 1897)

On the feast of the Assumption the illness took another turn. Thérèse suffered from her extreme difficulty in breathing. Her left side was very painful and her legs began to swell. On 17 August, in Dr de Cornière's absence, Mother Marie de Gonzague finally gave permission for Dr Francis La Néele to examine his cousin. Relations between the prioress, who was jealous of her authority, and the young outspoken doctor were strained. The diagnosis was very pessimistic. 'The right lung is completely gone, full of tubercles in process of softening. The lower third section of the left lung is affected. She is very emaciated, but her face still does her credit. The tuberculosis has reached its final stage.'[1] The dreaded word, taboo at the time, had finally been spoken. Perhaps Dr de Cornière had wanted to avoid using it, for on 8 July Sister Marie of the Eucharist had written to her parents: 'It is not tuberculosis, but an accident which has happened to the lungs, a real lung congestion.' Her brother-in-law, with his usual frankness, told the truth.

The disease had spread through the whole organism including the intestines. At the end of August the sufferings reached their climax. Thérèse gasped for breath, was suffocating, her functions blocked. *It's enough to make one go out of one's mind.*

LAST REMISSION (27 AUGUST TO 13 SEPTEMBER 1897)

On the afternoon of 27 August these great sufferings came to an end. There remained the fever (her temperature was never taken), the thirst, and above all the difficult respiration. She had only half the left lung with which to breathe.

So that she might see the garden in flower, her bed was moved to the middle of the infirmary with the window on her left. In front, framed by the curtains, she could see the Virgin of the Smile. *Look! She's watching for me!* She was—surprised

---

[1] Tuberculosis was the dreaded disease of the nineteenth century, and until about 1945. In France 150,000 persons a year contracted it. Calvados was among the departments most affected. In the Lisieux Carmel five nuns died of this disease between 1896 and 1914. Sister Marie-Antoinette, extern, November 1896, ten months before Thérèse. Sister Marie of the Eucharist, at thirty-four, 14 April 1905; Mother Marie-Ange in 1909, at twenty-eight, and Sister Isabelle of the Sacred Heart in 1914, at thirty-two.

that having loved Mary so much she had had such difficulty all her life saying her rosary.

In these days of remission Mother Agnès wrote down many of the sick nun's words. They are short sentences, skipping from one subject to another. Thérèse remained mistress of life, as much through her gestures as her words. She still joked to cheer up her sisters. At the stage when 'the outer man is wasting away and the inner man is being renewed day by day' (2 Cor. 4:16), Sister Thérèse appeared at peace, free, happy. Those around her were astonished. 'What did you do to reach such unshakable peace?' *I forgot self, and was careful not to seek myself in anything.*

She thought about Sister Geneviève who was having sleepless nights because of her. She was not at a loss for lively repartee. Mother Agnès, still anxious, said: 'Oh, how unfortunate it is when one is sick!' *No, we are not unfortunate when we are dying. Alas, how silly it is to be afraid of death! When one is married and has a husband and children, that's understandable, but I have nothing!*

On 30 August she went out on to the cloister on a movable bed which was placed in front of the open door of the chapel: it was her last visit to the Blessed Sacrament. She scattered rose petals for him. Sister Geneviève photographed her making this well-known gesture. On 14 September, scattering more petals, she said: *Gather up these petals carefully, sisters, they will be useful for you to do favours later on. Do not lose any of them.* This was one of her few prophetic utterances.

Aunt Guérin was ingenious at satisfying her craving for food, a result of her illness that surprised even Thérèse: she desired roast meat, thick soup, apple-charlotte, a chocolate éclair. *I have an appetite that's making up for my whole life. I have always eaten like a martyr and now I could devour everything. It seems to me that I'm dying of hunger.*

She spoke less and less. *Everything is said.* Her gaze often went to the garden; she counted nine pears on the pear tree near the window. *I love flowers very much, roses, red flowers and beautiful pink daisies.* But also: *Look! Do you see the black hole* (under the chestnut trees near the cemetery) *where we can see nothing; I am in a hole like that as far as my body and soul are concerned. Ah, yes, what darkness! But I am at peace there.*

When Dr de Cornière returned from holiday he found her

very emaciated, very weak (she had great difficulty making the sign of the cross). He could only say: 'She has fifteen days to live.' This time he was not mistaken.

IF THIS IS THE AGONY, WHAT IS DEATH (14–30 SEPTEMBER 1897)

Right to the end Thérèse's vitality astonished those around her. In the morning of 18 September the strong Sister Aimée took her in her arms while her bed was re-made. They thought she was dying. In the afternoon she declared: *I am better.* Mother Marie de Gonzague was called in to see how thin her back was. 'What is a little girl who is so thin?' *A skeleton!*[1] replied the sick nun.

What she had often feared came to pass. Her breathing became shorter and shorter. *Mother! earth's air is denied to me, when will God grant me the air of heaven?* Her great dread: suffocation. *Never will I know how to die.*

On Wednesday morning, 29th, she had the death-rattle in her chest. The community, summoned to the infirmary, recited in Latin the prayers for the dying, for almost an hour. The prioress sent the nuns away. They translated for the sick nun what had just been said. At midday she asked Mother Marie de Gonzague: *Mother, is this the agony? What must I do to die? I will never know how to die?* After the doctor's visit: *Is it today, Mother?* 'Yes, my little child.' . . . *I can't take any more! Ah, pray for me! Jesus! Mary! Yes, I will it, I really do will it . . . Oh, Mother, what this does to the nerves!*

In the evening, as the chaplain himself was seriously ill, Abbé Foucon came to hear her confession. As he left the infirmary he confided: 'What a beautiful soul! She seems confirmed in grace.'

The following night, for the first time, the prioress ordered Sister Marie of the Sacred Heart and Sister Geneviève to stay with their sister. They took it in turns. Mother Agnès slept in the next cell. It was a bad night for Thérèse – filled with nightmares. She prayed to the blessed Virgin. On the morning

[1] In the French there is a play on words: the prioress said: '*Qu*'est-ce *que* c'est *qu*'une petite fille aussi maigre?' Thérèse replied: 'Un *que*lette (squelette) (tr.).

of Thursday, an overcast and rainy day, the three Martin sisters stayed with her during the community mass. She said to them: *It is sheer agony, without any consolation.*

All day she was gasping for breath but, to the surprise of all, she moved about, sat up in bed, which she had not been able to do for a long time. *You see what strength I have today!* she said. *No, I'm not going to die! I still have enough strength for months, perhaps years!*

Mother Agnès took down her exclamations in between her gaspings for breath, which was growing shorter all the time. *If you knew what it is to suffocate! My God, have pity on your poor little child! Have pity on her!*

To Mother Marie de Gonzague: *O Mother, I assure you, the chalice is full right up to the brim! But God is not going to abandon me, for sure, he has never abandoned me.*

In the afternoon after vespers Mother Marie de Gonzague placed a picture of Our Lady of Mount Carmel on her knees. *O Mother, present me quickly to the blessed Virgin. I am a baby who can't take any more! Prepare me to die well.* She was told that she was ready. *Yes, it seems to me that I have never sought anything but the truth. Yes, I have understood humility of heart. It seems to me that I am humble.*

Everything I have written about my desires for suffering. Oh! it is true just the same. I'm not sorry for having surrendered myself to love. Oh! no, I'm not sorry, on the contrary.

Sister Marie of the Sacred Heart was so upset by her godchild's struggle that she was reluctant to go back into the infirmary. Mother Agnès, for her part, went and prayed in front of the statue of the Sacred Heart, on the first floor, that her sister might not despair in her last moments.

About five o'clock the bell rang to summon the community quickly to the infirmary. The dying nun welcomed the sisters with a smile. She was holding her crucifix firmly. A 'terrible death-rattle' tore her chest. Her face was flushed, her hands purplish, her feet cold; she was perspiring so much that the sweat soaked through the mattress. Time passed. The prioress dismissed the nuns.

After seven o'clock Thérèse managed to say: *Mother, isn't this the agony? Am I not going to die?* 'Yes, my poor little one, it's the agony, but God perhaps wills to prolong it for several hours.' *Well, all right! All right! I would not want to suffer for a shorter time.* She looked at her crucifix: *Oh! I love him! My God, I love you!*

Her head fell back. Mother Marie de Gonzague had the bell rung again: the community returned very quickly. The kneeling sisters saw her face become once again very peaceful, her gaze was fixed a little above the statue of the Virgin of the Smile, 'for the space of a creed'. Then she sank back on to the pillow, her eyes closed. She was smiling. She looked very beautiful and had the appearance of a very young girl. It was about twenty past seven.

Sister Geneviève, in tears, rushed out on to the cloister. It was raining. 'If only there were some stars in the sky!' She said to herself. A few moments later the clouds were swept away and stars twinkled in a sky which had become clear. The Guérins, returning home after spending the whole time of their niece's agony in the chapel of the Carmel, noticed this sudden change. An extern sister had just given them a note from Mother Agnès: 'My beloved Uncle and Aunt, my dearest Léonie, our angel is in heaven. She breathed her last sigh at seven o'clock clasping her crucifix to her heart and saying: "Oh, I love you!" She had raised her eyes to heaven; what was she seeing?!!!'

On a farewell picture given to her sisters in June, Sister Thérèse of the Child Jesus had written: *I see what I have believed. I possess what I have hoped for. I am united to the one whom I have loved with all the strength of my loving.*

The following day, Friday, Thérèse's body was placed in the choir, behind the grille. Sister Geneviève had taken a photograph of her in the infirmary. Until the Sunday evening the Martins, the Guérins, the La Néeles, the Maudelondes, priests, friends and the faithful filed past, as was the custom, and passed in rosaries and medals to touch the body.

The burial was arranged for Monday, 4 October at nine in the morning.

I AM NOT DYING, I AM ENTERING INTO LIFE

On Monday, 4 October a hearse drawn by two horses slowly climbed the steep slope which led to the city's cemetery, behind the hill overlooking the valley of the Orbiquet.

Léonie Martin led the mourners, surrounded by the Guérins, the La Néeles and a few friends. It was a 'very small funeral procession'. Uncle Isidore, confined to his bed with gout, was unable to be present at his niece's burial. He had never thought she would be the first to have a place in the plot he had bought for the Carmel.

The next day the Carmelites tidied up the infirmary, burnt the palliasse and her alpagates.[1] Sister Marie of the Sacred Heart had wanted to keep them; Sister Marthe opposed the idea: 'You are not going to keep those dirty things!' They were in fact in tatters.

Monastery life resumed its regular rhythm – based on prayer, work and community life exercises. The silence, which had been disturbed for a moment, descended once again on the Lisieux Carmel. For in these places, 'the life and death of a Carmelite is marked only by a slight change in the timetable of works and the offices of the day'.[2]

[1] Rope sandals worn by Carmelites. So as to keep some souvenirs of her sister, Mother Agnès suggested to Léonie that she should offer to buy Thérèse's homespun habit, white choir mantle, veils and another pair of alpagates. As the Carmel was poor, Mother Marie de Gonzague accepted. The lot was sold for 90F.

[2] From *Dialogues des Carmélites*, by Georges Bernanos, Act 2, Scene 8. In 1897 Bernanos was a nine-year-old boy. The President of the Republic, Félix Faure, had just returned from a triumphant visit to Russia to seal the alliance with Tsar Nicholas I. Captain Dreyfus, convicted of high treason, was imprisoned on Devil's Island. Maurice Barrès had just published *Les Déracinés*, and the young André Gide, *Les Nourritures terrestres*. Charles Péguy (born 1873) was correcting the proofs of his *Jeanne d'Arc*. On 14 October Clément Ader would fly his aeroplane 300m. above the ground. In Paris the Lumière brothers were successfully producing films. A few researchers were pursuing their studies in radio-activity. *We are in an age of inventions*, the unknown young Carmelite, who had just died at the threshold of the *Belle Epoque*, had remarked.

Life After Death: The Storm of Glory

A small spark, O mystery of life, is enough to start an immense fire.

Thus ends the story of Thérèse Martin.

And the amazing story of her life after death begins. We are not going to write it here. It would require a second volume. Let us simply recall some facts, some dates.

Beyond the small family circle, and despite the reservations of certain sisters, the Carmelites had esteemed and loved Sister Thérèse of the Child Jesus of the Holy Face. But when she died some of the nuns would no doubt have agreed with Sister Anne of the Sacred Heart, now back from Saigon; she had lived with Thérèse for seven years before going to Indo-China. 'There was nothing to say about her. She was very kind and very retiring, there was nothing conspicuous about her. I would never have suspected her sanctity.'

And yet the story of that very short life was going to echo throughout the world.

A tree is judged by its fruits. All these facts of recent past history enable us to prove that Sister Thérèse had not been experiencing 'the feverish dreams of a tubercular patient'. What she said and wrote has been shown, after her premature death, to be true and verifiable. Her courage in everyday life, and in her 'passion', proved the truth of her way of confidence and love, and so has her life after death.

PUBLICATION OF 'HISTOIRE D'UNE AME' (30 SEPTEMBER 1898)

Mother Agnès kept her word. But she did something quite unusual. The death-circular she had promised Thérèse on her sick bed became a bound volume of 475 pages, published by Imprimerie Saint-Paul at Bar-le-Duc. On 30 September 1898, a year to the day after her young sister's death, *Histoire d'une Ame* came out. Number of copies printed: 2,000. Price: 4F.

At the direction of Mother Marie de Gonzague who had insisted that all the manuscripts be addressed to her (which led to corrections), Mother Agnès divided her sister's exercise books into chapters, and corrected what seemed to her to be incorrect in these 'rough drafts' of a young girl who had difficulty with spelling. A born corrector, she availed herself without scruple of the mandate the sick nun had given her.[1] She corrected the exercise books as she used to correct Thérèse's school homework at Les Buissonnets. 'She practically rewrote the autobiography' (Father François de Sainte-Marie).

Father Godefroy Madelaine, prior of the Praemonstratensians at Mondaye, with pencil in hand, read through all this work, approved, and presented it to Mgr Hugonin for the imprimatur. He granted it verbally, without enthusiasm, on 7 March 1898. Uncle Guérin financed the venture and took charge of all the business arrangements.

All the French Carmels received a copy, as well as some churchmen. Brother Siméon in Rome was not forgotten. Two or three monasteries showed some reservations: 'Age and experience would have perhaps modified the views of this young sister about perfection.' But bishops, superiors of religious orders (Trappists, Eudists, Carmelites) expressed admiration, in writing, to the Carmel.

In May 1899 a second edition was brought out which included these letters of praise. M. Guérin, who carefully corrected the proofs, could not get over it. Mgr Amette, who had succeeded Mgr Hugonin, gave his favourable approval for this new edition, on 24 May 1899. The first translation was made into English (1901), and there followed translations into Polish (1902), Italian and Dutch (1904), and German, Portuguese, Spanish, Japanese and Russian (1905).

It has been said, and sometimes written, that this astonishing process of distribution was due to the industry of the Martin sisters who were experts in promoting their little

[1] See p. 196.

sister. This explanation does not hold when faced with facts and dates. The Carmelites had been the first to be bewildered by this tidal-wave. Mother Agnès said one day to her cousin Jeanne La Néele: 'Heavens above! What a business to come down on us in our old age! I could never have imagined even the smallest part of this universal conflagration when I timidly sent out the first spark in 1898.' It is true that they faced the situation with realism and a sense of organisation which was backed up by an enormous amount of work. Other Carmels would have been shipwrecked in that storm.

The way it spread was thus repeated thousands of times. Someone read *Story of a Soul*; that reading affected him very much. He prayed to 'little Sister Thérèse' and found his prayer answered. He wrote to the Lisieux Carmel for a memento, made a pilgrimage to the young Carmelite's grave, shared his enthusiasm with others, lent the book. In turn these readers' prayers were answered, they asked for relics, and so on. Thus the spark spread from one to another.

On 12 February 1899 Sister Marie of the Eucharist wrote to her cousin, Céline Pottier:

Everyone is speaking to us about this beloved angel who is doing so much good through her writings. Priests are comparing her to St Teresa and say she has opened up a whole new way to souls, the way of love. They are all enthusiastic, not only around us, but throughout France, and in most of their sermons they are quoting from the inspired passages of her manuscript. There are even men of the world, whom piety somewhat embarrasses, who are enthusiastic about it and have made it their favourite reading.

As a result of the translations[1] conversions and physical cures increased all over the world. These miracles have sometimes been accompanied by apparitions of the 'little sister' in brown homespun.

A young Scottish priest, Father Thomas Nimmo Taylor, ordained in 1897, read *The Little Flower of Jesus*. Overwhelmed by the young French Carmelite, he went to see Mother Marie

---

[1] Today *Histoire d'une Ame* has been translated into more than forty languages and dialects.

de Gonzague and the Martin sisters in the parlour in 1903. He spoke of Sister Thérèse's possible canonisation. The prioress answered, laughing: 'In that case, how many Carmelites would have to be canonised?' Neither Léonie nor the Guérins were in favour of such a proposition.

THE CANONISATION PROCESS (FROM 1909 TO 1917)

The press became involved. The famous Louis Veuillot disclosed in *l'Univers*, 9 July 1906, that Fr Prévost was busy in Rome preparing the cause of the Lisieux Carmelite. On 15 March 1907 Pius X himself expressed his wish for her glorification. In a private audience he did not hesitate to anticipate the future by calling her 'the greatest saint of modern times'.

The new Bishop of Bayeux-Lisieux, Mgr Lemonnier (Mgr Amette having been appointed to Paris) therefore with some reticence invited the Carmelites the following 15 October to write down their memories of Sister Thérèse of the Child Jesus. Some of them had not waited ten years to do so. Since 1898 everything concerning the one people were already calling 'the little saint' had been carefully preserved at the Carmel.

Thérèse had written to Jeanne La Néele: *I know that the Roman Curia has to take a long time to canonise saints*. But in her case, all the delays were shortened. The Roman Curia, which usually takes its time, found itself hurried. 'We must lose no time in crowning the little saint with glory, if we do not want the voice of the people to anticipate us,' declared Cardinal Vico, Prefect of the Congregation of Rites. In January 1909 Fr Rodriguo, a Carmelite in Rome, and Mgr de Teil[1] were appointed respectively postulator and vice-postulator of the cause. Just before the opening of the diocesan process, among the hundreds of miracles reported to Lisieux, an apparition of Sister Thérèse to the prioress of the Gallipoli Carmel (Italy) created a stir. Thérèse said to her: *La mia via è sicura, e non mi sono sbagliate seguendola*.[2]

---

[1] He had met Thérèse in the parlour in September 1896 (p. 131 n.2).
[2] *My way is sure, and I was not mistaken in following it.*

The diocesan beatification process opened on 3 August 1910; only thirteen years after her death. Thirty-seven witnesses, of whom nine were Carmelites who had lived with her, testified to the life of Sister Thérèse. It required one hundred and nine sittings.

Her body was exhumed at the Lisieux cemetery on 6 September 1910, in the presence of Mgr Lemonnier and several hundred persons. Doctors Francis La Néele and de Cornière made the customary statements. Her remains were placed in a lead coffin and transferred to another vault.

On 10 June 1914 Pius X signed the introduction of the cause and declared: 'It is very expedient that this cause for beatification be investigated as quickly as possible.'

The apostolic process which opened at Bayeux on 17 March 1915 was postponed by order of the new Pope, Benedict XV because of the First World War. But although hostilities made communication with Rome difficult, Sister Thérèse's renown did not cease to grow in the trenches, including on the German side. Even the 'limited' anthology of the Carmelite's interventions from 1914 to 1918 contains 592 pages of witnesses. The preface states that five volumes would have been needed to include them all. By 1915 the Carmel had sent out 211,515 copies of *Histoire d'une Ame*, 710,000 of *Vie abrégée (Abridged Life)*, and 110,000 copies of *Pluies de Roses (Showers of Roses)*.[1]

The apostolic process closed, on 30 October 1917 in Bayeux Cathedral, after ninety-one sessions. Benedict XV exempted the cause from the fifty years delay imposed by law for canonisation. On 14 August 1921 he promulgated the decree on the heroic quality of the virtues of Sister Thérèse of the Child Jesus.

His successor, Pius XI, made her 'the star of his pontificate'. Her picture and relics never left the office where he worked. After the investigation of two miracles, chosen from hundreds, the Pope presided at the beatification of Sister Thérèse of the Child Jesus in St Peter's Basilica, Rome on 29 April 1923. He saw in her a 'word of God' addressed to our century.

[1] Anthologies containing letters received by the Lisieux Carmel (50 a day in 1911, 500 in 1914, 800 to 1,000 in 1923–5). Seven volumes were published between 1911 and 1926 comprising some 3,200 pages.

SAINT THÉRÈSE OF LISIEUX (17 MAY 1925)

In that basilica, before 50,000 persons (500,000 were standing outside in St Peter's Square), in the presence of thirty-three cardinals and two hundred and fifty bishops on 17 May 1925, Pius XI inscribed little Thérèse Martin in the catalogue of saints. Two years later he proclaimed her 'Principal Patroness of the Universal Missions with St Francis Xavier'. It was an amazing paradox: the nun who had never left her cloister from the age of fifteen to twenty-four was put on an equal footing with the Spanish Jesuit who had given his life and gone as far as the borders of China.

Thérèse of Lisieux was universally known. After the beatification 600,000 pilgrims hastened to the little Norman city. They queued up in front of the chapel of the Carmel and at Les Buissonnets. Between 1898 and 1925, 30,328,000 pictures had been distributed. A great number of young girls asked to enter the Lisieux Carmel which was unable to receive them all. There were so many applicants that circulars had to be printed to reply to them. *Story of a Soul* inspired vocations in all the religious orders. The Theresian spirituality went far beyond Carmel. In 1933 the 'Oblates of St Thérèse' were founded who put themselves at the service of the new saint. Fr Martin set up a male congregation, the Missionaries of St Thérèse, in 1948.

She who had lived the end of her life in spiritual darkness, foretelling modern unbelief, also became patroness of the French missions. Cardinal Suhard, greatly disturbed by the dechristianisation of the masses, wrote in his personal diary on 8 September 1940:[1] 'I feel that part of the saint's mission is to be realised. When the work of La Mission de France begins the little saint will really be on her way, because there will be no end to the divine gifts. May I labour efficaciously at this work, and bring St Thérèse of the Child Jesus to work there.' The seminary of La Mission de France, which was founded on 24 July 1941, was set up at Lisieux in October 1942.

On 3 May 1944, just before the liberation of France, Pius XII (who as Legate had gone to Lisieux in 1937 to inaugurate

[1] Fiftieth anniversary of Thérèse's profession.

the basilica), proclaimed Thérèse 'Second Patroness of France with St Joan of Arc'. The two sisters were united. One month later Lisieux was ablaze under the D-day bombs. The seminarians of La Mission de France put out the fire which was beginning to take hold of the stairs in the cellar of the Carmel. The town became a furnace but the monastery was spared.

A SILENT REVOLUTION

Biographies and studies in all languages became numerous. Between 1898 and 1947 alone, Theresian biographies numbered 865 recorded works. Requests to read the original exercise books of *Histoire d'une Ame* became more and more pressing. Mother Agnès died on 28 July 1951, in her ninetieth year.[1] At Pius XII's order Father François de Sainte-Marie, a Carmelite, finally published in 1956 the *Manuscrits autobiographiques* in a photocopied edition. An album of photographs was brought out in 1961 which revealed the real face of Thérèse of Lisieux. It was then realised that there was no comparison between the insipid pictures which had been so widely distributed before by the Lisieux 'icon-painter' and Céline's authentic negatives. Céline, the last of the Martins, died on 25 February 1959 in her ninetieth year.

What an amazing adventure for that family! Throughout their life the sisters had pondered over the incredible transformation which had changed the 'baby of the family' into a universal saint. In 1939 Marie of the Sacred Heart was still astonished:

A short while ago as I was looking at the basilica I was thinking of Mamma. When she used to come to Lisieux my aunt would always take her to the cemetery. It was a beautiful spot; and then when members of the family were buried there Mamma loved to go there. If someone had said to her at that time: 'Do you see this beautiful little hill where we are now? Well, in fifty years a magnificent basilica will be built here in honour of your little Thérèse.' Poor

[1] Marie of the Sacred Heart died on 19 January 1940, in her eightieth year; Sister Françoise-Thérèse (Léonie) on 16 June 1941, at seventy-eight.

little Mother! She would have said: 'You are off your head!' She who had had so many sorrows would not have believed it. That's for sure!

The little Martin had slipped away from her family. She had become 'the cherished child of the world' (Pius XI). She belonged to it. Seventeen hundred churches throughout the world have been named in her honour.

From 1971 onwards the centenary edition began by publishing the original texts of the letters, poems, last conversations. The centenary of her birth (1973) gave new impetus to Theresian works. The Carmelites in Rome published between 1973 and 1976 the processes of beatification and canonisation, which had remained secret until then.

Since the beatification theologians have studied Thérèse's little exercise books and all her writings. One of the pioneers, Abbé Combes, believed Sister Thérèse of the Child Jesus of the Holy Face had brought about 'one of the greatest spiritual revolutions that the Holy Spirit has set in motion in the evolution of mankind. A silent and hidden revolution with innumerable fruits.' Fr Molinié, a Dominican theologian, was of the opinion that 'we had to wait for Thérèse of the Child Jesus to rediscover a movement of spirituality on a planetary scale which had all the fullness to fit exactly the dimensions of the Gospel'. Hans Urs Von Balthasar wrote: 'The theology of women has never been taken seriously, nor has it been received by the corpus. After the message of Lisieux, at last it will have to be taken into consideration in the present-day reconstruction of dogmatic theology.' Fr Congar saw in Thérèse (and in Charles de Foucauld), 'one of the beacons that the hand of God has lit at the threshold of the atomic century'.

It is true that anyone else but Thérèse Martin would have been utterly crushed by the obstacles and sufferings met along the way. A vitality and mad love urged her on. She had personally experienced salvation. At a time when soul-destroying Jansenism was still working havoc, when a narrow moralism threatened to reduce the image of God to that of a rigid lover of justice, she rediscovered the Gospel inspiration: God is the Father of Jesus. He gave his son who came for sinners, the poor, the little. She dared to name this God *Papa*, instinctively finding again the original *Abba* of Jesus.

The Second Vatican Council (1962–5), without naming Thérèse, owes much to her prophetic intuitions: the return to the word of God, the priority given to the theological virtues (faith, hope and charity) in everyday life, the Church seen as the body of Christ, the universal mission, the call of each baptised person to sanctity, fraternal attention paid to those who have different beliefs or who do not believe. Thérèse's spiritual trial of faith and hope has appeared as a herald of the twentieth century where unbelief has put Christians in the minority, when so many men and women come face to face with despair. One can add yet more: her idea of heaven as a dynamic place, her teaching on fraternal charity, her desire for daily communion, her Marian theology, and so on.

We can but hope that after Catherine of Siena (fourteenth century) and Teresa of Avila (sixteenth century), Thérèse of Lisieux, one day in the near future, might be proclaimed Doctor of the Church.[1]

THE UNIVERSAL SISTER

Her thought – Thérèse had never systematised anything! – has astonished French philosophers like Bergson, Guitton, Moré, Monnier, Thibou; politicians as opposite as Marc Sangnier and Charles Maurras. She has captivated writers as diverse as Paul Claudel, Henri Ghéon, Georges Bernanos, Lucie Delarue-Mardrus, Joseph Malègue, Edouard Estaunié, Giovanni Papini, René Schwob, Ida Görres, John Wu, Maxence Van der Meersch, Gilbert Cesbron, Stanislas Fumet, Julien Green, Maurice Clavel. It is a ridiculously short list which could easily be lengthened by taking into consideration the five continents of the world.

But finally who can express the profound appeal, the happy liberation that she has brought about in the hearts of the poor, the little, the 'voiceless' (her privileged friends) by revealing to them that evangelical sanctity is within their reach? Her life shows that emotional handicaps, neurosis, catastrophic

---

[1] *Despite my littleness, I would wish to enlighten souls like the doctors.*

heredity, various diseases, nothing can separate us from merciful love. By her 'loving boldness', by her 'brilliant fearlessness', she has chased away all fears. Ordinary everyday life has become once again the seed bed of possible holiness. *There will be something there for all tastes, except for those living in extraordinary ways.* She had prayed for the masses, those legions of 'little souls', those who came to Jesus beside the Lake of Tiberias. She was heard.

More than a million people pass through Lisieux each year, pilgrims and tourists of all ages, from all classes of society, from all countries. In the chapel of the Carmel, at Les Buissonnets, metal workers rub shoulders with lawyers, Japanese intellectuals with prostitutes from Pigalle, a North African Muslim with a Belgian missionary, the French country family with the South American theologian, a group of German pilgrims with Canadian religious. 'The only western saints the Russian Christians venerate after the Schism are Francis of Assisi and the little Thérèse,' declared Olivier Clément, quoting an Orthodox Christian.

The 'petite Thérèse'[1] of the French-speaking countries, 'the Little Flower' of the Anglo-Saxons, 'Teresinha' of Portugual, and 'Teresita' of the Spanish-speaking world, has friends everywhere. Many say: 'She is there. There is a presence. She is quite near us.'

The life stories of all these people will never be written. They are a secret between themselves and Thérèse. The real life after death of the saint of Lisieux is to be found at this depth. She eludes all surveys, all statistics.

In the end, her mystery eludes us. But is it not better that way?

A shooting star in the sky of holiness, in twenty-four years of earthly life she attained – while still young – the wisdom of the old. 'Saints hardly ever grow old,' said John Paul II at Lisieux. 'They never become figures of the past, men and women "of yesterday". On the contrary, they are always men and women of the evangelical future, witnesses of the "future world".'

The Polish Pope wanted to end his visit to France with a

---

[1] She was asked: 'What shall we call you after your death?' *You will call me 'little Thérèse'.*

pilgrimage to Lisieux (2 June 1980). On the Esplanade of the Basilica he spoke in front of a crowd of a hundred thousand:

> Of Thérèse of Lisieux, one can say with conviction that the Spirit of God let her heart reveal directly to the men and women of our day *the fundamental mystery*, the fundamental reality of the Gospel: the fact that we have really received 'a spirit of adoption which makes us cry out: Abba! Father!' The little way is the way of 'holy childhood'. In that way, there is both confirmation and renewal of the most fundamental and most universal truth. What truth of the Gospel message is indeed more fundamental and more universal than this: God is our Father and we are his children?

John Paul II wanted to go and pray in the infirmary where Thérèse had died after so much suffering. To the contemplative nuns of different orders who had gathered in the chapel of the Carmel he said: 'The density and the radiance of your life hidden in God must challenge the men and women of

31 Pope John Paul II in the infirmary where Thérèse died (2 June 1980)

today who are so often searching for the meaning of their lives.'

These few pages of the life after death of the Carmelite of Lisieux cover eighty-five years of history: they illustrate imperfectly 'the density and the radiance of (her) life hidden in God'.

This radiance continues. It will continue.

Yes, I want to spend my life doing good on earth . . . I do not want to rest as long as there are souls to save. But when the angel says: 'Time is no more', then I will take my rest.

Some Testimonies Selected from the Tens of Thousands

I would want to preach the Gospel on all the five continents simultaneously, and even to the remotest isles.

I love St Thérèse of Lisieux very much because she has simplified things: in our relationship with God she has done away with the mathematics . . . In the spiritual life, she has restored to the Holy Spirit the place which directors had taken from him.

Cardinal Bourne (1912)
Archbishop of Westminster

When I was in Haiti, a friend passed me a small book, *Story of a Soul*. So I opened it absent-mindedly and glanced through the first pages without any great interest. It did not seem to have been written for me, or to be of any use to me. Then I came to the episode of the basket where Thérèse, invited by Léonie to choose some remnants or braids, replied: *I choose all*. Instantly, my soul was completely enlightened. An unknown emotion came over me, inundated me: fire, joy, tears of joy; I was carried away into another world . . . For a moment, it seemed that 'little Thérèse' [she was not yet beatified], was near me, that she was opening the eyes of my soul . . . No, it was not an illusion. After forty-eight years, the effect of that striking grace still influences my life . . .

Jean Le Cour-Grandmaison (1914)
Naval officer, Deputy of Loire-Atlantique,
died at Kergonan Abbey, 1974.

St Thérèse of Lisieux is my patron saint. The white roses which I planted in front of her [her statue in the garden] flower almost all the year round.

Alain Mimoun (1970)
Olympic marathon champion

The Coptic Monastery at Wadi El Natroon was founded by Matta El Meskeen nearly twenty-five years ago. Matta El Maskeen was an Egyptian, a pharmaceutical student belonging to the Coptic-Orthodox faith. In his youth he felt called to the religious life. He retired into the desert of Upper Egypt and began living as a hermit, after the example of St Macarius, one of the Fathers of Coptic monasticism. St Thérèse of the Child Jesus' writing, which had been translated into Arabic in 1964, deeply moved Matta El Meskeen and became the rule of life for him and his monks. It is now being used as a basis for renewal at Wadi El Natroon.

Informations carmélitaines (SIC, 1981)

I was a student in the sixties. I took part in Catholic groups. Several times a chaplain spoke to us about Thérèse of Lisieux. The girls laughed, and the boys wondered what it had to do with their struggle for peace in Algeria, and against torture. We were too serious, too committed to be interested in that good little sister. Then came May 1968 and the years of intense political action which followed. I cut all ties with a Church which was ineffective and incapable of opening up a human future.

1975: I had gained nothing through efficiency and had lost the hope of being able to change anything in this sad world. At the home of my fiancée's parents I found Thérèse Martin's autobiography. It was a revelation, the staggering discovery of the Gospels read by the demanding voice of a child. I was overwhelmed, shattered, for a week. And then like a poor beggar I tried to pray. I have rediscovered God, and hope in action when it is inspired by love. My life is transformed.

D. L. (1979)

We wished to build a monastery, but you well know that

it is impossible. The law categorically forbids it. Then we discovered *Story of a Soul*. It has become our cloister. For everyone can follow the 'little way' of spiritual childhood, even when official religious institutions are not allowed, even when nothing religious is permitted.

Russian Orthodox Christians (1977)
Moscow

This book is a tribute. The enthusiastic tribute from an unbeliever to the Carmelite-apparition which miraculously appeared, roses in hand, in the midst of an era which grieves and terrifies poets . . . Thérèse Martin is my fellow-countrywoman, and almost my contemporary. I do not wish to let her glorious entry into sanctity pass by without honouring her in my own way. And besides, she is henceforth public property. We wish to share in it.

Lucie Delarue-Mardrus (1926)
writer

I am writing a little note to you, for I am in prison and I think about you very much. I have not been here long, it was not a serious crime. I went to see you not long ago with my wife and as soon as I can, I will come back to see you again with my son who is four months old. I wear around my neck a medal of you and my Jesus Christ. I am to leave prison on 24 March. I am doing a sketch for you which, I hope, will please you. St Thérèse, I leave you with a big kiss, and one from my son and my wife.

Serge X (1979)
prisoner

My name is Thérèse B. I live in America. Recently I finished reading the book *Mr Martin an Ideal Father*. I have also read *Story of a Soul*. I must say that nothing I have read in the forty-two years of my life has ever touched me so much before. Although I am a Catholic and my name is Thérèse, I never knew a great deal about this saint who is so powerful and who saves souls. In January 1981 I was at the lowest point of my life and one day went into a church where there was a statue. At the foot of it there was a picture with a prayer: 'Why not, since everything else has failed?' My faith was strengthened to such an extent that I cannot believe I am the same person, I who thought only of suicide.

Mrs Thérèse Bremer (1981)

I can still see that Buddhist priest in his saffron robe, his head shaven, seated on a small stool after visiting St Thérèse's bedroom. There he said to the visitors he had brought with him: 'Now we are going to say the Our Father', and he added: 'St Thérèse, pray for the visitors who will pass through here.' He was a Buddhist who had studied with the Jesuits in India. He greatly appreciated Thérèse's openness of spirit because she had never been against anyone, but had loved much. For him, a non-Christian, she combined concern with her own spirituality with that of universal love.

Sister Colette Barthélemy (1973)
at Les Buissonnets

There is hardly a day here at the school of Thérèse of Lisieux when I do not admit all sorts of people, thanks to her writings or to what has been written about her: that goes for the prostitute and the young girl in search of a religious vocation, for the priest who has become a tramp as a result of a very sad past, the former prisoner on a pension who admits he took the wrong path; from the mother of a family who can hardly read French, but who knows intuitively what St Thérèse has said, to the divorced father who feels himself 'pardoned' in the very special light of St Thérèse's God of mercy. I glean these from the pile of true small miracles, thanks to her.

A parish priest (1982)
at Lyons

Jesus is very near me. He is drawing me more and more to himself, and I can only adore him in silence, desiring to die of love. I would wish, like little St Thérèse of the Child Jesus, to renew with each beat of my heart that offering to become 'a sacrifice to his merciful love'. I am waiting in darkness,

and in peace . . . I am waiting for Love! In five hours, I will
see Jesus!

Jacques Fesch (30 September 1957)
Written on the sixtieth anniversary of Thérèse's death, the night
before his execution. He was twenty-seven years old.

At the time when the cruel trial which I have just passed
through came upon me, I received, from an unknown hand,
a small pamphlet about Sister Thérèse of the Child Jesus. I
had scarcely begun reading it when I became aware of a very
gentle consolation, a sort of inner prompting to become very
little and to abandon myself to God's will as Sister Thérèse
had done. May Thérèse from on high support us and show
us how to be more one with Jesus.

Marc Sangnier (15 September 1910)
Founder of Sillon.
Letter to Mother Agnès.

I owe her a great deal . . . St Thérèse has been my 'good
angel'. I have a relic of her bones which never leaves me. It
was given to me by Mother Agnès with whom I corresponded
until her death . . . *Story of a Soul* contains treasures of
wisdom.

Charles Maurras (1952)
Founder of Action Française

I know that my daughter Reine, aged four and a half, on 11
January 1906 contracted a disease of the eyes which the
doctors declared incurable. After six months of useless treatment my wife carried our blind child to Sister Thérèse of the
Child Jesus' grave and we began a novena to this little saint.
On the second day, 26 May 1908, two days before the feast
of the Ascension, while my wife was at the six o'clock mass
little Reine, after a violent attack, suddenly recovered her
sight. My wife was the first to become aware of this, and then
I did. In witness whereof, with much gratitude for the miracle
worked for us, we sign the present certificate with witnesses.

[There follow eleven signatures and the remarks of the doctor who had diagnosed the condition as phlyctenular keratitis.][1]

A. Fauquet (12 December 1908)
Little Reine Fauquet went to see the Lisieux Carmelites in the
parlour.

At the end of these two works, of this long tramp of fifteen years with Thérèse, the feeling that I am walking beside an original, indefinable personality is even stronger . . . 'But then, who is Thérèse?' the surprised and perplexed reader will ask. 'Come and see,' he will be told. Do you want the author to give you a key? It is the story of love, there is then no key, the door stands open. The door to death and to life, as always in a love story.

Jean-François Six (1973)
biographer of Thérèse

Dear little Thérèse
I was seventeen when I read your autobiography. It struck me forcibly. You called it *The Story of a Little White Spring Flower.* To me the willpower, courage and decisiveness it showed made it seem more like the story of a piece of steel. Once you had chosen the path of complete dedication to God, nothing could stop you: not illness, nor opposition from outside, nor the mists or inner darkness.

Albino Luciani (1973)
afterwards Pope John Paul I

Shortly after her birth Edith developed a cataract. It was not even noticed! She was blind for almost three years. Her grandmother, Louise, took her to Lisieux. She saw. It was a real miracle for Edith. She always believed this. Since that time she had a real devotion to St Thérèse of the Child Jesus. Not only did she wear her medal for a long time, but she always had a small picture of the saint on her bedside table.

Simone Berteaut (1969)
Edith Piaf's sister

---

[1] At the time tuberculosis was widespread and the child's condition may well have been a tubercular allergy (tr.).

With Thérèse one can always begin again, no matter how low one has fallen. To begin to love again, to begin to live again. Thérèse always appears as one who breaks through misfortune, who makes you enter into the resurrection. She unnails you from the wrong and false cross, that of fear, remorse and despair, that you may kneel at the foot of the true one. As for me, in this town where I have all but been engulfed, never can I thank Thérèse enough for having saved me from revolt. Nevertheless I feel I still have everything to learn from her, and I ask her to free me from everything which so often blocks my way.

H.M. (1982)
Loiret

Genealogies of the Martin and Guérin Families

ON THE SIDE OF THÉRÈSE'S FATHER LOUIS MARTIN

b 22 August 1823   *d* 29 July 1894

The grandparents were:
Pierre-François Martin   *b* 16 April 1777   *d* 26 June 1865
Fanie Bourear   *b* 12 January 1800   *d* 8 April 1883
They had three daughters and two sons, the lastborn Louis.

ON THE SIDE OF THÉRÈSE'S MOTHER AZÉLIE GUÉRIN

b 23 December 1831   *d* 28 August 1877

The grandparents were:
Isidore Guérin   *b* 6 July 1789   *d* 3 September 1868
Louise-Jeanne Macé   *b* 11 July 1805   *d* 9 September 1859

They had three children:

Marie-Louise   *b* 31 May 1829   *d* 24 February 1877 Sr Marie-
Dosithée of the Visitation, Le Mans.
Azélie-Marie. Thérèse's mother.
Isidore   *b* 2 January 1841   *d* 28 September 1909
Thérèse's uncle, a chemist of Lisieux.
m 11 September 1866 Elisa-Céline Fournet   *b* 15 March
1847   *d* 13 February 1900

They had three children:

Jeanne   *b* 24 February 1868   *d* 25 April 1938
m 1 October 1890 Dr Francis La Néele   *b* 18 October
1858   *d* 19 March 1916
Marie   *b* 22 August 1870   *d* 14 April 1905
Thérèse's cousin. Sr Marie of the Eucharist, Lisieux Carmel.
Paul   *b* 16 October 1871   *d* at birth

THE MARTIN FAMILY

Louis Martin *m* 13 July 1858 Azélie Guérin

They had nine children:

Marie-Louise   *b* 22 February 1860   *d* 19 January 1940
Thérèse's godmother. Sr Marie of the Sacred Heart, Lisieux
Carmel.
Marie-Pauline   *b* 7 September 1861   *d* 28 July 1951
Sr then M Agnès of Jesus, Lisieux Carmel.
Marie-Léonie   *b* 3 June 1863   *d* 16 June 1941
Sr Françoise-Thérèse of the Visitation, Caen, 1899.
Marie-Hélène   *b* 3 October 1864   *d* 22 February 1870
Marie-Joseph   *b* 20 September 1866   *d* 14 February 1867
Marie-Jean Baptiste   *b* 19 December 1867   *d* 24 August 1868
Marie-Céline   *b* 28 April 1869   *d* 25 February 1959
Sr Geneviève of Sainte-Thérèse, Lisieux Carmel.
Marie-Mélanie-Thérèse   *b* 16 August 1870   *d* 8 October 1870
Marie-Françoise-Thérèse   *b* 2 January 1873   *d* 30 September
1897
Sr THÉRÈSE OF THE CHILD JESUS, Lisieux Carmel.

b   born   Sr   Sister
d   died   M   Mother
m   married

Bibliography

Clarke, John, OCD (tr.), *General Correspondence*, vol. I. ICS Publications, Washington, DC, 1982.

    Last Conversations. Thérèse's conversations with her sisters. ICS Publications, Washington, DC, 1977.

    Story of a Soul. The three autobiographical MSS of St Thérèse. ICS Publications, Washington, DC, 1976.

Sheed, F. J. (tr.), *The Collected Letters of Saint Thérèse of Lisieux*. Sheed and Ward, London, 1949.